The Unbound Journey

The Practice Companion to Heart Unbound 2.0

Dr John McSwiney

https://www.timetotransform.world

McSwiney, Dr John (author)

Title: *The Unbound Journey: The Practice Companion to Heart Unbound 2.0* / Dr John McSwiney, author.

Illustrations: Canva

ISBN: 978-0-6486101-6-8

Emotional intelligence workbook

Leadership and self development

Mindfulness and resilience guide

Heart centred living book

Authentic leadership training

Personal growth transformation

Mental health and wellbeing

DEDICATION

For anyone who has felt too much, *may you discover it is your gift.*

For those learning to trust your breath, your body, and your story, *may you find ground.*

For every quiet heart who keeps choosing kindness, *may you know your courage.*

And

For you, holding these pages, you are not alone; your tenderness lights the way.

FRONT COVER

Yes, the name has changed, but the invitation is the same. I have kept the original photograph because it still captures the soul of the work: a lone figure at the brink of the known, standing on rough rock with arms open to what is next. In *The Unbound Journey*, that image now appears in black and white. The shift to monochrome is deliberate: without the distraction of colour, the essentials come forward, form, contrast, texture, and truth.

Rock, sea, sky, light, now as tones, not tints.

The weathered outcrop reads as discipline and daily practice; the ocean becomes the field of feeling and possibility; the sky holds spacious awareness; the faint mountains keep purpose on the horizon. In grayscale, each element is distilled to its structure, solid ground beneath, vastness ahead, so you can project your own colours: your lived experience.

An open posture, not a raised fist.

The figure's stance is consent, not conquest: a commitment to meet reality with presence rather than performance. Vulnerability remains the doorway to courage and connection.

The horizon as threshold.

Where sea meets sky you find the line between what has been and what could be, the exact latitude of this program. The black-and-white palette underscores integration: grounding and expansion, emotion and intention, steadiness and vision.

A quiet map of the journey.

- *Breath, Ground, Ease:* feet on rock, lungs open.

- *Identity, Mirror, Heart-voice:* honest pause before the step.

- *Stillness, Reflection:* space that clarifies right action.

- *Homecoming, Invitations to Live:* belonging to self, then to the world.

The cover does not sell a fantasy. It shows a human at a real edge, steady, available, and ready. That is *The Unbound Journey:* a year of small, repeatable practices that let you meet the vastness of your life with your feet on stone and your heart unguarded.

CONTENTS

ACKNOWLEDGMENTS

To every client, participant, reader, and friend, thank you for trusting me with your stories; your courage is the heartbeat of *The Unbound Journey*.

To my family and close friends, your steadiness made this possible.

To mentors, colleagues, and collaborators, your wisdom and craft shaped these pages with care.

To the places and communities that held me, thank you for your quiet teaching, and to you, dear reader, and to the Mystery that moved this work, may these words meet you where you are and guide you home..

WHY THE UNBOUND JOURNEY WAS WRITTEN

Heart Unbound 2.0 emerged from a 30-module emotional-intelligence program developed across 2024-2025 to help people turn inward, heal, learn, and grow, so they can live and lead from authentic heartspace. The intent has always been clear: provide a **robust, legitimate, and credible pathway** for life transformation, not as sentiment, but as disciplined practice.

To strengthen that intent, the program and book were **mapped to nationally recognised Australian frameworks**, including the Australian Qualifications Framework (AQF), Australian Skills Quality Authority (ASQA) guidance, National Safety and Quality Health Service (NSQHS) Standards, and the Australian Public Sector (APS) Capability Framework.

This alignment does not imply endorsement; it ensures that participants are building capabilities consistent with established benchmarks for professional growth and personal mastery, the same qualities sought by leaders, carers, and changemakers across Australia and beyond.

The Unbound Journey was written to take the next essential step: **scholarly validation**. Where *Heart Unbound 2.0* introduces the practices, the companion volume provides the **evidence architecture** that legitimises them for professional and academic audiences to ensure that the program stands up in boardrooms, classrooms, clinics, and peer-review.

What this companion delivers

- **Thirty analytical articles**, one per Heart Unbound chapter, each functioning as a concise social-scientific paper: theory lens, evidence map, practical protocol, and implications.

- **Crosswalks to national capability and quality frameworks**, clarifying how each practice builds assessable competencies.

- **Translates evidence** from neuroscience, psychology, and leadership studies into short, implementable protocols.

- **Legitimises practice** through citations, logic models, and outcome measures suitable for evaluation and publication.

- **Measurement guidance** (recommended psychometrics and optional physiological indices such as HRV), fidelity checklists, and ethically informed, trauma-aware delivery notes.

- **Enables continuous improvement** with light-touch, validated tools (e.g., WHO-5, PANAS, PSS-10; optional HRV).

- **Implementation and evaluation tools**: logic model, outcomes rubrics, data dictionary, and reporting templates to support replication, quality assurance, and peer review.

In short, *The Unbound Journey* exists to **validate, strengthen, and legitimise** *Heart Unbound 2.0*. It equips leaders, educators, clinicians, and researchers with the language, methods, and measures to implement the program with **rigour, replicability, and credibility**, so a heart-led transformation can stand confidently in professional and academic settings.

Welcome to the next chapter of your heart's unfolding.

From my heart to yours,

Dr John McSwiney

THE
UNBOUND
JOURNEY

1 - "Breathing" as the Bridge Between Mind, Body, and Heart: An Integrative Perspective on Self-Regulation and Emotional Intelligence

Rationale for the Article

This article is foundational to *Heart Unbound 2.0* because it provides the **scientific and philosophical grounding** for the programs opening practice, conscious breathing. Transformation cannot begin without safety, presence, and self-regulation; the breath is the most accessible and evidence-based tool to achieve this. By bridging **ancient wisdom and modern neuroscience**, the article validates why breathing is more than relaxation, it is the **physiological gateway to emotional intelligence, resilience, and heart-centred living**. Establishing this rigour at the outset gives participants confidence that the program is both **deeply human and scientifically sound**, creating a strong platform for the self-discovery and leadership development that follow.

Abstract

Breathing is both an automatic physiological process and a conscious practice with profound implications for emotional regulation, resilience, and leadership. Ancient contemplative traditions have long recognised the breath as a pathway to self-awareness and healing, while contemporary neuroscience and psychophysiology confirm its ability to regulate autonomic arousal and build emotional intelligence. This paper critically examines the role of breath as the foundational practice in *Heart Unbound 2.0*, a personal transformation and leadership development program, and synthesises evidence from neurocardiology, vagal tone research, and emotional intelligence frameworks. It argues that conscious breathing is not merely a relaxation technique but an evidence-informed intervention for emotional stability, cognitive clarity, and transformative leadership.

Keywords: breathing, vagus nerve, emotional intelligence, self-regulation, leadership, neurocardiology

Introduction

Breath is lifes most immediate act, yet often goes unnoticed. In ancient traditions such as **prāṇāyāma**, Taoist qìgōng, and Buddhist mindfulness, breath is revered as a bridge between physical survival and spiritual presence (Brown & Gerberg, 2005). In modern society, many individuals habitually engage in shallow, rapid breathing, unconsciously sustaining stress and emotional reactivity (Russo, Santarelli, & O'Rourke, 2017).

Heart Unbound 2.0, an evidence-informed program for personal and organisational transformation, begins with the chapter *"Breathing - The Bridge Between Your Mind, Body and Heart."* This pedagogical choice reflects an emerging consensus: intentional breath regulation is fundamental to psychological resilience, emotional intelligence, and leadership effectiveness.

Neuroscience and Psychophysiology of Breath

Autonomic Regulation and the Parasympathetic Response

Slow, deep breathing (approximately 6–10 breaths per minute) stimulates the **parasympathetic nervous system** via the vagus nerve, counteracting the sympathetic fight-or-flight response. This activation lowers heart rate and blood pressure, reduces cortisol production, and improves **heart rate variability** (HRV), a key biomarker of stress resilience (Porges, 2011; Lehrer & Gevirtz, 2014).

Vagal Tone and Emotional Recovery

The **vagus nerve**, the bodys longest cranial nerve, provides a bidirectional communication pathway between the brain and organs such as the heart and gut. High **vagal tone** correlates with quicker emotional recovery, flexible executive functioning, and prosocial emotional states such as compassion and empathy (Kok & Fredrickson, 2010). Practices that promote vagal stimulation, including diaphragmatic breathing, humming, chanting, and mindfulness, strengthen this adaptability.

Heart–Brain Coherence

Research from neurocardiology demonstrates that rhythmic, diaphragmatic breathing promotes **heart–brain coherence**, a state of smooth, ordered heart rhythm patterns that support clarity, problem solving, and emotional balance (McCraty & Shaffer, 2015). This coherence reflects what *Heart Unbound 2.0* describes as heart intelligence, the alignment of physiology and emotion to enable wise, grounded action.

Breath, Emotional Intelligence, and Leadership

Emotional intelligence (EI) models consistently identify **self-awareness and self-regulation** as core competencies for effective leadership (Goleman, 2021). Conscious breathing trains both by offering a **real-time feedback loop**: noticing breath reveals emotional states, and intentionally shifting breath transforms them (Barrett & Gross, 2001).

In high-stakes leadership environments, such as my own work directing **technical training reform for the Royal Australian Navy**, breath-based practices helped teams remain adaptive and psychologically safe amid change. This aligns with leadership research showing that physiological self-regulation improves empathy, decision-making, and cultural influence (Boyatzis, Smith, & Beveridge, 2013).

Clinical and Wellbeing Outcomes

Breathing-based interventions reduce anxiety, depression, and post-traumatic stress (Seppälä et al., 2014; Hopper, Murray, Ferrara, & Singleton, 2019). Slow, intentional breathing enhances **digestion, detoxification, and cellular oxygenation** while promoting a shift from sympathetic hyperarousal to parasympathetic restoration (Russo et al., 2017). These benefits extend to cognitive performance: breath-anchored mindfulness improves focus, working memory, and emotional stability (Zeidan et al., 2010).

Application in *Heart Unbound 2.0*

The first chapter of *Heart Unbound 2.0* operationalises this evidence by introducing **practical, reflective, and physiological breathing exercises**:

- **Learning objectives** guide participants to understand breath's role in emotional regulation, master heart-centred breathing techniques, and develop sustainable self-soothing rituals.
- Reflection prompts help participants become aware of breath patterns, emotional responses, and subtle somatic shifts.
- Micro-practices such as the *3-Minute Detox & Reset Breath* teach individuals to pause, regulate, and reconnect in real time.

By starting with breath, the program builds the **physiological foundation** for later emotional intelligence and leadership modules.

Implications for Education and Organisational Culture

Integrating conscious breathing into educational and professional contexts can:

- **Reduce burnout and decision fatigue** by improving autonomic recovery.
- **Enhance learning outcomes** by reducing performance anxiety and increasing attentional control.
- **Model emotionally intelligent culture** by equipping leaders to regulate collective stress and respond with presence.

Residential learning environments such as **Mannix College** can particularly benefit: students navigating transition and high cognitive load may find in breathwork a low-cost, high-impact resilience tool.

Conclusion

Breathing is a **neurobiological, psychological, and spiritual anchor**, a unifying practice bridging ancient wisdom and modern science. By centring the *Heart Unbound 2.0* journey on breath awareness and regulation, the program embodies a rigorously evidence-based approach to self-leadership and cultural transformation. In a time of rising stress and complexity, conscious breathing remains one of the most **accessible, scientifically validated, and transformative practices** for individuals and organisations alike.

References

Barrett, L. F., & Gross, J. J. (2001). Emotional intelligence: A process model of emotion representation and regulation. *Cognition & Emotion, 15*(2), 263–299

Boyatzis, R. E., Smith, M. L., & Beveridge, A. J. (2013). Coaching with compassion: Inspiring health, well-being, and development in organizations. *The Journal of Applied Behavioral Science, 49*(2), 153–178.

Brown, R. P., & Gerbarg, P. L. (2005). Sudarshan Kriya yogic breathing in the treatment of stress, anxiety, and depression. *Journal of Alternative and Complementary Medicine, 11*(4), 711–717.

Goleman, D. (2021). *Emotional Intelligence: Why It Can Matter More Than IQ.* Bantam.

Hopper, S. I., Murray, S. L., Ferrara, L. R., & Singleton, J. K. (2019). Effectiveness of diaphragmatic breathing for reducing physiological and psychological stress in adults: A meta-analysis. *Health Psychology Review, 13*(2), 113–132.

Kok, B. E., & Fredrickson, B. L. (2010). Upward spirals of the heart: Autonomic flexibility, vagal tone, and social connectedness. *Biological Psychology, 85*(3), 432–436.

Lehrer, P. M., & Gevirtz, R. (2014). Heart rate variability biofeedback: How and why does it work? *Frontiers in Psychology, 5,* 756.

McCraty, R., & Shaffer, F. (2015). Heart rate variability: New perspectives on physiological mechanisms, assessment of self-regulatory capacity, and health risk. *Frontiers in Psychology, 6,* 86.

Porges, S. W. (2011). *The Polyvagal Theory: Neurophysiological Foundations of Emotions, Attachment, Communication, and Self-Regulation.* Norton.

Russo, M. A., Santarelli, D. M., & O'Rourke, D. (2017). The physiological effects of slow breathing in the healthy human. *Breathe, 13*(4), 298–309.

Seppälä, E. M., Nitschke, J. B., Tudorascu, D. L., Hayes, A., Goldstein, M.

R., Nguyen, D. T., Perlman, D., & Davidson, R. J. (2014). Breathing-based meditation decreases posttraumatic stress disorder symptoms in U.S. military veterans: A randomized controlled longitudinal study. *Journal of Traumatic Stress, 27*(4), 397–405.

Zeidan, F., Johnson, S. K., Diamond, B. J., David, Z., & Goolkasian, P. (2010). Mindfulness meditation improves cognition: Evidence of brief mental training. *Consciousness and Cognition, 19*(2), 597–605.

THE
UNBOUND
JOURNEY

2 - "Gratitude" as a Catalyst for Heart-Led Living

Rationale for the Article

Gratitude is a foundational practice for the *Heart Unbound 2.0* journey because it provides the **emotional and psychological grounding** needed to move from self-awareness into sustained heart-led living. While breathing (Chapter 1) anchors safety and presence, gratitude (Chapter 2) cultivates a positive emotional climate that strengthens resilience, empathy, and authentic connection.

Research across **psychology, neuroscience, and leadership studies** shows that gratitude reshapes the brain's reward and emotional regulation systems (Emmons & McCullough, 2003; Fox et al., 2015), improves mental health and life satisfaction (Wood et al., 2010), and enhances prosocial behaviour and trust in teams (Algoe, 2012). In leadership contexts, gratitude is linked to stronger engagement, reduced burnout, and cultures of psychological safety (Fehr, Fulmer, Awtrey, & Miller, 2017).

By presenting gratitude as both an **ancient spiritual practice** and a **scientifically validated intervention**, this article reinforces the program's integrity, ensuring participants, whether individuals or organisational leaders, understand why gratitude is not just *"feel good,"* but a **strategic capacity for thriving, leading, and transforming culture**.

Abstract

Gratitude is increasingly recognised as a core competency for emotional intelligence, psychological well-being, and effective leadership. While frequently framed as a personal virtue, emerging research demonstrates that gratitude produces measurable neural, physiological, and relational benefits and can transform organisational culture. This article explores gratitude as the second chapter of the *Heart Unbound 2.0* program, situating it within ancient wisdom traditions, contemporary neuroscience, and leadership studies. It argues that gratitude functions not merely as an affective state but as a deliberate, trainable practice that grounds heart-led living, enhances resilience, and fosters compassionate leadership. Practical implications are discussed for individuals and organisations seeking to cultivate gratitude as a strategic and humanising force.

Keywords: gratitude, emotional intelligence, leadership, neuroscience, resilience, Heart Unbound

Introduction

Gratitude has long been celebrated across philosophical and spiritual traditions as a pathway to moral integrity and flourishing (Cicero, trans. 2019). In modern psychology, it is increasingly understood as a powerful driver of well-being, prosocial behaviour, and resilience (Emmons & McCullough, 2003; Wood, Froh, & Geraghty, 2010). For leaders, gratitude is not only personally restorative but socially transformative, shaping trust and engagement within teams (Fehr, Fulmer, Awtrey, & Miller, 2017).

Within *Heart Unbound 2.0*, a 28-part journey into heart-centred living and leadership, gratitude emerges as the essential next step after breathing. Breathing (Chapter 1) cultivates physiological safety and presence; gratitude (Chapter 2) directs that presence toward meaning, appreciation, and positive relational energy. This sequencing reflects evidence that emotional regulation is strengthened when safety precedes reflective appreciation (Siegel, 2020).

Gratitude in Ancient Wisdom Traditions

Ancient thought viewed gratitude as more than politeness. Cicero called it the *"mother of all virtues"* because it recognises goodness and compels reciprocity (Cicero, trans. 2019). In Judeo-Christian spirituality, gratitude shapes prayer, community, and resilience under suffering (Emmons & Stern, 2013). In Islam, *shukr* anchors faith in divine provision and humility (Nasr, 2002). Buddhist practice frames gratitude as awareness of interdependence, softening ego and fostering compassion (Nhat Hanh, 1998). These traditions converge on one theme: gratitude orients the self beyond fear and entitlement toward connection and service.

Neuroscience and Physiology of Gratitude

Contemporary neuroscience validates these ancient intuitions. Functional MRI studies show that gratitude activates the **ventromedial prefrontal cortex, anterior cingulate cortex,** and **limbic structures,** areas associated with reward, moral cognition, and emotional regulation (Fox et al., 2015; Kini et al., 2016). This activation supports neuroplasticity and positive affective states.

Physiologically, gratitude is associated with **parasympathetic nervous system activation,** improved **heart rate variability (HRV),** and lower cortisol (Mills et al., 2015; Kok et al., 2013). Such shifts enhance resilience by reducing allostatic load and increasing capacity to return to calm after stress. These findings align with *Heart Unbound*'s emphasis on heart-brain coherence: intentional gratitude stabilises autonomic rhythms, creating internal safety and clarity.

Gratitude as a Psychological Intervention

Gratitude interventions, journaling, expressive writing, or direct appreciation, have been shown to reduce depressive symptoms and anxiety (Seligman, Steen, Park, & Peterson, 2005), improve sleep quality (Wood et al., 2009), and increase life satisfaction (Emmons & McCullough, 2003). Importantly, gratitude works not by denying hardship but by reframing attention toward what is sustaining. This attentional shift interrupts rumination and promotes adaptive coping (Lambert, Graham, Fincham, & Stillman, 2009).

Heart Unbound 2.0 integrates this evidence through reflective journaling, embodied practices such as *"Heartful Gratitude Moments,"* and presence-based challenges that train the brain to seek what is life-giving even under pressure.

Gratitude in Leadership and Organisational Culture

In leadership studies, gratitude has been linked to enhanced **employee engagement, psychological safety,** and **team performance** (Fehr et al.,

2017; Owens & Hekman, 2016). Leaders who express genuine appreciation foster trust and relational energy, counteracting burnout and cynicism (Cameron, 2012). At the cultural level, gratitude rituals, such as public recognition and shared storytelling, promote belonging and shared purpose.

This resonates strongly with *Heart Unbound 2.0*'s ambition to transform not only individuals but organisational systems. When leaders practise daily gratitude, they model humility and connection, creating climates where people feel valued and inspired.

Application in Heart Unbound 2.0

Turn the chapter into lived practice. Choose one micro-reset for your day and one ritual for your team. Keep it simple, body-first, heart-led.

Rapid resets (60–120 seconds)

- **Coherent Breathing** - Inhale 4–5, exhale 6–8 (≈6 breaths/min). Use before hard conversations, after tough emails, or between meetings to stabilise HRV and mood.

- **5–4–3–2–1 Orientation (eyes open)** - Name 5 things you *see*, 4 you can *touch*, 3 you *hear*, 2 you can *smell*, 1 truth you *know*. Trauma-sensitive, no forced eye closure.

- **Feet–Seat–Breath Scan** - Feel the soles, feel the seat, follow one full breath. Decide only after this scan.

Short daily rituals (3–10 minutes)

- **Nature Micro-Ritual** - Step outside for an "attention reset." Notice sky, ground, air on skin. Barefoot optional. Pair with three slow exhales.

- **Weighted Exhale** - Hands on ribs or belly; lengthen your out-breath till the shoulders drop. Repeat for 8–10 cycles.

- **Grounding Object** - Keep a stone, ring, or mug at your desk. Each touch = one settling breath and the inner cue, *"I'm here."*

Leadership applications

- **Meeting Bookend** - Open with one collective breath; close with one concrete "next step." Keeps bodies present and minds aligned.

- **Embodied Decision Check** - Before approving/declining: Feet–Seat–Breath → *What changes in my body when I choose A vs B?* Note sensation, then act.

- **HRV Micro-Biofeedback (optional)** - 2 minutes of paced breathing with a basic HRV app to train steadiness under pressure.

Guardrails (inclusive, trauma-aware)

- Always opt-in; eyes-open alternatives offered.

- No forced touch or sharing.

- Grounding complements emotion, never bypass it. Make room for what is here.

Sustain & measure (lightweight)

- **Daily tick**: Did I ground before my hardest task? Y/N.

- **Weekly pulse** (1–5): calm, clarity, connection.

- Leaders: notice meeting tone when a 60–120s reset is used vs skipped.

Bottom line: Grounding turns theory into reliable, repeatable regulation, personally restorative and professionally transferable for emerging and senior leaders committed to authentic, values-aligned self-leadership.

Practical Implications for Heart-Led Living

The *Heart Unbound* approach treats gratitude as a **deliberate daily discipline**, not a fleeting feeling. Recommended practices include:

- **Gratitude Journaling:** Recording three specific daily blessings trains attentional bias toward positivity.

- **Heart-Centred Reflection:** Placing a hand on the heart and breathing into appreciation activates parasympathetic calming.

- **Relational Gratitude:** Verbalising appreciation strengthens empathy and social bonds.

- **Leadership Rituals:** Integrating gratitude into team meetings or project milestones reinforces culture.

These methods reflect evidence that consistent micro-practices can rewire neural pathways and reshape emotional climates (Fredrickson, 2013).

Conclusion

Gratitude stands at the intersection of ancient virtue, modern neuroscience, and transformative leadership. As the second step in *Heart Unbound 2.0*, it builds on the safety and presence cultivated through conscious breathing and directs it toward appreciation, empathy, and meaning. For individuals, it fosters emotional intelligence and resilience; for leaders, it becomes a quiet yet powerful strategy to create cultures of trust and hope. In a time of disruption and disconnection, gratitude is not sentimental, it is strategic, evidence-based, and deeply human.

References

Algoe, S. B. (2012). Find, remind, and bind: The functions of gratitude in everyday relationships. *Social and Personality Psychology Compass, 6*(6), 455–469. https://doi.org/10.1111/j.1751-9004.2012.00439.x

Cameron, K. S. (2012). *Positive leadership: Strategies for extraordinary performance.* Berrett-Koehler.

Cicero, M. T. (2019). *On gratitude* (R. Crisp, Trans.). Princeton University Press.

Emmons, R. A., & McCullough, M. E. (2003). Counting blessings versus burdens: An experimental investigation of gratitude and subjective well-being. *Journal of Personality and Social Psychology, 84*(2), 377–389. https://doi.org/10.1037/0022-3514.84.2.377

Emmons, R. A., & Stern, R. (2013). Gratitude as a psychotherapeutic intervention. *Journal of Clinical Psychology, 69*(8), 846–855. https://doi.org/10.1002/jclp.22020

Fehr, R., Fulmer, A., Awtrey, E., & Miller, J. A. (2017). The grateful workplace: A multilevel model of gratitude in organizations. *Academy of Management Review, 42*(2), 361–381. https://doi.org/10.5465/amr.2014.0374

Fox, G. R., Kaplan, J., Damasio, H., & Damasio, A. (2015). Neural correlates of gratitude. *Frontiers in Psychology, 6,* 1491. https://doi.org/10.3389/fpsyg.2015.01491

Fredrickson, B. L. (2013). *Love 2.0: Creating happiness and health in moments of connection.* Plume.

Kini, P., Wong, J., McInnis, S., Gabana, N., & Brown, J. W. (2016). The effects of gratitude expression on neural activity. *Frontiers in Psychology, 7*, 956. https://doi.org/10.3389/fpsyg.2016.00956

Kok, B. E., Coffey, K. A., Cohn, M. A., Catalino, L. I., Vacharkulksemsuk, T., Algoe, S. B., … Fredrickson, B. L. (2013). How positive emotions build physical health: Perceived positive social connections account for the upward spiral between positive emotions and vagal tone. *Psychological Science, 24*(7), 1123–1132. https://doi.org/10.1177/0956797612470827

Lambert, N. M., Graham, S. M., Fincham, F. D., & Stillman, T. F. (2009). A changed perspective: How gratitude can affect relationship maintenance. *Journal of Personality and Social Psychology, 96*(1), 60–78. https://doi.org/10.1037/a0013470

Mills, P. J., Redwine, L., Wilson, K., Pung, M. A., Chinh, K., Greenberg, B. H., … Chopra, D. (2015). The role of gratitude in spiritual well-being in asymptomatic heart failure patients. *Spirituality in Clinical Practice, 2*(1), 5–17. https://doi.org/10.1037/scp0000050

Nasr, S. H. (2002). *The heart of Islam: Enduring values for humanity.* HarperOne.

Nhat Hanh, T. (1998). *Teachings on love.* Parallax Press.

Owens, B. P., & Hekman, D. R. (2016). How does leader humility influence team performance? Exploring the mechanisms of contagion and collective promotion focus. *Academy of Management Journal, 59*(3), 1088–1111. https://doi.org/10.5465/amj.2013.0660

Seligman, M. E. P., Steen, T. A., Park, N., & Peterson, C. (2005). Positive psychology progress: Empirical validation of interventions. *American Psychologist, 60*(5), 410–421. https://doi.org/10.1037/0003-066X.60.5.410

Siegel, D. J. (2020). *The developing mind: How relationships and the brain interact to shape who we are* (3rd ed.). Guilford.

Wood, A. M., Froh, J. J., & Geraghty, A. W. (2010). Gratitude and well-being: A review and theoretical integration. *Clinical Psychology Review, 30*(7), 890–905. https://doi.org/10.1016/j.cpr.2010.03.005

Wood, A. M., Joseph, S., Lloyd, J., & Atkins, S. (2009). Gratitude influences sleep through the mechanism of pre-sleep cognitions. *Journal of Psychosomatic Research, 66*(1), 43–48. https://doi.org/10.1016/j.jpsychores.2008.09.002

THE UNBOUND JOURNEY

3 - "I Am": The Science of Self-Affirmation and Heart-Led Leadership

Rationale for the Article

The *I Am* chapter sits at the heart of **Heart Unbound 2.0 – The Journey Expands**, inviting readers to consciously reclaim and rewrite their inner narrative. Research in psychology and neuroscience demonstrates that **self-affirmation** practices influence brain regions associated with self-processing and emotional regulation (Cascio et al., 2016; Critcher & Dunning, 2015), while leadership literature shows that a strong, authentic sense of identity enhances resilience, empathy, and values-based action (Avolio & Gardner, 2005; Ibarra, 2015).

This article is critical because it provides the **scholarly foundation** for the transformative work in this chapter, bridging ancient spiritual wisdom about "I Am" identity with modern evidence on **neuroplasticity, self-compassion, and adaptive leadership**. By validating the practice of "I am" statements through rigorous, referenced research, the article strengthens the credibility of *Heart Unbound 2.0* as a **professional development and wellbeing resource**. It affirms that cultivating authentic self-identity is not just self-help, it is a scientifically grounded process that improves mental health, emotional intelligence, and heart-led leadership.

Abstract

The capacity to define and affirm one's identity through intentional self-statements, "I am…", is a profound psychological, physiological, and leadership practice. Based in ancient spiritual traditions and validated by modern neuroscience, self-affirmation practices rewire the brain, regulate the nervous system, and cultivate resilience. This article examines the theoretical and empirical foundations underpinning the *I Am* chapter of *Heart Unbound 2.0 – The Journey Expands*, exploring its contribution to self-awareness, emotional regulation, and authentic leadership. By synthesising insights from psychology, neurobiology, and leadership studies, the article positions the *I Am* practice as a core mechanism for heart-led transformation in both personal growth and leadership development.

Keywords: self-affirmation, identity, emotional intelligence, neuroplasticity, heart-led leadership, self-compassion, resilience

Introduction

In an increasingly complex and high-pressure world, many individuals and leaders experience disconnection from their authentic selves (Brown, 2018; Kegan & Lahey, 2016). The *Heart Unbound 2.0* program responds to this challenge by integrating ancient wisdom with contemporary psychological and leadership science to cultivate authenticity, resilience, and emotional intelligence. Chapter Three, **"I Am"**, invites participants to reclaim the narratives they hold about their identity through self-affirmation and heart-led awareness.

This article explores the theoretical and empirical validity of the *I Am* framework, connecting its reflective exercises to the growing body of research on self-affirmation theory, neuroplasticity, emotional regulation, and authentic leadership. The chapter's invitation, to consciously redefine one's self-story, emerges as both timeless and timely.

The Power of "I Am" Across Cultures and Traditions

The phrase "I Am" is deeply embedded in human spiritual and cultural history. In the **Hebrew Bible**, God names Himself "I AM WHO I AM" (Exodus 3:14), symbolising eternal presence and identity. **Eastern traditions** such as Hinduism use affirmations like *Aham Brahmasmi* ("I am Brahman") to express unity with divine consciousness (Radhakrishnan, 1990). In **Sufi mysticism**, the statement "Ana al-Haqq" ("I am the Truth") expresses transcendent union with the Divine (Nasr, 2007). Even in ancient **Egyptian**

texts, affirmations such as "I am yesterday, today, and tomorrow" anchored identity to timeless wisdom (Assmann, 2001).

These traditions frame *I Am* as more than personal affirmation; it is a spiritual practice of presence, truth, and belonging. *Heart Unbound 2.0* translates this ancient insight into a contemporary, emotionally intelligent approach to self-identity and healing.

Self-Affirmation Theory: Psychological Foundations

Self-affirmation theory (Steele, 1988) proposes that individuals are motivated to maintain a sense of self-integrity and adapt better when their core values are affirmed. Experimental studies demonstrate that self-affirmation reduces defensiveness, improves problem-solving under stress, and buffers against threats to self-concept (Sherman & Cohen, 2006). For example, Creswell et al. (2005) found that self-affirmed participants showed lower cortisol responses to stress tasks.

Practising *I Am* statements such as "I am worthy of love" or "I am resilient" functions as an intentional self-affirmation, allowing participants to confront fear and reframe limiting beliefs. This shift nurtures **self-compassion** (Neff, 2003), enabling individuals to respond to setbacks with understanding rather than self-criticism.

Neuroplasticity and the Brain's Response to Affirmation

Neuroscience confirms that the brain is malleable; repeated thought patterns can change neural wiring (Davidson & McEwen, 2012). Self-affirmation activates the **ventromedial prefrontal cortex (vmPFC)**, a region involved in self-referential processing, reward, and positive valuation (Falk et al., 2015). This activation creates new, adaptive pathways that replace shame and fear-driven narratives.

Balanced heart-focused breathing, introduced earlier in *Heart Unbound*, complements this by calming the autonomic nervous system and stimulating the vagus nerve (Porges, 2011). Together, these practices create the physiological conditions for identity transformation: safety, self-compassion, and open-hearted presence.

Emotional Intelligence and Identity Work

Emotional intelligence (EI) is widely recognised as essential for wellbeing and leadership (Goleman, 1995; Mayer et al., 2016). The *I Am* chapter cultivates the **core EI domains**:

- **Self-awareness:** noticing and naming internal experience with clarity.
- **Self-regulation:** responding with intentional calm rather than reactive impulse.
- **Motivation:** aligning with intrinsic, heart-led purpose.
- **Empathy and self-compassion:** offering kindness to oneself and others.
- **Relationship management:** building authenticity and trust through honest self-expression.

By shifting inner narratives from self-criticism to heart-led affirmation, participants increase resilience and relational intelligence, skills critical to both personal growth and leadership effectiveness.

Leadership Implications: Authenticity, Resilience, and Impact

Modern leadership research emphasises **authenticity** as a driver of trust, engagement, and sustainable performance (Avolio & Gardner, 2005; George, 2015). Leaders who understand and articulate their core identity are better equipped to navigate ambiguity, inspire teams, and foster psychological safety.

The *I Am* practice acts as an identity anchor for leaders. By affirming values and worth, leaders build inner stability and courage. Neuroplasticity supports this process: intentional self-affirmations create durable shifts that help leaders remain centred under pressure (Boyatzis et al., 2015). Furthermore, emotionally intelligent leaders, those able to regulate their own emotions and model vulnerability, are associated with higher organisational trust and innovation (Cherniss & Goleman, 2001).

Application in Heart Unbound 2.0

The *I Am* chapter integrates theory into accessible, heart-led practice:

- **Mirror Work & Voice Activation:** participants speak affirmations aloud while connecting physically to the heart space.

- **Identity Journaling:** uncovering and rewriting limiting self-beliefs.

- **Daily Affirmation Rituals:** cultivating neural and emotional resilience through repetition.

- **Leadership Alignment:** translating self-affirmation into values-driven action.

The program's design ensures these practices are both personally healing and professionally transformative, applicable to emerging leaders, seasoned executives, and anyone seeking authentic self-leadership.

Discussion

Bridging spiritual wisdom, psychological science, and leadership development, *I Am* offers a profound mechanism for change. Its impact is twofold: it **heals internal narratives** fractured by fear, trauma, or external expectation; and it **equips leaders** to show up authentically in complex, high-stakes environments. This integration of heart and evidence is rare in leadership and wellbeing programs, making *Heart Unbound 2.0* a distinctive contribution to transformative education.

Conclusion

The *I Am* practice is far more than positive self-talk; it is a rigorously supported pathway to self-integration, resilience, and heart-centred leadership. Drawing from spiritual heritage, psychological research, and neurobiology, *Heart Unbound 2.0* provides an actionable, credible framework for identity transformation. For individuals and leaders alike, reclaiming one's "I Am" is a vital step in living and leading with authenticity, courage, and compassion.

References

Assmann, J. (2001). *The search for God in ancient Egypt*. Cornell University Press.

Avolio, B. J., & Gardner, W. L. (2005). Authentic leadership development: Getting to the root of positive forms of leadership. *The Leadership Quarterly, 16*(3), 315–338. https://doi.org/10.1016/j.leaqua.2005.03.001

Boyatzis, R. E., Rochford, K., & Taylor, S. N. (2015). The role of emotional and social intelligence competencies in leadership effectiveness. *Journal of Management Development, 34*(9), 822–836. https://doi.org/10.1108/JMD-02-2014-0023

Brown, B. (2018). *Dare to lead: Brave work. Tough conversations. Whole hearts.* Random House.

Cherniss, C., & Goleman, D. (2001). *The emotionally intelligent workplace: How to select for, measure, and improve emotional intelligence in individuals, groups, and organizations.* Jossey-Bass.

Creswell, J. D., Welch, W. T., Taylor, S. E., Sherman, D. K., Gruenewald, T. L., & Mann, T. (2005). Affirmation of personal values buffers neuroendocrine and psychological stress responses. *Psychological Science, 16*(11), 846–851. https://doi.org/10.1111/j.1467-9280.2005.01624.x

Davidson, R. J., & McEwen, B. S. (2012). Social influences on neuroplasticity: Stress and interventions to promote well-being. *Nature Neuroscience, 15*(5), 689–695. https://doi.org/10.1038/nn.3093

Falk, E. B., O'Donnell, M. B., Cascio, C. N., Tinney, F., Kang, Y., Lieberman, M. D., & Taylor, S. E. (2015). Self-affirmation alters the brain's response to health messages and subsequent behavior change. *Proceedings of the National Academy of Sciences, 112*(7), 1977–1982. https://doi.org/10.1073/pnas.1500247112

George, B. (2015). *Discover your true north*. Wiley

Goleman, D. (1995). *Emotional intelligence: Why it can matter more than IQ.* Bantam Books.

Kegan, R., & Lahey, L. L. (2016). *An everyone culture: Becoming a deliberately developmental organization.* Harvard Business Review Press.

Mayer, J. D., Salovey, P., & Caruso, D. R. (2016). The ability model of emotional intelligence: Principles and updates. *Emotion Review, 8*(4), 290–300. https://doi.org/10.1177/1754073916639667

Nasr, S. H. (2007). *The garden of truth: The vision and promise of Sufism, Islam's mystical tradition.* HarperOne.

Neff, K. D. (2003). Self-compassion: An alternative conceptualization of a healthy attitude toward oneself. *Self and Identity, 2*(2), 85–101. https://doi.org/10.1080/15298860309032

Porges, S. W. (2011). *The polyvagal theory: Neurophysiological foundations of emotions, attachment, communication, and self-regulation.* W. W. Norton & Company.

Sherman, D. K., & Cohen, G. L. (2006). The psychology of self-defense: Self-affirmation theory. *Advances in Experimental Social Psychology, 38,* 183–242. https://doi.org/10.1016/S0065-2601(06)38004-5

Steele, C. M. (1988). The psychology of self-affirmation: Sustaining the integrity of the self. *Advances in Experimental Social Psychology, 21,* 261–302. https://doi.org/10.1016/S0065-2601(08)60229-4

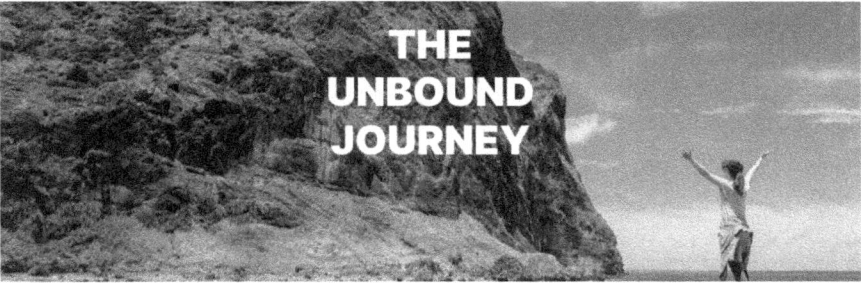

4 - "Meditation" as a Catalyst for Emotional Intelligence and Heart-Led Leadership: An Integrative Review

---

Rationale for the Article

The *Meditation* chapter is central to *Heart Unbound 2.0* because it provides the psychological, physiological, and leadership-based grounding that transforms meditation from a wellness trend into an evidence-informed practice for emotional intelligence and heart-led living. By synthesising ancient contemplative traditions with modern neuroscience and organisational psychology, this article validates meditation as a tool that improves self-awareness, emotional regulation, resilience, and compassionate leadership, skills essential for thriving in complex personal and professional environments. Establishing this scholarly foundation strengthens the program's credibility, supports its alignment with leadership development and wellbeing frameworks, and empowers participants to engage in meditation with confidence, knowing it is both timeless and scientifically robust.

Abstract

Meditation has shifted from an esoteric spiritual practice to a mainstream, evidence-based intervention supporting psychological health, physiological resilience, and adaptive leadership. This article critically examines meditation through the lens of *Heart Unbound 2.0 – The Journey Expands*, validating its inclusion as a foundational chapter for cultivating emotional intelligence (EI) and heart-led living. Integrating historical contemplative traditions with contemporary neuroscience, psychophysiology, and leadership studies, we demonstrate how meditation enhances self-awareness, self-regulation, empathy, and social connectedness while improving cardiovascular health and stress adaptation. Implications are offered for personal transformation and leadership development programs.

Keywords: meditation, emotional intelligence, neuroplasticity, heart-led leadership, mindfulness, psychophysiology

Introduction

The *Heart Unbound 2.0* program positions meditation as a core competency for cultivating presence, resilience, and authentic leadership. While meditation has ancient spiritual roots, modern psychological and physiological evidence now substantiates its role in mental health (Keng et al., 2011), stress reduction (Goyal et al., 2014), and leadership effectiveness (Reitz et al., 2020). This article validates the inclusion of meditation within a transformational framework, connecting its historical context to current empirical findings and demonstrating its relevance for individuals seeking heart-centred personal growth and leadership impact.

Historical and Spiritual Roots of Meditation

Meditation appears across global traditions as a method of cultivating presence and transcending ego.

- **Hinduism:** Dhyāna, described in the Upanishads and integrated into Rāja Yoga, emphasises stilling the mind to realise Atman as one with Brahman (Feuerstein, 2013).

- **Buddhism:** Vipassanā and Samatha practices develop mindful awareness and compassion, core to the Eightfold Path (Analayo, 2010).

- **Taoism:** Taoist meditation encourages alignment with the Tao, cultivating softness and effortless action (wu wei) (Kohn, 2008).

- **Christianity:** Contemplative prayer and lectio divina invite surrender and divine presence (Keating, 2009).

- **Modern mindfulness:** Jon Kabat-Zinn's Mindfulness-Based Stress Reduction (MBSR) adapted these ancient principles to clinical and organisational contexts (Kabat-Zinn, 2013).

These traditions converge on a single insight: presence transforms the inner life and supports ethical, compassionate action.

Psychological Foundations: Self-Awareness and Self-Regulation

Meditation enhances key EI capacities (Goleman, 1995; Schutte & Malouff, 2011). Regular practice develops **meta-awareness**, the ability to notice thoughts and emotions without fusing with them (Brown et al., 2007). Mindfulness interventions reduce rumination, anxiety, and depressive symptoms while improving emotion regulation (Hölzel et al., 2011).

Self-affirmation models also intersect with meditative presence. Affirmations practiced within meditation activate the ventromedial prefrontal cortex, reinforcing positive self-concepts and buffering stress (Cascio et al., 2016). This supports *Heart Unbound 2.0's* aim to help participants replace self-criticism with self-compassion and resilience.

Physiological Benefits: The Brain–Heart Connection

Meditation positively influences autonomic balance by enhancing parasympathetic activity and improving heart rate variability (HRV), a marker of stress resilience and cardiovascular health (Thayer et al., 2012). Meta-analytic evidence shows mindfulness and loving-kindness meditation reduce blood pressure and cortisol (Pascoe et al., 2017).

Functional neuroimaging studies show decreased amygdala reactivity and strengthened prefrontal regulation during mindfulness practice (Hölzel et al., 2011; Tang et al., 2015). These neural changes underpin calmer responses under pressure, critical for leadership and wellbeing.

Meditation and Empathy-Centred Leadership

Heart-centred leadership requires attunement to self and others. Meditation, particularly compassion-focused forms, activates neural circuits supporting empathy (anterior insula, anterior cingulate cortex) and increases prosocial behaviour (Lutz et al., 2008; Weng et al., 2013).

In organisational studies, leaders engaging in mindfulness report greater emotional regulation, authentic presence, and ethical decision-making (Reitz et al., 2020). Such findings validate *Heart Unbound 2.0's* use of meditation as a leadership capability builder, not merely a stress-management tool.

Practical Application Within Heart Unbound 2.0

This chapter equips participants with accessible practices: breath-anchored mindfulness, loving-kindness meditation, and movement-based options (e.g., walking meditation) to suit different temperaments. Emphasis is placed on:

- **Self-awareness:** noticing thought/emotion patterns.

- **Self-regulation:** responding rather than reacting.

- **Empathy & social connection:** fostering compassionate presence.

- **Resilience:** engaging the parasympathetic nervous system to recover from stress.

Such tailoring reflects current best practice in program design, which emphasises individual fit and sustained habit formation (Creswell, 2017).

Implications for Leadership and Organisational Culture

Organisations adopting meditation as part of leadership and culture transformation can expect improvements in psychological safety, relational trust, and adaptive decision-making (Good et al., 2016). Embedding meditative practice within *Heart Unbound 2.0* aligns with emotional intelligence frameworks and modern leadership development models that emphasise presence, authenticity, and compassion under complexity.

Conclusion

Meditation is far more than a personal wellness tool; it is a scientifically validated pathway to self-awareness, emotional regulation, empathy, and resilient leadership. By integrating ancient wisdom with rigorous psychological and physiological research, *Heart Unbound 2.0* offers participants a credible, transformative approach to living and leading from the heart.

References

Analayo, B. (2010). *Satipatthana: The direct path to realization*. Windhorse Publications.

Brown, K. W., Ryan, R. M., & Creswell, J. D. (2007). Mindfulness: Theoretical foundations and evidence for its salutary effects. *Psychological Inquiry, 18*(4), 211–237. https://doi.org/10.1080/10478400701598298

Cascio, C. N., et al. (2016). Self-affirmation activates brain systems supporting self-related processing and reward. *Social Cognitive and Affective Neuroscience, 11*(4), 621–629. https://doi.org/10.1093/scan/nsv136

Creswell, J. D. (2017). Mindfulness interventions. *Annual Review of Psychology, 68*, 491–516. https://doi.org/10.1146/annurev-psych-042716-051139

Feuerstein, G. (2013). *The yoga tradition: Its history, literature, philosophy and practice*. Hohm Press.

Goleman, D. (1995). *Emotional intelligence: Why it can matter more than IQ*. Bantam Books.

Good, D. J., et al. (2016). Contemplating mindfulness at work: An integrative review. *Journal of Management, 42*(1), 114–142. https://doi.org/10.1177/0149206315617003

Goyal, M., et al. (2014). Meditation programs for psychological stress and well-being: A systematic review and meta-analysis. *JAMA Internal Medicine, 174*(3), 357–368. https://doi.org/10.1001/jamainternmed.2013.13018

Hölzel, B. K., et al. (2011). Mindfulness practice leads to increases in regional brain gray matter density. *Psychiatry Research: Neuroimaging, 191*(1), 36–43. https://doi.org/10.1016/j.pscychresns.2010.08.006

Kabat-Zinn, J. (2013). *Full catastrophe living* (2nd ed.). Bantam Books.

Keating, T. (2009). *Open mind, open heart*. Continuum.

Keng, S. L., Smoski, M. J., & Robins, C. J. (2011). Effects of mindfulness on psychological health: A review. *Clinical Psychology Review, 31*(6), 1041–1056. https://doi.org/10.1016/j.cpr.2011.04.006

Kohn, L. (2008). *Chinese healing exercises: The tradition of daoyin*. University of Hawai'i Press.

Lutz, A., et al. (2008). Regulation of the neural circuitry of emotion by compassion meditation: Effects of meditative expertise. *PLoS ONE, 3*(3), e1897. https://doi.org/10.1371/journal.pone.0001897

Pascoe, M. C., et al. (2017). Mindfulness mediates the physiological markers of stress: A meta-analysis. *Psychoneuroendocrinology, 82*, 57–68. https://doi.org/10.1016/j.psyneuen.2017.05.003

Reitz, M., Chaskalson, M., & Waller, L. (2020). Mindful leadership: A review of theory and practice. *Leadership & Organization Development Journal, 41*(6), 741–757. https://doi.org/10.1108/LODJ-11-2019-0485

Schutte, N. S., & Malouff, J. M. (2011). Emotional intelligence mediates the relationship between mindfulness and subjective well-being. *Personality and Individual Differences, 50*(7), 1116–1119. https://doi.org/10.1016/j.paid.2011.01.037

Tang, Y. Y., et al. (2015). The neuroscience of mindfulness meditation. *Nature Reviews Neuroscience, 16*(4), 213–225. https://doi.org/10.1038/nrn3916

Thayer, J. F., Åhs, F., Fredrikson, M., Sollers, J. J., & Wager, T. D. (2012). A meta-analysis of heart rate variability and neuroimaging studies: Implications for HRV as a marker of stress and health. *Neuroscience & Biobehavioral Reviews, 36*(2), 747–756. https://doi.org/10.1016/j.neubiorev.2011.11.009

Weng, H. Y., et al. (2013). Compassion training alters altruism and neural responses to suffering. *Psychological Science, 24*(7), 1171–1180. https://doi.org/10.1177/0956797612469537

5 - "Mirror" Work and the Science of Seeing the Self: Psychological, Physiological, and Leadership Bases for the Mirror

---

Rationale for the Article

Mirror operationalises the program's promise to move from insight to embodiment. It translates robust mechanisms, self-affirmation, reappraisal, compassion, and paced exposure, into a brief, repeatable ritual that increases self-awareness, steadies the nervous system, and reduces defensive reactivity. These outcomes directly support heart-led leadership and psychologically safe cultures. By grounding a simple daily practice in rigorous science, the chapter strengthens the integrity, credibility, and impact of *Heart Unbound 2.0* for individuals and organisations alike.

Abstract

"Mirror work", the intentional practice of meeting one's gaze and speaking with accuracy, kindness, and commitment, features in Chapter 5 (*Mirror*) of *Heart Unbound 2.0*. This article examines its plausibility and utility through convergent evidence from psychology (self-affirmation, cognitive reappraisal, self-compassion, exposure and inhibitory learning), psychophysiology (autonomic balance and heart–brain pathways), and leadership science (authentic and values-based leadership, psychological safety). Empirical findings indicate that practices closely aligned with mirror work can reduce defensiveness, reshape maladaptive self-narratives, increase self-compassion, and improve emotion regulation, capacities associated with resilient, trustworthy leadership. Neural and physiological studies implicate the ventromedial prefrontal cortex (vmPFC), insula, amygdala, and heart-rate variability (HRV) in these changes. We outline an evidence-informed protocol for *Heart Unbound 2.0*, note limitations, and propose research directions. Taken together, mirror work is theoretically coherent, ethically practicable, and organisationally relevant when delivered with adequate safeguards.

Keywords: mirror work, self-affirmation, self-compassion, emotion regulation, heart-rate variability, authentic leadership, psychological safety

Introduction

Chapter 5 of *Heart Unbound 2.0* invites participants to "face themselves with love." While the modality is simple, eye contact with one's reflection paired with truthful statements, the mechanisms are multi-determinant. The practice intersects with self-affirmation theory (Steele, 1988), cognitive change processes (Beck, 1979; Gross, 2015), compassion-based interventions (Neff, 2003; Gilbert, 2009), and exposure/inhibitory learning (Craske et al., 2014). Its promised outcomes, greater self-awareness, emotional steadiness, and kinder inner dialogue, are core to emotional intelligence (Mayer et al., 2016) and to contemporary leadership effectiveness (Avolio & Gardner, 2005; Edmondson, 2018). This article synthesises the most relevant evidence to validate the chapter's claims and to situate mirror work within a rigorous, ethically sound framework.

Conceptualising "Mirror Work"

Contemporary mirror work popularised by Hay (1984) involves intentional eye-gazing and affirming self-statements. In research terms, it is best framed as a *compound intervention* comprising:

1. **Self-affirmation** (values-consistent statements),
2. **Cognitive reappraisal** (updating appraisals of self and events),
3. **Compassion practices** (warmth toward self), and

4. **Graduated exposure** to self-focused cues (face, eyes, voice) that may evoke shame or avoidance. This composite view enables alignment with tested mechanisms rather than relying on intuition alone.

Psychological Mechanisms

1. Self-affirmation and identity integrity

Self-affirmation theory proposes that affirming personally important values maintains self-integrity and reduces threat-based defensiveness (Steele, 1988; Sherman & Cohen, 2006). Laboratory and field studies show improved problem-solving under stress and greater receptivity to feedback following self-affirmation (Creswell et al., 2005). Neuroimaging demonstrates vmPFC activation during affirmation, a hub for self-relevance and valuation (Cascio et al., 2016). When mirror work uses truthful, values-anchored statements ("I am committed to…", "I choose…"), it likely recruits the same circuitry.

2. Cognitive reappraisal and negative self-talk

Cognitive therapy established that identifying and restructuring maladaptive self-statements reduces distress (Beck, 1979). Reappraisal, a cornerstone of emotion regulation, reliably decreases negative affect and amygdala reactivity while engaging prefrontal control regions (Gross, 2015). Speaking revised statements while *seeing* oneself can increase salience and memory consolidation of the new appraisal.

3. Self-compassion and shame resilience

Self-compassion, mindfulness, common humanity, and self-kindness, buffers shame and predicts well-being (Neff, 2003; Neff & Germer, 2013). Compassion-focused therapy similarly targets self-criticism as a threat-focused strategy (Gilbert, 2009). Eye-contact with one's own image can initially heighten shame; when paired with kind language and paced exposure, it cultivates "caring motivation" toward the self.

4. Exposure and inhibitory learning

Mirror-based exposure is used in body-image treatment: systematic mirror viewing decreases avoidance, reduces distress, and improves body satisfaction (Delinsky & Wilson, 2006; Jarry & Ip, 2005). The mechanism is *inhibitory learning*: new, non-fearful associations compete with older threat memories (Craske et al., 2014). For many leaders and professionals, the "feared stimulus" is not the body but *the evaluative gaze*, including one's own.

Mirror work operationalises graded, supported contact with that stimulus.

Neurobiological and Physiological Correlates

Heart–brain pathways and autonomic regulation

Practices that combine breath, attention, and soothing self-talk increase parasympathetic tone and HRV, a biomarker of flexible emotion regulation and cardiovascular health (Thayer et al., 2012). Polyvagal theory highlights how cues of warmth and safety down-shift defensive states and support social engagement (Porges, 2011). If mirror work is delivered with slow breathing and kind prosody, it plausibly engages these pathways.

Neural systems for self and emotion

Self-referential processing involves medial prefrontal cortex networks (Northoff et al., 2006). Interoceptive and affective awareness rely on anterior insula and anterior cingulate (Craig, 2009). Compassion meditation alters activity in overlapping regions and reduces amygdala reactivity (Lutz et al., 2008; Weng et al., 2013). These findings explain why repeated, warm self-address may gradually "quiet" threat circuits and strengthen regulatory control.

Evidence From Adjacent Interventions

- **Affirmation studies:** Reduced cortisol and improved performance under stress (Creswell et al., 2005); vmPFC engagement (Cascio et al., 2016).

- **Body-image mirror exposure:** Decreases body dissatisfaction and avoidance (Delinsky & Wilson, 2006; Jarry & Ip, 2005).

- **Self-compassion training:** Increases well-being and reduces self-criticism (Neff & Germer, 2013).

- **Mindfulness/compassion practices:** Structural and functional changes in regions linked to attention and emotion (Hölzel et al., 2011; Tang et al., 2015). While direct randomised trials of "mirror work" per se are sparse, these converging findings support the constituent processes *Heart Unbound 2.0* deploys.

Relevance for Leadership and Culture

<u>Authentic and values-based leadership</u>

Authentic leadership predicts trust, engagement, and ethical action (Avolio & Gardner, 2005; George, 2015). Identity work, examining who I am, what I value, and how I show up, is central to sustaining authenticity amid pressure (Ibarra, 2015). Mirror work is a structured micro-practice for daily identity work, reinforcing coherence between espoused and enacted values.

<u>Psychological safety and relational presence</u>

Teams thrive when interpersonal risk-taking is safe (Edmondson, 2018). Leaders who regulate threat responses and model compassionate candor foster that safety. By reducing self-criticism and defensive reactivity, mirror work supports the relational behaviors, listening, owning impact, repairing ruptures, that build high-trust climates.

An Evidence-Informed Protocol for *Heart Unbound 2.0*

1. **Preparation (2–3 min):** Slow nasal breathing (e.g., 4–6 breaths/min) to prime parasympathetic tone.

2. **Gaze & Ground (30–60 s):** Soft eye-contact with one's reflection; hand over heart to supply a safety cue.

3. **Truthful Statements (2–3 min):** One values-anchored affirmation (self-affirmation), one reappraisal (updating a frequent self-criticism), one compassion phrase (e.g., "May I be kind to myself"). All stated *accurately* and *specifically*.

4. **Reflect (1–2 min):** Noting sensations/emotions without judgment (mindful meta-awareness).

5. **Close & Record (1 min):** Brief journaling of the statement that felt most *true*; commit to one aligned behavior (identity-consistent action). **Cadence:** 5–8 minutes, 5 days/week for 4–8 weeks. **Safeguards:** Offer alternatives (eyes-closed imagery) for participants with trauma histories; integrate referral pathways; never force prolonged eye-contact.

Limitations and Ethical Considerations

Evidence is indirect; rigorous RCTs on composite mirror work in diverse samples are needed. Individuals with acute trauma, eating disorders, or severe self-criticism may require clinician-guided protocols (Craske et al., 2014). Programs should avoid overstating claims, maintain voluntary participation, and embed practices within broader psychological safety and wellbeing strategies.

Conclusion

Mirror work, when defined as a structured blend of self-affirmation, reappraisal, compassion, and paced exposure, rests on robust psychological and physiological mechanisms and aligns with the leadership capabilities *Heart Unbound 2.0* seeks to cultivate. Practiced ethically, it helps participants replace harsh self-narratives with accurate, values-anchored identities, improves emotion regulation, and strengthens the relational presence required for trustworthy, heart-led leadership.

References

Avolio, B. J., & Gardner, W. L. (2005). Authentic leadership development: Getting to the root of positive forms of leadership. *The Leadership Quarterly, 16*(3), 315–338. https://doi.org/10.1016/j.leaqua.2005.03.001

Beck, A. T. (1979). *Cognitive therapy of depression.* Guilford.

Cascio, C. N., O'Donnell, M. B., Tinney, F., Lieberman, M. D., Taylor, S. E., Strecher, V., & Falk, E. B. (2016). Self-affirmation activates brain systems supporting self-related processing and reward. *Social Cognitive and Affective Neuroscience, 11*(4), 621–629. https://doi.org/10.1093/scan/nsv136

Craig, A. D. (2009). How do you feel—now? The anterior insula and human awareness. *Nature Reviews Neuroscience, 10*(1), 59–70. https://doi.org/10.1038/nrn2555

Craske, M. G., Treanor, M., Conway, C. C., Zbozinek, T., & Vervliet, B. (2014). Maximizing exposure therapy: An inhibitory learning approach. *Behaviour Research and Therapy, 58*, 10–23. https://doi.org/10.1016/j.brat.2014.04.006

Creswell, J. D., Welch, W. T., Taylor, S. E., Sherman, D. K., Gruenewald, T.

L., & Mann, T. (2005). Affirmation of personal values buffers neuroendocrine and psychological stress responses. *Psychological Science, 16*(11), 846–851. https://doi.org/10.1111/j.1467-9280.2005.01624.x

Delinsky, S. S., & Wilson, G. T. (2006). Mirror exposure for the treatment of body image disturbance. *International Journal of Eating Disorders, 39*(2), 108–116. https://doi.org/10.1002/eat.20207

Edmondson, A. C. (2018). *The fearless organization: Creating psychological safety in the workplace for learning, innovation, and growth.* Wiley.

George, B. (2015). *Discover your true north* (Extended ed.). Wiley.

Gilbert, P. (2009). *The compassionate mind.* Constable.

Gross, J. J. (2015). Emotion regulation: Current status and future prospects. *Psychological Inquiry, 26*(1), 1–26. https://doi.org/10.1080/1047840X.2014.940781

Hay, L. (1984). *You can heal your life.* Hay House.

Hölzel, B. K., Lazar, S. W., Gard, T., Schuman-Olivier, Z., Vago, D. R., & Ott, U. (2011). How does mindfulness meditation work? Proposing mechanisms of action from a conceptual and neural perspective. *Perspectives on Psychological Science, 6*(6), 537–559. https://doi.org/10.1177/1745691611419671

Ibarra, H. (2015). *Act like a leader, think like a leader.* Harvard Business Review Press.

Jarry, J. L., & Ip, K. (2005). The effectiveness of a stand-alone body-image cognitive dissonance intervention. *Body Image, 2*(4), 363–370. https://doi.org/10.1016/j.bodyim.2005.08.001

Mayer, J. D., Salovey, P., & Caruso, D. R. (2016). The ability model of emotional intelligence: Principles and updates. *Emotion Review, 8*(4), 290–300. https://doi.org/10.1177/1754073916639667

Neff, K. D. (2003). Self-compassion: An alternative conceptualization of a healthy attitude toward oneself. *Self and Identity, 2*(2), 85–101. https://doi.org/10.1080/15298860309032

Neff, K. D., & Germer, C. K. (2013). A pilot study and randomized controlled trial of the Mindful Self-Compassion program. *Journal of Clinical Psychology, 69*(1), 28–44. https://doi.org/10.1002/jclp.21923

Northoff, G., Heinzel, A., de Greck, M., Bermpohl, F., Dobrowolny, H., &

Panksepp, J. (2006). Self-referential processing in our brain—A meta-analysis of imaging studies on the self. *NeuroImage, 31*(1), 440–457. https://doi.org/10.1016/j.neuroimage.2005.12.002

Porges, S. W. (2011). *The polyvagal theory: Neurophysiological foundations of emotions, attachment, communication, and self-regulation.* Norton.

Sherman, D. K., & Cohen, G. L. (2006). The psychology of self-defense: Self-affirmation theory. *Advances in Experimental Social Psychology, 38*, 183–242. https://doi.org/10.1016/S0065-2601(06)38004-5

Steele, C. M. (1988). The psychology of self-affirmation: Sustaining the integrity of the self. *Advances in Experimental Social Psychology, 21*, 261–302. https://doi.org/10.1016/S0065-2601(08)60229-4

Tang, Y.-Y., Hölzel, B. K., & Posner, M. I. (2015). The neuroscience of mindfulness meditation. *Nature Reviews Neuroscience, 16*(4), 213–225. https://doi.org/10.1038/nrn3916

Thayer, J. F., Åhs, F., Fredrikson, M., Sollers, J. J., & Wager, T. D. (2012). A meta-analysis of heart rate variability and neuroimaging studies: Implications for HRV as a marker of stress and health. *Neuroscience & Biobehavioral Reviews, 36*(2), 747–756. https://doi.org/10.1016/j.neubiorev.2011.11.009

Weng, H. Y., Fox, A. S., Shackman, A. J., et al. (2013). Compassion training alters altruism and neural responses to suffering. *Psychological Science, 24*(7), 1171–1180. https://doi.org/10.1177/0956797612469537

THE
UNBOUND
JOURNEY

6 - "Dance" as Emotion in Motion: Validating Dance

Rationale for the Article

In *Heart Unbound 2.0*, Dance is not decoration, it is a simple, repeatable way to help the body lead the mind back to balance. The article translates clear evidence from neuroscience, psychology, and dance-movement therapy into everyday practice: brief, rhythmic movement down-regulates stress, improves heart-rate variability, lifts mood, and widens the bandwidth for thinking and feeling. We keep it practical. Participants are invited into short 90–180-second movement bursts with clear pacing and safety cues so facilitators can deliver the practice consistently while everyone keeps full choice and agency.

Leadership programs often ignore the body, we make Dance directly useful at work. Micro-rituals, before a meeting, between agenda items, after a tough conversation, teach attunement, co-regulation, empathy, and even gentle repair. The practice is accessible by design: no gear, no choreography, and body-inclusive options (standing, seated, or subtle/silent variants) that fit any culture and any level, from emerging talent to the C-suite.

Psychological safety is non-negotiable. Participation is opt-in, there's no forced touch or being "on show," and everyone is encouraged to stay within their window of tolerance. To keep the practice honest and improvable, we use light check-ins and validated scales (e.g., PANAS, WHO-5, PSS-10, quick psychological-safety pulses; optional HRV in pilots) so teams can see and iterate on real outcomes.

Finally, we make it stick. Simple habit loops, cue → 90–180 seconds of movement → notice the shift, embed Dance into busy, hybrid schedules. The practice also weaves naturally with earlier modules (Breathing, Gratitude, I Am, Meditation), turning insight into embodied action. In short, this article gives the program a rigorous, humane, and measurable pathway to convert movement into everyday emotional intelligence, for personal regulation and collective cohesion.

Abstract

Dance is a universal, embodied practice that integrates emotion, physiology, and social connection. This article evaluates and extends Chapter 6 ("Dance") of *Heart Unbound 2.0* by synthesising evidence from psychology, neuroscience, physiology, and leadership studies. We review meta-analytic findings on dance/movement therapy (DMT), mechanisms linking movement with affect regulation (polyvagal theory, interoception, heart-rate variability), and social/reward processes (synchrony, endorphins, mirror-neuron systems). We then translate these mechanisms into practical, low-barrier micro-practices for personal wellbeing and heart-led leadership. Evidence indicates that dance reliably improves mood, reduces depression and anxiety, enhances social bonding, increases parasympathetic tone, and supports executive function and adaptive leadership behaviors. We conclude that structured and improvisational dance practices constitute a rigorous, evidence-informed pathway for developing emotional intelligence, resilience, and relational capacity, core aims of *Heart Unbound 2.0*.

Keywords: dance, embodiment, emotional regulation, polyvagal theory, synchrony, leadership, heart-rate variability, dance/movement therapy

Introduction

The "Dance" chapter of *Heart Unbound 2.0* positions movement as a direct route to presence, expression, and connection. This framing aligns with a rapidly growing evidence base showing that dance and DMT deliver measurable psychological and physiological benefits (Koch et al., 2019; Meekums et al., 2015) and that collective movement shapes trust, cohesion, and prosociality (Wiltermuth & Heath, 2009; Tarr et al., 2015). Situating dance within an integrated biopsychosocial model clarifies **why** it works and

how to implement it as a repeatable practice for individual flourishing and human-centered leadership.

Psychological Mechanisms: From Affect to Agency

Emotion regulation and mood

Meta-analytic evidence shows small-to-moderate effects of dance and DMT on depression, anxiety, and overall wellbeing across age groups and settings (Koch et al., 2019). A Cochrane review found preliminary but promising benefits for depressive symptoms (Meekums et al., 2015). These outcomes map to core emotional-intelligence skills, self-awareness and self-regulation, emphasised throughout *Heart Unbound 2.0*.

Broaden-and-build

Dance reliably induces positive affect, which broadens attention and cognitive repertoires, catalysing durable personal resources (Fredrickson, 2001). In practice, short "joy sets" (2–5 minutes of free movement) can shift state affect and widen behavioral options before difficult conversations or creative work.

Embodied cognition and interoception

Emotions are enacted in and through the body (Niedenthal, 2007). Rhythmic movement increases interoceptive accuracy, the felt sense of internal states, supporting wiser self-regulation and choice. This gives empirical ballast to the chapter's invitation to "let the body speak."

Physiological Mechanisms: Vagal Regulation and HRV

Polyvagal theory proposes that social safety and calm are mediated by the myelinated vagus (Porges, 2007). Slow, rhythmic movement entrained to breath can enhance vagal activity, reflected in higher heart-rate variability (HRV), a biomarker of flexibility and stress resilience (Laborde et al., 2017). Exercise-based dance programs in older adults and clinical groups report HRV improvements alongside gains in balance and mood (e.g., Hackney & Earhart, 2009). These data substantiate the chapter's claim that dance is a regulatory practice, not only an expressive one.

Social and Neural Mechanisms: Synchrony, Reward, and Empathy

Synchrony and bonding

Moving in synchrony predicts cooperation and generosity (Wiltermuth & Heath, 2009) and elevates pain thresholds, an endorphin proxy, while increasing social bonding (Tarr et al., 2015). Group dance therefore naturally cultivates psychological safety and cohesion.

Action observation and motor resonance

Expertise-specific activation of premotor and parietal circuits while watching dance demonstrates sensorimotor resonance, the neural basis of "feeling with" others (Calvo-Merino et al., 2005; Gazzola & Keysers, 2009). Practically, leader-facilitated mirroring and call-and-response sequences can enhance empathic attunement in teams.

Health, Aging, and Cognitive Outcomes

Beyond mood, longitudinal and clinical findings suggest broader neurocognitive and functional benefits. In a prospective cohort, frequent social dancing was associated with lower dementia risk in older adults compared with other leisure activities (Verghese et al., 2003). Tango-based interventions improve gait, balance, and quality of life in Parkinson's disease (Hackney & Earhart, 2009). The World Health Organisation's evidence synthesis concludes that arts-in-health, including dance, improves mental and physical outcomes across the lifespan (Fancourt & Finn, 2019).

Implications for Leadership and Culture

Embodied leadership

Leadership is enacted, not merely decided. Embodiment approaches emphasise presence, attunement, and ethical use of power through somatic awareness (Ladkin & Taylor, 2010). Dance-based practices train the very micro-skills leaders need: grounded stance, breath-paced speaking, reading the room, and repairing ruptures through synchrony and pacing.

From "me" to "we"

Positive affect (Fredrickson, 2001) and synchrony (Wiltermuth & Heath, 2009) scale from individual state shifts to collective norms: curiosity over reactivity, generosity over defensiveness. Short warm-ups (90–180 seconds) embedded at the start of meetings can measurably change tone, participation, and psychological safety.

Application in *Heart Unbound 2.0* - Dance

The **Dance** chapter turns insight into simple, heart-led practice:

- **Somatic Arrival:** 60–90 seconds of breath-led sway to down-shift stress and arrive in the body.

- **Emotion-to-Motion:** Free movement to name and gently release a chosen emotion (joy, grief, tension).

- **Synchrony & Connection:** Dyad mirroring and brief group rhythms to build attunement and trust.

- **Choice & Safety:** Always opt-in; seated/standing variants, low-stimulus music or silence, cameras-off option.

- **Leadership Transfer:** 90-second movement openers before meetings, "repair" mirroring after conflict, one-song creativity sprints.

- **Light Measurement:** One-word mood check-ins (pre/post); optional HRV or breath-rate snapshot.

Designed for aspiring and seasoned leaders alike, these micro-rituals are personally regulating and professionally connecting, turning movement into everyday emotional intelligence.

Practice Framework: Micro-Rituals That Travel

1. **90-Second Reset (solo):** two slow shoulder rolls, sway to a four-count, exhale longer than inhale; repeat 6–8 cycles (vagal down-shift).

2. **Leader–Follower (pairs):** 60 seconds of silent mirroring at chest height; swap roles (motor resonance, empathy).

3. **Circle Pulse (teams):** 2–3 minutes of simple synchronised steps or claps (synchrony, bonding).

4. **Joy Set (anywhere):** one song, eyes soft, attention on feet and breath (broaden-and-build).

These are inclusive (no choreography), trauma-aware (opt-in, eyes optional), and time-efficient.

Limitations and Research Gaps

Heterogeneity in dance modalities, session length, and populations complicates meta-analytic precision (Koch et al., 2019). More high-quality randomised trials with physiological endpoints (e.g., HRV, inflammatory markers) and organisational outcomes (e.g., turnover, error rates) are needed. Nevertheless, converging evidence across disciplines warrants applied use with appropriate consent and accessibility considerations.

Conclusion

Dance operationalises the *Heart Unbound 2.0* commitment to heart-led living by uniting affect regulation, bodily wisdom, and social connection in a single, scalable practice. The literature affirms that even brief, low-threshold movement can improve mood, enhance vagal regulation, deepen empathy, and strengthen the cultural fabric of teams. In short: dance is evidence-based medicine for the nervous system and a practical pedagogy for humane leadership.

References

Calvo-Merino, B., Glaser, D. E., Grèzes, J., Passingham, R. E., & Haggard, P. (2005). Action observation and acquired motor skills: An fMRI study with expert dancers. *Cerebral Cortex, 15*(8), 1243–1249. https://doi.org/10.1093/cercor/bhi007

Fancourt, D., & Finn, S. (2019). *What is the evidence on the role of the arts in improving health and well-being? A scoping review.* World Health Organization, Regional Office for Europe.

Fredrickson, B. L. (2001). The role of positive emotions in positive psychology: The broaden-and-build theory of positive emotions. *American Psychologist, 56*(3), 218–226. https://doi.org/10.1037/0003-066X.56.3.218

Gazzola, V., & Keysers, C. (2009). The observation and execution of actions share motor and somatosensory voxels in all tested subjects: Single-subject analyses of unsmoothed fMRI data. *Cerebral Cortex, 19*(6), 1239–1255. https://doi.org/10.1093/cercor/bhn181

Hackney, M. E., & Earhart, G. M. (2009). Health-related quality of life and alternative forms of exercise in Parkinson disease. *Parkinsonism & Related Disorders, 15*(9), 644–648. https://doi.org/10.1016/j.parkreldis.2009.03.003

Koch, S. C., Riege, R., Tisborn, K., Biondo, J., Martin, L., & Beelmann, A. (2019). Effects of dance movement therapy and dance on health-related psychological outcomes: A meta-analysis update. *Frontiers in Psychology, 10*, 1806. https://doi.org/10.3389/fpsyg.2019.01806

Laborde, S., Mosley, E., & Thayer, J. F. (2017). Heart rate variability and cardiac vagal tone in psychophysiological research—Recommendations for experiment planning, data analysis, and data reporting. *Frontiers in Psychology, 8*, 213. https://doi.org/10.3389/fpsyg.2017.00213

Ladkin, D., & Taylor, S. S. (2010). Enacting the 'somatic': Leadership through embodied practice. *Leadership, 6*(3), 235–263. https://doi.org/10.1177/1742715010368768

Meekums, B., Karkou, V., & Nelson, E. A. (2015). Dance movement therapy for depression. *Cochrane Database of Systematic Reviews, 2015*(2), CD009895. https://doi.org/10.1002/14651858.CD009895.pub2

Niedenthal, P. M. (2007). Embodying emotion. *Science, 316*(5827), 1002–1005. https://doi.org/10.1126/science.1136930

Porges, S. W. (2007). The polyvagal perspective. *Biological Psychology, 74*(2), 116–143. https://doi.org/10.1016/j.biopsycho.2006.06.009

Tarr, B., Launay, J., Cohen, E., & Dunbar, R. (2015). Synchrony and exertion during dance independently raise pain threshold and encourage social bonding. *Biology Letters, 11*(10), 20150767. https://doi.org/10.1098/rsbl.2015.0767

Verghese, J., Lipton, R. B., Katz, M. J., Hall, C. B., Derby, C. A., Kuslansky, G., Ambrose, A. F., Sliwinski, M., & Buschke, H. (2003). Leisure activities and the risk of dementia in the elderly. *New England Journal of Medicine, 348*(25), 2508–2516. https://doi.org/10.1056/NEJMoa022252

Wiltermuth, S. S., & Heath, C. (2009). Synchrony and cooperation. *Psychological Science, 20*(1), 1–5. https://doi.org/10.1111/j.1467-9280.2008.02253.x

THE
UNBOUND
JOURNEY

7 - "Self-Love" as the Ground of Heart-Led Development: Psychological, Physiological, and Leadership Evidence

Rationale for the Article

Self-love is the system-driver for the entire curriculum. The capacities introduced in earlier chapters (breath, gratitude, "I am," meditation, mirror work, dance) reliably deepen when participants relate to themselves with warmth and truthfulness. Evidence shows that compassionate self-regard down-regulates threat physiology (Creswell et al., 2005), improves vagal flexibility (Svendsen et al., 2016), and expands prosocial motivation (Neff & Pommier, 2013), the exact conditions needed for heart-led living and leadership. Placing self-love at the program's core ensures the practices are not performative but restorative, turning insight into durable identity change and ethical action.

Abstract

Self-love, defined as a steady, compassionate regard for one's own humanity, functions as the substrate for emotional intelligence and sustainable leadership. This article synthesises theory and evidence from self-compassion science, self-affirmation, psychophysiology, and organisational behavior to validate Chapter 7 ("Self-Love") of *Heart Unbound 2.0*. We distinguish mature self-love from selfishness and narcissism; map mechanisms through which compassionate self-regard alters threat processing, stress biology, and cognitive control; and translate findings into leader behaviors that protect well-being while improving team climate. Convergent data show that self-compassion reliably predicts lower anxiety and depression, healthier cortisol dynamics, higher vagally mediated heart-rate variability (HRV), better problem-solving under stress, and prosocial tendencies, all antecedents of ethical, resilient leadership. We conclude with brief, evidence-aligned practices (values affirmations, self-kindness scripts, boundary rituals) suitable for personal development and leadership programs.

Keywords: self-love, self-compassion, self-affirmation, vagal tone, heart-rate variability, leadership, psychological safety, emotional intelligence

Introduction

Across traditions, from Greek *philautia* to contemporary self-compassion research, wise care for self is framed as prerequisite to caring for others (Aristotle, trans.). In modern contexts of volatility and burnout, cultivating self-love is not indulgence but risk management for minds, bodies, and organisations. This paper consolidates high-quality evidence that positions self-love as a measurable, trainable capability that supports heart-led living and leadership.

Conceptual foundations: From *Philautia* to self-compassion

Classical writers distinguished virtuous self-love from egoic self-exaltation; the former underwrites character and civic contribution. Contemporary psychology operationalises this stance as **self-compassion**, mindful awareness of suffering, self-kindness, and recognition of common humanity (Neff, 2003). Unlike contingent self-esteem, self-compassion is associated with stable well-being and less defensiveness (Neff & Vonk, 2009).

Differentiating self-love from selfishness and narcissism

Self-love centers honest care and responsibility; narcissism centers superiority and external validation. Empirically, narcissism predicts aggression when ego is threatened (Bushman & Baumeister, 1998), whereas self-compassion predicts humility, forgiveness, and other-oriented concern (Neff & Pommier, 2013). Programs that raise self-compassion do not inflate entitlement; they reduce shame and fear of failure (Neff & Germer, 2013).

Mechanisms: What changes when we practice compassionate self-regard?

A. Threat regulation and neuroendocrine load

Affirming core values buffers cortisol and subjective stress responses during evaluative threats (Creswell et al., 2005) and recruits brain regions for reward and self-relevance (ventromedial prefrontal cortex; Cascio et al., 2016). Meta-analytic work shows compassion-based interventions lower distress and increase well-being (Kirby et al., 2017).

B. Vagal pathways and the heart

Polyvagal theory links feelings of safety to parasympathetic dominance and social engagement (Porges, 2007). Higher vagally mediated HRV, an index of flexible emotion regulation, is robustly associated with better executive control and resilience (Thayer & Lane, 2000). Compassion imagery can raise HRV and modulate cortisol (Rockliff et al., 2008), and trait self-compassion correlates positively with resting HRV (Svendsen et al., 2016). Positive emotions cultivated through kind self-relating broaden attention and build biological resources, including vagal tone (Fredrickson, 2001; Kok et al., 2013).

C. Cognition, motivation, and behavior

Self-affirmation improves problem solving under pressure (Cohen & Sherman, 2014) and reduces defensiveness, permitting learning. Self-compassion supports intrinsic motivation and persistence after failure (Neff, 2003), aligning with self-determination theory's competence-autonomy-relatedness triad (Deci & Ryan, 2000).

Leadership relevance: From inner stance to outer climate

Leader well-being and presence shape climates of learning and psychological safety (Edmondson, 1999). Compassion toward self predicts less burnout and greater caring for others in caring professions (Duarte et al., 2016) and complements the "Positive Emotional Attractor" pathway of resonant leadership (Boyatzis et al., 2013). Mindfulness-related capacities, often co-trained with self-compassion—are linked to better leader self-regulation and ethical decision-making (Good et al., 2016). Practically, self-love enables: (a) values-aligned boundary setting; (b) steadier feedback conversations (lower threat reactivity); and (c) prosocial norms via modeling humane self-talk and sustainable pace.

Application in *Heart Unbound 2.0*

- **Self-Kindness Micro-Practice:** pause → name the struggle → remember common humanity → offer a caring phrase ("May I meet this with kindness").

- **Heart-Breath & Hand-on-Heart:** 6-breaths/minute with gentle chest contact to regulate the nervous system and embed warmth toward self.

- **Mirror Compassion Ritual:** 60–90 seconds of eye contact + one truth ("I will not abandon you") to soften shame and stabilise self-worth.

- **Boundaries in Action:** one-sentence boundary + recovery ritual to translate self-respect into clear, prosocial behaviour.

Designed for brevity and repetition, these practices are personally restorative and professionally transferable, strengthening resilience, authenticity, and psychologically safe leadership.

Evidence-aligned practices

1. **Values Affirmation (2–3 minutes).** Write and silently re-affirm a personally central value before evaluative tasks (Creswell et al., 2005; Cohen & Sherman, 2014).

2. **Self-Kindness Script.** In difficult moments: "This is hard. Struggle is human. May I respond with care." Rehearse daily; integrate breath to prolong exhale (parasympathetic cue).

3. **HRV Hygiene.** 5 minutes/day of paced breathing (≈ 6 breaths/min) while evoking appreciation to support vagal tone (Porges, 2007; Kok et al., 2013).

4. **Boundary Rituals.** Define one daily "stop time" and one protected recovery micro-ritual; communicate both to stakeholders (leader energy conservation; Good et al., 2016).

5. **Compassion Training.** Dose-response evidence supports structured programs such as Mindful Self-Compassion (Neff & Germer, 2013) to reduce shame and increase prosociality (Kirby et al., 2017).

Limitations and future directions

Most studies rely on WEIRD samples and self-report; more longitudinal and cross-cultural research with objective biomarkers (e.g., ambulatory HRV, diurnal cortisol) is warranted. Leadership field trials that embed self-compassion within systemic interventions (workload, role clarity) are needed to isolate individual- versus context-level effects.

Conclusion

Self-love, operationalised as self-compassion and values-affirmation, reliably improves affective stability, stress biology, executive function, and prosocial behavior. Far from indulgent, it is the ethical foundation of heart-led living and leadership. Programs that teach people to relate to themselves with warmth and truthfulness are scientifically justified and practically urgent.

References

Boyatzis, R. E., Smith, M. L., & Beveridge, A. J. (2013). Coaching with compassion: Inspiring health, well-being, and development in organisations. *Journal of Applied Behavioral Science, 49*(2), 153–178.

Bushman, B. J., & Baumeister, R. F. (1998). Threatened egotism, narcissism, self-esteem, and direct and displaced aggression: Does self-love or self-hate lead to violence? *Journal of Personality and Social Psychology, 75*(1), 219–229.

Cascio, C. N., O'Donnell, M. B., Tinney, F. J., Lieberman, M. D., Taylor, S. E., Strecher, V. J., & Falk, E. B. (2016). Self-affirmation activates brain systems associated with self-related processing and reward. *Psychosomatic Medicine, 78*(5), 491–499.

Cohen, G. L., & Sherman, D. K. (2014). The psychology of change: Self-affirmation and social psychological intervention. *Annual Review of Psychology, 65*, 333–371.

Creswell, J. D., Welch, W. T., Taylor, S. E., Sherman, D. K., Gruenewald, T. L., & Mann, T. (2005). Affirmation of personal values buffers neuroendocrine and psychological stress responses. *Psychological Science, 16*(11), 846–851.

Deci, E. L., & Ryan, R. M. (2000). The "what" and "why" of goal pursuits: Human needs and the self-determination of behavior. *Psychological Inquiry, 11*(4), 227–268.

Duarte, J., Pinto-Gouveia, J., & Cruz, B. (2016). Relationships between nurses' empathy, self-compassion and dimensions of professional quality of life: A cross-sectional study. *International Journal of Nursing Studies, 60*, 1–11.

Edmondson, A. (1999). Psychological safety and learning behavior in work teams. *Administrative Science Quarterly, 44*(2), 350–383.

Fredrickson, B. L. (2001). The role of positive emotions in positive psychology: The broaden-and-build theory. *American Psychologist, 56*(3), 218–226.

Gilbert, P. (2009). *The compassionate mind.* Constable.

Good, D. J., Lyddy, C. J., Glomb, T. M., Bono, J. E., Brown, K. W., Duffy, M. K., … Lazar, S. W. (2016). Contemplating mindfulness at work. *Annual Review of Organisational Psychology and Organisational Behavior, 3*, 189–210.

Kirby, J. N., Tellegen, C. L., & Steindl, S. R. (2017). A meta-analysis of compassion-based interventions. *Clinical Psychology Review, 47*, 40–58.

Kok, B. E., Coffey, K. A., Cohn, M. A., Catalino, L. I., Vacharkulksemsuk, T., Algoe, S. B., … Fredrickson, B. L. (2013). How positive emotions build physical health. *Proceedings of the National Academy of Sciences, 110*(38), 13684–13689.

Neff, K. D. (2003). Self-compassion: An alternative conceptualisation of a healthy attitude toward oneself. *Self and Identity, 2*(2), 85–101.

Neff, K. D., & Germer, C. K. (2013). A pilot study and randomised controlled trial of the Mindful Self-Compassion program. *Journal of Clinical Psychology, 69*(1), 28–44.

Neff, K. D., & Pommier, E. (2013). The relationship between self-compassion and other-focused concern among college undergraduates, community adults, and practicing meditators. *Self and Identity, 12*(2), 160–176.

Neff, K. D., & Vonk, R. (2009). Self-compassion versus global self-esteem. *Journal of Personality, 77*(1), 23–50.

Porges, S. W. (2007). The polyvagal perspective. *Biological Psychology, 74*(2),

116–143.

Rockliff, H., Gilbert, P., McEwan, K., Lightman, S., & Glover, D. (2008). A pilot exploration of HRV and salivary cortisol responses to compassion-focused imagery. *British Journal of Medical Psychology, 81*(1), 83–96.

Svendsen, J. L., Osnes, B., Binder, P.-E., Dundas, I., Visted, E., Nordby, H., & Schanche, E. (2016). Trait self-compassion reflects emotional flexibility through an association with high vagally mediated HRV. *Mindfulness, 7*(5), 1103–1113.

Thayer, J. F., & Lane, R. D. (2000). A model of neurovisceral integration in emotion regulation and dysregulation. *Journal of Affective Disorders, 61*(3), 201–216.

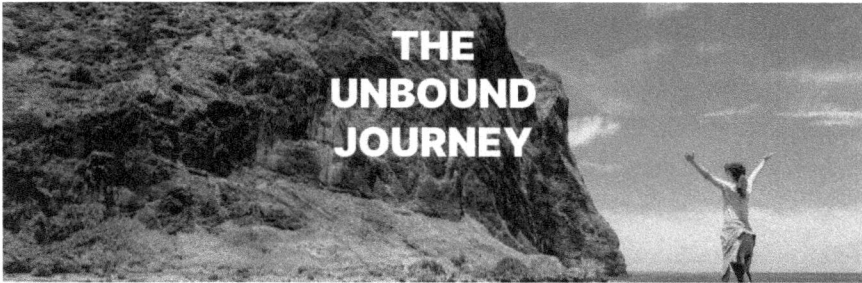

THE UNBOUND JOURNEY

8 - "Nutrition" as an Engine of Emotional Intelligence and Heart-Led Leadership

Rationale for the Article

Heart-led living is embodied. This article demonstrates, across rigorous clinical, mechanistic, and leadership literatures, that the way we eat is inseparable from how we feel, think, relate, and lead. By translating robust findings on Mediterranean-style patterns, hydration, micronutrients, mindful eating, and the gut–brain axis into simple daily practices, Chapter 8 gives participants a controllable lever for emotional steadiness and ethical presence. For *Heart Unbound 2.0*, nutrition is not an adjunct wellness tip; it is the metabolic ground on which gratitude, self-love, meditation, and compassionate leadership can reliably stand.

Abstract

Nutrition, conceived as daily dietary patterns plus mindful, values-aligned eating, provides the physiological ground for emotional intelligence and heart-led leadership. This article synthesises evidence from nutritional psychiatry, psychophysiology, microbiome science, hydration research, and organisational behaviour to validate Chapter 8 ("Nutrition") of *Heart Unbound 2.0*. We differentiate self-nourishment from restrictive, perfectionistic "dieting," and map mechanisms linking food to affect and cognition: glycaemic stability, neuroinflammation, neurotransmitter and micronutrient sufficiency (e.g., omega-3s, B-vitamins), gut–brain signalling, and hydration.

Convergent findings associate higher-quality, Mediterranean-lean patterns with lower depressive symptoms, better cognitive performance, improved sleep and energy, and markers of autonomic balance, precursors to compassionate presence and ethical decision-making at work. We conclude with brief, evidence-aligned practices, mindful-eating rituals, a simple plate template, hydration scheduling, fibre/fermented-food targets, and carbohydrate-protein pairing, suitable for personal development and leadership programs.

Keywords: nutrition; emotional intelligence; gut-brain axis; mindful eating; hydration; leadership; self-care; Heart Unbound 2.0

Introduction

Heart Unbound 2.0 proposes that inner coherence, physiological, emotional, and ethical, is the substrate of heart-led living and leadership. This article validates the Nutrition chapter by demonstrating how daily nourishment shapes mood, cognition, relational presence, and leadership behaviour through well-characterised biological and psychosocial mechanisms.

Nutrition and Emotional Functioning: Evidence Base

Dietary patterns and mood

Meta-analytic and trial evidence shows that improving diet quality reduces depressive symptoms (Firth et al., 2019) and that adherence to healthy dietary indices (e.g., Mediterranean patterns rich in plants, legumes, and olive oil) is prospectively associated with lower depression risk (Lassale et al., 2019). Randomised trials such as SMILES found clinically meaningful symptom reduction following structured dietary support (Jacka et al., 2017). Parallel cardiometabolic benefits are robust (Estruch et al., 2013), indirectly supporting brain and emotional health.

Specific nutrients and hydration

Omega-3 long-chain polyunsaturated fatty acids (EPA/DHA) modulate neuroinflammation and membrane fluidity and can reduce depressive symptoms in some populations (Grosso et al., 2014). B-vitamins (B6, B9, B12), iron, zinc, and magnesium are cofactors in monoamine synthesis and stress physiology; inadequacy is linked to fatigue and low mood (Sarris et al., 2015). Even mild dehydration impairs mood and cognition (Ganio et al., 2011; Pross et al., 2013), underscoring the role of fluid intake as a simple affect-regulation tool.

The gut–brain axis

Microbial metabolites (e.g., short-chain fatty acids) and vagal signalling link diet, microbiota composition, and emotional functioning (Cryan & Dinan, 2012; Sarkar et al., 2016). Diets rich in fibre and fermented foods support microbial diversity with downstream cognitive-affective benefits.

Psychological Mechanisms: From Mindful Eating to Self-Determination

Mindfulness-based eating programs improve binge-eating, emotional eating, and interoceptive awareness (Kristeller et al., 2014). Self-determination theory clarifies why restrictive, externally controlled diets erode adherence, whereas autonomous, values-congruent changes enhance vitality and persistence (Deci & Ryan, 2000). Nutrition thus becomes a daily practice of self-attunement, not moral perfectionism, a stance that aligns with compassion-based approaches central to *Heart Unbound*.

Physiological Coherence and Heart-Led Presence

Nourishment shapes physiological stability (glycaemic variability, inflammatory tone, sleep quality), which scaffolds executive function and emotion regulation. Such "body-to-mind" effects are prerequisites for empathy and perspective-taking, cornerstones of emotional intelligence.

Leadership Implications

Leaders transmit affective states and norms. Health-oriented leadership frameworks show that leaders' own self-care behaviours predict their health, their transformational leadership, and follower wellbeing (Franke et al., 2014, 2017; Kaluza et al., 2020). Authentic leadership emphasises self-awareness and self-regulation (Avolio & Gardner, 2005); nutrition is a tractable lever for both. Within Job Demands Resources theory, food quality, hydration, and regularity constitute personal resources that buffer stress and sustain engagement (Bakker & Demerouti, 2007).

Evidence-Informed Practice Framework

1. **Pattern first.** Emphasise a Mediterranean-style template: vegetables/fruit, legumes, whole grains, nuts/seeds, extra-virgin olive oil; fish 2–3× weekly; minimal ultra-processed foods (Estruch et al., 2013).

2. **Glycaemic steadiness.** Pair carbohydrates with protein/fat; prioritise fibre to reduce mood-relevant energy crashes.

3. **Brain-supportive nutrients.** Ensure omega-3s, B-vitamins, iron, zinc, and magnesium via food-first strategies; consider evidence-based supplementation if deficient (Sarris et al., 2015; Grosso et al., 2014).

4. **Hydration habits.** Scheduled fluid intake across the day; front-load before cognitively demanding or relationally intense tasks (Ganio et al., 2011).

5. **Gut-friendly practices.** Daily fibre variety ("eat the rainbow"), fermented foods, and gradual changes to support microbial resilience (Cryan & Dinan, 2012).

6. **Mindful eating micro-practices.** 60–120-second pre-meal pause (breath, gratitude, intention), device-free first five bites; hunger/fullness check-ins (Kristeller et al., 2014).

Application in Heart Unbound 2.0

The Nutrition chapter turns science into accessible, heart-led practice:

- **Mindful Eating Rituals:** 3-breath pause, gratitude, first-five-bites awareness to strengthen interoception and emotion regulation.

- **Mediterranean-Lean Plate Builder:** simple visual template for everyday meals; weekly "colour count" for fibre diversity.

- **Hydration & Energy Map:** personalised schedule tied to peak relational/leadership moments.

- **Gut–Brain Support:** "3-2-1 rule" (3 cups veg, 2 fermented servings, 1 legume/whole-grain choice daily). These practices are designed to be personally restorative and professionally portable, suited to emerging leaders and executives seeking stable energy, clearer thinking, and compassionate presence.

Limitations and Future Directions

Nutrition science is probabilistic and individual responses vary (genetics, microbiome, culture). More trials should examine multi-component interventions that combine diet, mindfulness, and leadership training, with mechanistic biomarkers (inflammation, microbiota, HRV) and workplace outcomes (ethical decision-making, burnout).

Conclusion

Nutrition is a daily, repeatable act of self-leadership that shapes emotional tone, cognitive clarity, and relational capacity. By embedding mindful, Mediterranean-lean nourishment, hydration, and gut-supportive habits, *Heart Unbound 2.0* grounds heart-led living in physiology and offers leaders a practical pathway to show up with steadiness, compassion, and integrity.

References

Avolio, B. J., & Gardner, W. L. (2005). Authentic leadership development: Getting to the root of positive forms of leadership. *The Leadership Quarterly, 16*(3), 315–338. https://doi.org/10.1016/j.leaqua.2005.03.001

Bakker, A. B., & Demerouti, E. (2007). The Job Demands–Resources model: State of the art. *Journal of Managerial Psychology, 22*(3), 309–328. https://doi.org/10.1108/02683940710733115

Cryan, J. F., & Dinan, T. G. (2012). Mind-altering microorganisms: The impact of the gut microbiota on brain and behaviour. *Nature Reviews Neuroscience, 13*(10), 701–712. https://doi.org/10.1038/nrn3346

Deci, E. L., & Ryan, R. M. (2000). The "what" and "why" of goal pursuits: Human needs and the self-determination of behavior. *Psychological Inquiry, 11*(4), 227–268. https://doi.org/10.1207/S15327965PLI1104_01

Estruch, R., Ros, E., Salas-Salvadó, J., et al. (2013). Primary prevention of cardiovascular disease with a Mediterranean diet. *The New England Journal of Medicine, 368*(14), 1279–1290. https://doi.org/10.1056/NEJMoa1200303

Firth, J., Marx, W., Dash, S., et al. (2019). The effects of dietary improvement on symptoms of depression and anxiety: A meta-analysis of randomised controlled trials. *Psychosomatic Medicine, 81*(3), 265–280.

https://doi.org/10.1097/PSY.0000000000000673

Franke, F., Felfe, J., & Pundt, A. (2014). Gesundheitsförderliche Führung [Health-oriented leadership]. *Gruppe. Interaktion. Organisation. (GIO), 45*, 285–296. https://doi.org/10.1007/s11612-014-0241-6

Franke, F., Felfe, J., & Pundt, A. (2017). The impact of health-oriented leadership on follower health: Development and test of a new instrument. *Journal of Personnel Psychology, 16*(2), 57–67. https://doi.org/10.1027/1866-5888/a000176

Ganio, M. S., Armstrong, L. E., Casa, D. J., et al. (2011). Mild dehydration impairs cognitive performance and mood of men. *British Journal of Nutrition, 106*(10), 1535–1543. https://doi.org/10.1017/S0007114511002005

Grosso, G., Pajak, A., Marventano, S., et al. (2014). Role of omega-3 fatty acids in the treatment of depressive disorders: A comprehensive meta-analysis. *PLOS ONE, 9*(5), e96905. https://doi.org/10.1371/journal.pone.0096905

Jacka, F. N., O'Neil, A., Opie, R., et al. (2017). A randomised controlled trial of dietary improvement for adults with major depression (the 'SMILES' trial). *BMC Medicine, 15*, 23. https://doi.org/10.1186/s12916-017-0791-y

Kaluza, A. J., Weber, H., van Dick, R., & Junker, N. M. (2020). Why self-care matters for leaders' well-being: An investigation of leader self-care, transformational leadership, and health. *Journal of Occupational Health Psychology, 25*(4), 296–306. https://doi.org/10.1037/ocp0000172

Kristeller, J. L., Wolever, R. Q., & Sheets, V. (2014). Mindfulness-based eating awareness training (MB-EAT) for binge eating: A randomised clinical trial. *Journal of Consulting and Clinical Psychology, 82*(5), 861–873. https://doi.org/10.1037/a0036833

Lassale, C., Batty, G. D., Baghdadli, A., et al. (2019). Healthy dietary indices and risk of depressive outcomes: A systematic review and meta-analysis of observational studies. *Molecular Psychiatry, 24*, 965–986. https://doi.org/10.1038/s41380-018-0237-8

Pross, N., Demazières, A., Girard, N., et al. (2013). Effects of changes in water intake on mood of high and low drinkers. *British Journal of Nutrition, 109*(2), 313–321. https://doi.org/10.1017/S0007114512001159

Sarkar, A., Harty, S., Lehto, S. M., et al. (2016). The microbiome in psychology and cognitive neuroscience. *Trends in Cognitive Sciences, 20*(9), 611–

623. https://doi.org/10.1016/j.tics.2016.07.002

Sarris, J., Logan, A. C., Akbaraly, T. N., et al. (2015). Nutritional medicine as mainstream in psychiatry. *The Lancet Psychiatry, 2*(3), 271–274. https://doi.org/10.1016/S2215-0366(14)00051-0

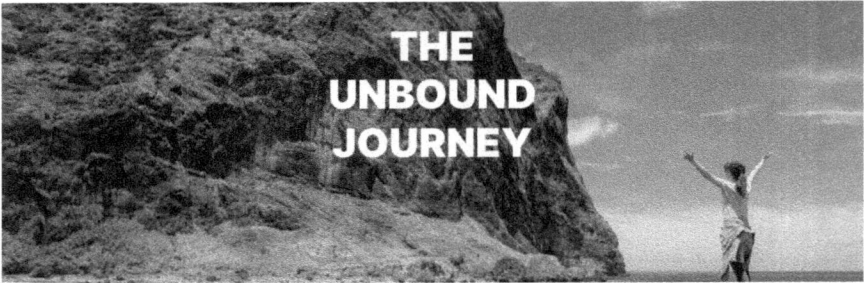

THE
UNBOUND
JOURNEY

9 - "Nothingness": The Sacred Pause as a Mechanism for Emotional Regulation, Creativity, and Ethical Leadership

> **Rationale for the Article**
>
> This article is necessary because the chapter's central claim, that deliberate non-doing is transformative, runs counter to prevailing productivity norms. By grounding "nothingness" in neuroscience, psychophysiology, and leadership science, we provide the conceptual legitimacy and practical dosing guidance required for adoption in personal development and executive contexts. The result is a defensible, teachable protocol that protects participant well-being while improving reflective judgment and team climate.

Abstract

"Nothingness", periods of deliberate, wakeful non-doing, supports emotional regulation, cognitive renewal, and leader effectiveness. This article validates Chapter 9 ("Nothingness") of *Heart Unbound 2.0* by integrating evidence from affective neuroscience, psychophysiology, cognitive psychology, and organisational research. We define nothingness as intentional stillness (distinct from avoidance), review mechanisms involving the default mode network, parasympathetic activation, vagally mediated heart-rate variability, and cortisol down-regulation, and summarise effects on memory consolidation, creative insight, and stress recovery. We translate these findings into leader practices (micro-pauses, white-space scheduling, reflective detachment) and provide a brief, evidence-aligned protocol for program delivery.

Keywords: stillness, default mode network, heart-rate variability, recovery, creativity, leadership, mindfulness, wakeful rest

Introduction

Contemporary work cultures privilege constant availability and rapid output, yet a robust literature shows that *pauses*, periods of intentional stillness without instrumental goals, improve well-being and performance (Sonnentag & Fritz, 2015; Wendsche & Lohmann-Haislah, 2017). Chapter 9 of *Heart Unbound 2.0* proposes "nothingness" as a core practice for heart-led living and leadership. Here we (a) distinguish nothingness from passivity, (b) summarise psychological and physiological mechanisms, (c) review effects on cognition and leadership, and (d) offer brief, program-ready practices.

Conceptualising "Nothingness"

We define nothingness as *wakeful rest*: deliberate, non-instrumental awareness marked by reduced external input and minimal goal pursuit (Dewar et al., 2012; Smallwood & Schooler, 2015). It differs from procrastination or apathy (avoidant inaction) by its intentionality and present-moment orientation. As such, it is aligned with contemplative micro-practices (Keng et al., 2011) and psychological detachment in recovery theory (Sonnentag & Fritz, 2007).

Psychological Mechanisms

Default Mode Network and Integrative Processing

During wakeful rest the default mode network (DMN) becomes prominent, supporting autobiographical memory, perspective-taking, and meaning-making (Raichle et al., 2001; Andrews-Hanna et al., 2014). DMN engagement during undemanding intervals facilitates consolidation and integration, precisely the functions required for values-aligned action and identity coherence.

Emotion Regulation and Cognitive Control

Brief stillness practices reduce perseverative cognition and bolster top-down regulation, reflected in improved executive control and less reactivity (Keng et al., 2011). By interrupting habitual stimulus–response loops, pauses create a window for sensemaking (Weick et al., 2005) and compassionate self-talk, central to *Heart Unbound*'s heart-led ethos.

Physiological Mechanisms

Parasympathetic Activation and HRV

Intentional stillness increases parasympathetic tone, indexed by vagally mediated heart-rate variability (HRV), which predicts better emotion regulation and stress recovery (Laborde et al., 2017; Thayer & Lane, 2000). HRV improvement is associated with calmer affect and greater cognitive flexibility, key resources for resilient leadership.

Stress Biology

Mindfulness-type resting practices reduce cortisol and perceived stress (Pascoe et al., 2017) and can improve autonomic balance (Goessl et al., 2017). Over time these changes support sleep, immune function, and sustained energy, foundations of ethical decision quality and prosocial behavior (Good et al., 2016).

Cognitive Outcomes: Memory and Creativity

Wakeful rest after learning enhances memory consolidation (Dewar et al., 2012), and undirected mind-wandering during quiet intervals facilitates creative incubation (Baird et al., 2012). Leaders who protect white space thus not only recover but also generate novel, integrative solutions.

Leadership Implications

Recovery research shows that detachment, relaxation, mastery, and control predict lower exhaustion and better performance (Sonnentag & Fritz, 2007, 2015). Field studies link leader mindfulness to follower well-being and performance (Reb et al., 2014) and to more ethical, resonant leadership climates (Avolio & Gardner, 2005; Boyatzis & McKee, 2005). Micro-pauses and scheduled stillness create conditions for reflective sensemaking (Weick et al., 2005), temper amygdala-driven urgency, and improve interpersonal presence.

Application in *Heart Unbound 2.0*

The Nothingness chapter converts evidence into brief, heart-led practices:

- **Five-Minute Sacred Pause:** timed, eyes-open/closed wakeful rest to restore parasympathetic balance and attention control.

- **White-Space Scheduling:** daily 2–3 protected "no-task" blocks for DMN-supported integration and creative incubation.

- **Breath-Anchored Micro-breaks:** 60–90-second box-breathing or open-monitoring between meetings to reset HRV and reduce reactivity.

- **Reflect–Then–Respond Ritual:** leaders take a 3-breath pause before high-stakes replies; pairs with a values cue ("What serves the whole?").

- **Evening Detachment Cue:** device-free wind-down (10–20 min) to support recovery, sleep, and next-day self-regulation.

These practices are brief, scalable, and suitable for individual development and leadership cohorts.

Distinguishing Nothingness from Laziness

Laziness reflects avoidant inaction and disengagement; nothingness is intentional non-doing for regulation and integration. Empirically, micro-breaks and recovery experiences predict *higher* subsequent task engagement and performance (Wendsche & Lohmann-Haislah, 2017) rather than sloth.

Practical Protocol (Evidence-Aligned)

1. **Dose:** 2–3 micro-pauses/day (60–120 s) + one 5–10 min white-space block.

2. **Technique:** quiet posture; attention rests on breath or ambient sounds; allow thoughts to pass.

3. **Transfer:** after the pause, name one value-aligned next step (sensemaking link; Weick et al., 2005).

4. **Metrics:** brief check-ins on perceived stress, HRV (if available), and evening detachment to track benefits.

Conclusion

Intentional stillness is not indulgence; it is a biologically and psychologically efficient intervention. By engaging integrative brain networks, strengthening parasympathetic tone, and enabling reflective sensemaking, "nothingness" enhances well-being, creativity, and ethical leadership. As a core practice in *Heart Unbound 2.0*, it operationalises presence into repeatable skills.

References

Andrews-Hanna, J. R., Smallwood, J., & Spreng, R. N. (2014). The default network and self-generated thought: Component processes, dynamic control, and clinical relevance. *Annals of the New York Academy of Sciences, 1316*(1), 29–52. https://doi.org/10.1111/nyas.12360

Avolio, B. J., & Gardner, W. L. (2005). Authentic leadership development: Getting to the root of positive forms of leadership. *The Leadership Quarterly, 16*(3), 315–338. https://doi.org/10.1016/j.leaqua.2005.03.001

Baird, B., Smallwood, J., Mrazek, M. D., Kam, J. W. Y., Franklin, M. S., & Schooler, J. W. (2012). Inspired by distraction: Mind wandering facilitates creative incubation. *Psychological Science, 23*(10), 1117–1122. https://doi.org/10.1177/0956797612446024

Boyatzis, R. E., & McKee, A. (2005). *Resonant leadership: Renewing yourself and connecting with others through mindfulness, hope, and compassion.* Harvard Business School Press.

Creswell, J. D. (2017). Mindfulness interventions. *Annual Review of Psychology, 68*, 491–516. https://doi.org/10.1146/annurev-psych-042716-051139

Dewar, M. T., Alber, J., Butler, C., Cowan, N., & Della Sala, S. (2012). Brief wakeful resting boosts new memories over the long term. *Psychological Science, 23*(9), 955–960. https://doi.org/10.1177/0956797612441220

Goessl, V. C., Curtiss, J. E., & Hofmann, S. G. (2017). The effect of heart rate variability biofeedback training on stress and anxiety: A meta-analysis. *Psychological Medicine, 47*(15), 2578–2586. https://doi.org/10.1017/S0033291717001003

Good, D. J., Lyddy, C. J., Glomb, T. M., Bono, J. E., Brown, K. W., Duffy, M. K., ... & Lazar, S. W. (2016). Contemplating mindfulness at work. *Journal of Management, 42*(1), 114–142. https://doi.org/10.1177/0149206315617003

Keng, S.-L., Smoski, M. J., & Robins, C. J. (2011). Effects of mindfulness on psychological health: A review. *Clinical Psychology Review, 31*(6), 1041–1056. https://doi.org/10.1016/j.cpr.2011.04.006

Laborde, S., Mosley, E., & Thayer, J. F. (2017). Heart rate variability and cardiac vagal tone in psychophysiological research—Recommendations for experiment planning, data analysis, and data reporting. *Frontiers in Psychology, 8*, 213. https://doi.org/10.3389/fpsyg.2017.00213

Pascoe, M. C., Thompson, D. R., Jenkins, Z. M., & Ski, C. F. (2017). Mindfulness mediates the physiological markers of stress: Systematic review and meta-analysis. *Journal of Psychiatric Research, 95*, 156–178. https://doi.org/10.1016/j.jpsychires.2017.08.004

Raichle, M. E., MacLeod, A. M., Snyder, A. Z., Powers, W. J., Gusnard, D. A., & Shulman, G. L. (2001). A default mode of brain function. *Proceedings of the National Academy of Sciences, 98*(2), 676–682. https://doi.org/10.1073/pnas.98.2.676

Reb, J., Narayanan, J., & Chaturvedi, S. (2014). Leading mindfully: Two studies on the influence of supervisor trait mindfulness on employee well-being and performance. *Mindfulness, 5*(1), 36–45. https://doi.org/10.1007/s12671-012-0144-z

Smallwood, J., & Schooler, J. W. (2015). The science of mind wandering: Empirically navigating the stream of consciousness. *Annual Review of Psychology, 66*, 487–518. https://doi.org/10.1146/annurev-psych-010814-015331

Sonnentag, S., & Fritz, C. (2007). The recovery experience questionnaire: Development and validation. *Journal of Occupational Health Psychology, 12*(3), 204–221. https://doi.org/10.1037/1076-8998.12.3.204

Sonnentag, S., & Fritz, C. (2015). Recovery from job stress: The stressor-detachment model as an integrative framework. *Journal of Organisational Behavior, 36*(S1), S72–S103. https://doi.org/10.1002/job.1924

Thayer, J. F., & Lane, R. D. (2000). A model of neurovisceral integration in emotion regulation and dysregulation. *Journal of Affective Disorders, 61*(3), 201–216. https://doi.org/10.1016/S0165-0327(00)00338-4

Weick, K. E., Sutcliffe, K. M., & Obstfeld, D. (2005). Organising and the process of sensemaking. *Organisation Science, 16*(4), 409–421. https://doi.org/10.1287/orsc.1050.0133

Wendsche, J., & Lohmann-Haislah, A. (2017). A meta-analysis on the benefits of micro-breaks. *International Journal of Environmental Research and Public Health, 14*(8), 919. https://doi.org/10.3390/ijerph14080919

THE
UNBOUND
JOURNEY

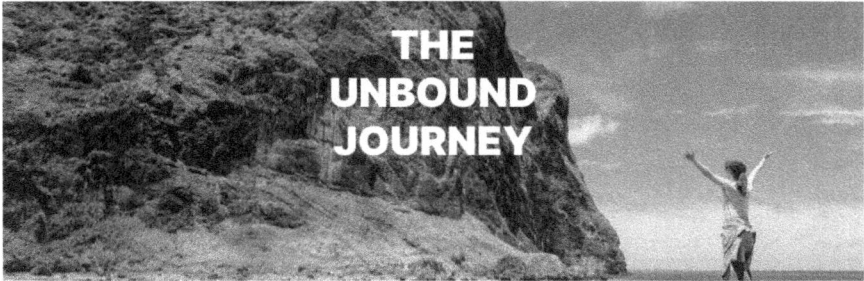

10 - "Forgiveness" as Inner Liberation: Psychological, Physiological, and Leadership Foundations for *Forgiveness*

Rationale for the Article

Forgiveness is the hinge that converts insight into durable freedom. Across studies, it lowers symptom burden, down-regulates stress physiology, and enables values-aligned action, the precise capacities *Heart Unbound 2.0* seeks to cultivate. Embedding rigorously tested protocols (REACH/Enright), clarifying boundaries (forgiveness ≠ excusing), and translating them into leader behaviours ensures the program develops not only calmer nervous systems but also kinder, more accountable cultures.

Abstract

Forgiveness, defined as an intentional, prosocial release of resentment without excusing wrongdoing, predicts robust gains in mental health, stress physiology, and relational functioning. This article synthesises evidence from clinical trials, psychophysiology, and organisational behaviour to validate Chapter 10 ("Forgiveness") of *Heart Unbound 2.0*. Meta-analytic data show that structured forgiveness interventions (e.g., REACH, Enright process) reliably reduce anger, anxiety, and depression while increasing well-being (Wade et al., 2014). Laboratory studies demonstrate lower cardiovascular reactivity and faster physiological recovery when individuals adopt forgiving versus ruminative appraisals (Witvliet et al., 2001). At work, forgiveness norms and leader responses to transgressions are associated with trust, cohesion, and citizenship behaviours (Fehr et al., 2010; Cameron & Caza, 2002). We clarify distinctions between forgiveness, excusing, and reconciliation; outline mechanisms (rumination reduction, reappraisal, parasympathetic activation); and translate findings into brief practices and leader routines. The convergent literature supports forgiveness as a learnable capability that protects health, restores agency, and strengthens ethical, resilient leadership.

Keywords: forgiveness; self-forgiveness; psychophysiology; rumination; emotional intelligence; leadership; REACH model

Introduction

Across traditions and disciplines, forgiveness is treated not as denial but as an evidence-based route to psychological release and relational repair (Worthington & Wade, 2020). Contemporary researchers define interpersonal forgiveness as a motivational shift away from avoidance/retaliation toward benevolence while maintaining appropriate boundaries and justice claims (McCullough et al., 2013). This article integrates the strongest empirical strands, clinical, physiological, and organisational, to ground the *Heart Unbound 2.0* chapter "Forgiveness - Releasing the Past."

Conceptual Foundations

What Forgiveness Is, and Is Not

Forgiveness is an intrapersonal process; it does **not** require forgetting, condoning, or reconciling (Enright & Fitzgibbons, 2015). Distinguishing decisional forgiveness (behavioural intent to treat the offender differently) from emotional forgiveness (replacement of negative with positive other-directed emotions) clarifies pathways to change and relapse risks (Worthington & Scherer, 2004).

Self-Forgiveness

Self-forgiveness involves accepting responsibility while releasing self-condemnation and committing to value-consistent change; when misapplied, it can become pseudo-absolution (Woodyatt et al., 2017). Properly practiced, it predicts lower shame and greater prosocial reengagement (Thompson et al., 2005; Woodyatt et al., 2017).

Mechanisms Linking Forgiveness to Health

Cognitive–Affective Mechanisms

Unforgiveness is sustained by rumination and threat appraisals. Forgiveness training introduces reappraisal and compassion, reducing perseverative cognition that amplifies stress (Worthington & Wade, 2020). Meta-analysis confirms medium-to-large reductions in anger, depression, and anxiety following structured interventions (Wade et al., 2014).

Psychophysiology

When participants recall offenses with unforgiving intent, they exhibit heightened heart rate, blood pressure, skin conductance, and corrugator EMG; adopting forgiving imagery attenuates these responses and speeds recovery (Witvliet et al., 2001). Reviews link trait forgiveness to healthier stress biology and downstream physical health (Toussaint et al., 2015).

Evidence-Based Interventions

Two widely tested models demonstrate efficacy:

- **REACH Forgiveness** - Recall the hurt, Empathise with the offender, offer an Altruistic gift of forgiveness, Commit, and Hold to the forgiveness (Worthington & Wade, 2020).

- **Enright Process Model** - Uncover anger, decide to forgive, work (e.g., reframing, empathy), and discover release/meaning (Enright & Fitzgibbons, 2015).

Across delivery formats and populations, randomised and controlled trials show reliable benefits (Wade et al., 2014).

Forgiveness in Leadership and Organisations

Positive organisational scholarship positions forgiveness as a core virtue that amplifies trust and resilience after transgressions (Cameron & Caza, 2002). Meta-analytic evidence indicates that apology, empathy, and justice cues increase forgiveness and reduce retaliation, supporting healthier team climates (Fehr et al., 2010; Aquino et al., 2006). Leaders who model boundary-honoring forgiveness, separating accountability from dehumanisation, facilitate psychological safety and ethical learning.

Integrative Model for *Heart Unbound 2.0*

1. **Trigger** (offense) → 2. **Appraisal** (threat + moral injury) → 3. **Unforgiveness Loop** (rumination, anger, avoidance) → 4. **Intervention** (REACH or Enright; compassion practices; values affirmation) → 5. **Physiological Shift** (parasympathetic activation; reduced reactivity) → 6. **Behavioural Outcomes** (boundary-aligned contact or dignified distance) → 7. **Leadership Spillover** (trust restoration, learning).

Application in *Heart Unbound 2.0*

Short, practice-ready integrations for cohorts and leaders:

- **REACH Micro-Practices:** 10-minute guided cycles to move from decisional to emotional forgiveness.

- **Self-Forgiveness Letters:** Responsibility + repair plan + compassionate release.

- **Rumination Interrupts:** 90-second breath reset, then values-based reappraisal script.

- **Boundary & Accountability Scripts:** "Forgive and **hold** the line", clear requests, consequences, and check-backs.

- **Restorative Conversations:** Brief, structured dialogues (harm named → needs → agreements) to rebuild trust.

These practices are brief enough for daily use, scalable for programs, and appropriate from emerging leaders to executives.

Conclusion

The multidisciplinary evidence converges: forgiveness is a learnable self-regulation skill that restores agency, improves health, and strengthens leadership. Properly framed and practiced, it frees individuals from the past without erasing justice, and equips teams to recover ethically after harm. *Heart Unbound 2.0* can therefore treat forgiveness not as inspiration but as an empirically grounded capability.

References

Aquino, K., Tripp, T. M., & Bies, R. J. (2006). Getting even or moving on? Power, procedural justice, and types of offense as predictors of revenge, forgiveness, reconciliation, and avoidance. *Journal of Applied Psychology, 91*(3), 653–668. https://doi.org/10.1037/0021-9010.91.3.653

Cameron, K. S., & Caza, A. (2002). Organisational and leadership virtues and the role of forgiveness. *Journal of Leadership & Organisational Studies, 9*(1), 33–48. https://doi.org/10.1177/107179190200900103

Enright, R. D., & Fitzgibbons, R. P. (2015). *Forgiveness therapy: An empirical guide for resolving anger and restoring hope* (2nd ed.). American Psychological Association.

Fehr, R., Gelfand, M. J., & Nag, M. (2010). The road to forgiveness: A meta-analytic synthesis of its situational and dispositional correlates. *Journal of Applied Psychology, 95*(2), 356–392. https://doi.org/10.1037/a0018628

McCullough, M. E., Kurzban, R., & Tabak, B. A. (2013). Cognitive systems for revenge and forgiveness. *Behavioural and Brain Sciences, 36*(1), 1–15. https://doi.org/10.1017/S0140525X11002160

Thompson, L. Y., Snyder, C. R., Hoffman, L., Michael, S. T., Rasmussen, H. N., Billings, L. S., Heinze, L., Neufeld, J. E., Shorey, H. S., Roberts, J. C., & Roberts, D. E. (2005). Dispositional forgiveness of self, others, and situations. *Journal of Personality, 73*(2), 313–359. https://doi.org/10.1111/j.1467-6494.2005.00311.x

Toussaint, L., Worthington, E. L., Jr., & Williams, D. R. (Eds.). (2015). *Forgiveness and health: Scientific evidence and theories.* Springer.

Wade, N. G., Hoyt, W. T., Kidwell, J. E., & Worthington, E. L., Jr. (2014). Efficacy of psychotherapeutic interventions to promote forgiveness: A meta-analysis. *Journal of Consulting and Clinical Psychology, 82*(1), 154–170. https://doi.org/10.1037/a0035268

Witvliet, C. V. O., Ludwig, T. E., & Vander Laan, K. L. (2001). Granting forgiveness or harboring grudges: Implications for emotion, physiology, and health. *Psychological Science, 12*(2), 117–123. https://doi.org/10.1111/1467-9280.00320

Woodyatt, L., Worthington, E. L., Jr., Wenzel, M., & Griffin, B. J. (Eds.).

(2017). *Handbook of the psychology of self-forgiveness*. Springer.

Worthington, E. L., Jr., & Scherer, M. (2004). Forgiveness is an emotion-focused coping strategy that can reduce health risks and promote health resilience: Theory, review, and hypotheses. *Journal of Clinical Psychology, 60*(11), 1145–1162. https://doi.org/10.1002/jclp.20049

Worthington, E. L., Jr., & Wade, N. G. (Eds.). (2020). *Handbook of forgiveness* (2nd ed.). Routledge.

THE
UNBOUND
JOURNEY

11 - "Grounding" the Heart: Psychophysiological and Leadership Foundations for Grounding

Rationale for the Article

This chapter operationalises a non-stigmatisng, evidence-aligned skill that participants can deploy anywhere,at a desk, in a corridor, or outdoors, to stabilise physiology and widen choice. By coupling slow breathing, sensory anchors, and nature-based resets with leadership routines, the program addresses both individual well-being (HRV, sleep, affect) and relational impact (psychological safety, ethical clarity). Grounding thus functions as the program's "reset lever," enabling all subsequent chapters (forgiveness, self-love, purpose) to be practiced from a regulated nervous system and a steady heart.

Abstract

Grounding—defined as deliberate, body-based orienting to the present moment, has emerged as a practical bridge between affect regulation, health physiology, and ethical leadership. This article synthesises evidence from stress neurobiology, interoception, heart-rate variability (HRV), mindfulness/somatic therapies, nature exposure, and organisational behaviour to validate the intent of Chapter 11 ("Grounding") of *Heart Unbound 2.0*. Mechanistically, grounding down-regulates threat circuits and restores prefrontal control via parasympathetic activation (polyvagal and neurovisceral integration models), increases vagally mediated HRV through slow-paced breathing and sensory anchoring, and improves attentional stability through interoceptive awareness. Empirically, randomised and quasi-experimental studies show that HRV-biofeedback and slow breathing (~6 breaths/min) reduce anxiety and cortisol, improve executive function and sleep; brief mindfulness/somatic practices enhance emotion regulation; and contact with natural environments reduces rumination and stress markers. In leadership contexts, grounded presence supports decision quality, psychological safety, and prosocial influence via emotion contagion pathways. We distill trauma-sensitive implementation guidance and program elements aligned to *Heart Unbound 2.0*. Collectively, convergent data indicate that grounding is an evidence-aligned, low-cost, portable method that protects well-being while enabling steady, values-based leadership.

Keywords: grounding; parasympathetic regulation; interoception; heart-rate variability; mindfulness; leadership; nature exposure

Introduction: What Grounding Is, and Is Not

Grounding refers to intentional, body-anchored practices that orient attention to current sensory, motor, and interoceptive signals (e.g., breath, pressure through the feet, tactile contact, environmental cues). Unlike avoidance or suppression, grounding increases *contact* with present-moment experience to interrupt stress reactivity and restore choice (Briere & Scott, 2014; Hayes et al., 2011). Across contemplative, indigenous, and clinical traditions, grounding is framed as a return to safety, place, and agency (Kabat-Zinn, 2013; van der Kolk, 2014).

Psychophysiological Mechanisms

Stress, Autonomic Balance, and Executive Control

Chronic stress biases the sympathetic branch, elevating cortisol and narrowing attentional scope (McEwen, 2007). Grounding recruits the parasympathetic system, especially vagal pathways, lowering arousal and re-engaging prefrontal networks for planning, perspective-taking, and inhibition (Porges, 2011; Thayer & Lane, 2009). The neurovisceral integration model links higher vagal tone (indexed by HRV) with better self-regulation and emotion management (Thayer et al., 2012).

Interoception and Emotion Regulation

Interoceptive awareness,the capacity to sense internal bodily states, supports labeling of affect and adaptive regulation (Craig, 2002; Khalsa et al., 2018). Grounding practices (body scan, breath-sensing, contact with surfaces) improve interoceptive accuracy and reduce maladaptive rumination (Hölzel et al., 2011).

Slow Breathing and HRV

Slow, diaphragmatic breathing near the baroreflex resonance (~0.1 Hz; ~6 breaths/min) increases vagally mediated HRV, improves gas exchange, and down-shifts threat appraisal (Lehrer & Gevirtz, 2014; Laborde et al., 2017). HRV-biofeedback and paced breathing reliably decrease anxiety and enhance sleep and cognitive flexibility (Lehrer & Gevirtz, 2014).

Empirical Evidence for Grounding Modalities

Somatic and Mindfulness-Based Techniques

Brief mindfulness and compassion practices reduce negative affect, enhance attentional control, and improve coping in high-demand settings (Tang et al., 2007; Shapiro et al., 2005; Good et al., 2016). Body-based grounding (e.g., 5-4-3-2-1 sensory orientation, posture/pressure cues) is a first-line, trauma-sensitive skill to stabilise arousal without revisiting trauma content (Briere & Scott, 2014; van der Kolk, 2014).

Nature Exposure and "Being of the Earth"

Experimental and field studies show that contact with natural environments improves mood, reduces stress biomarkers, and supports attention restoration (Ulrich, 1984; Berman et al., 2008; Bratman et al., 2015). These effects dovetail with culturally grounded practices that reconnect people with land and seasonality.

Earthing/Direct Ground Contact (Preliminary)

A small but growing literature suggests that direct skin contact with the earth may modulate inflammation and subjective stress; findings remain preliminary and should be framed cautiously (Chevalier et al., 2012).

Grounding, Leadership, and Teams

Grounded leaders regulate their own arousal, which shapes team climate through emotion contagion and behavioural modeling (Barsade, 2002). Mindful, embodied presence is associated with better judgment under uncertainty, ethical conduct, and enhanced psychological safety (Karelaia & Reb, 2015; Edmondson, 2018; Good et al., 2016). Vagal tone has been linked to prosocial orientation and social connectedness, offering a plausible pathway from physiologic steadiness to relational leadership (Kok & Fredrickson, 2010; Thayer et al., 2012).

Implications.

- **Decision quality:** Grounding re-engages prefrontal oversight, reducing threat-biased decisions.

- **Psychological safety:** A regulated leader presence de-escalates conflict and normalises reflective pauses (Edmondson, 2018).

- **Sustainable performance:** Routine recovery via micro-grounding limits allostatic load (McEwen, 2007).

Implementation, Safety, and Equity Considerations

Grounding is brief, portable, and low-cost, but it should be delivered with trauma awareness: offer opt-in, eyes-open options, external sensory anchors, and clear stop rules (Briere & Scott, 2014). In occupational settings, normalise micro-practices (30–90 seconds) before/after meetings and critical incidents; pair with HRV-biofeedback where feasible (Lehrer & Gevirtz, 2014). Ensure cultural humility, invite participants to adapt practices to their traditions (e.g., nature connection, prayer, walking).

Application in *Heart Unbound 2.0*

Grounding integrates theory into concise, heart-led practice:

- **Paced Breathing & HRV Moments:** 60–120 seconds at ~6 breaths/min before difficult conversations or transitions.

- **Sensory Orientation (5-4-3-2-1):** Rapid de-escalation using sight/touch/sound anchors; eyes-open, trauma-sensitive.

- **Nature Micro-Rituals:** Daily 5–10 minute outdoor "attention resets" (barefoot optional), linking presence to place.

- **Embodied Leadership Checks:** "Feet, seat, breath" scan before decisions; brief HRV-biofeedback for leaders.

The design makes practices personally restorative and professionally transferable for emerging and senior leaders seeking authentic, values-aligned self-leadership.

Conclusion

Grounding is not a metaphor but a measurable alteration in autonomic balance and attentional control that scales from individual calm to collective climate. Across converging literatures, brief, body-based presence practices reduce stress, improve HRV and executive control, and strengthen prosocial leadership. Implemented with cultural and trauma sensitivity, grounding is a credible, scalable cornerstone for *Heart Unbound 2.0.*

References

Barsade, S. G. (2002). The ripple effect: Emotional contagion and its influence on group behaviour. *Administrative Science Quarterly, 47*(4), 644–675.

Berman, M. G., Jonides, J., & Kaplan, S. (2008). The cognitive benefits of interacting with nature. *Psychological Science, 19*(12), 1207–1212.

Bratman, G. N., Hamilton, J. P., & Daily, G. C. (2015). The impacts of nature experience on human cognitive function and mental health. *Annals of the New York Academy of Sciences, 1249*(1), 118–136.*

Briere, J. N., & Scott, C. (2014). *Principles of trauma therapy* (2nd ed.). Sage.

Chevalier, G., Sinatra, S. T., Oschman, J. L., Delany, R. M., & Forys, K. (2012). Earthing: Health implications of reconnecting the human body to the Earth's surface electrons. *Journal of Environmental and Public Health*, 2012, 291541.

Craig, A. D. (2002). How do you feel? Interoception: The sense of the physiological condition of the body. *Nature Reviews Neuroscience, 3*(8), 655–666.

Edmondson, A. C. (2018). *The fearless organisation: Creating psychological safety in the workplace for learning, innovation, and growth.* Wiley.

Good, D. J., Lyddy, C. J., Glomb, T. M., Bono, J. E., Brown, K. W., Duffy, M. K., ... Lazar, S. W. (2016). Contemplating mindfulness at work: An integrative review. *Annual Review of Organisational Psychology and Organisational Behaviour, 3*, 89–135.

Hays, S. C., Strosahl, K. D., & Wilson, K. G. (2011). *Acceptance and commitment therapy* (2nd ed.). Guilford.

Hölzel, B. K., Lazar, S. W., Gard, T., Schuman-Olivier, Z., Vago, D. R., & Ott, U. (2011). How does mindfulness meditation work? Proposing mechanisms of action. *Perspectives on Psychological Science, 6*(6), 537–559.

Kabat-Zinn, J. (2013). *Full catastrophe living* (Rev. ed.). Bantam. (Original work published 1990)

Karelaia, N., & Reb, J. (2015). Improving decision making through mindfulness. In J. Reb & P. W. B. Atkins (Eds.), *Mindfulness in organisations* (pp. 163–189). Cambridge University Press.

Khalsa, S. S., Adolphs, R., Cameron, O. G., Critchley, H. D., Davenport, P. W., Feinstein, J. S., … Zucker, N. (2018). Interoception and mental health. *Trends in Cognitive Sciences, 22*(6), 488–506.

Kok, B. E., & Fredrickson, B. L. (2010). Upward spirals of the heart: Autonomic flexibility, as indexed by vagal tone, reciprocally and prospectively predicts positive emotions and social connectedness. *Biological Psychology, 85*(3), 432–436.

Laborde, S., Mosley, E., & Thayer, J. F. (2017). Heart rate variability and cardiac vagal tone in psychophysiological research. *Frontiers in Psychology, 8*, 213.

Lehrer, P. M., & Gevirtz, R. (2014). Heart rate variability biofeedback: How and why it works. *Frontiers in Psychology, 5*, 756.

McEwen, B. S. (2007). Physiology and neurobiology of stress and adaptation: Central role of the brain. *Physiological Reviews, 87*(3), 873–904.

Porges, S. W. (2011). *The polyvagal theory: Neurophysiological foundations of emotions, attachment, communication, and self-regulation*. Norton.

Shapiro, S. L., Astin, J. A., Bishop, S. R., & Cordova, M. (2005). Mindfulness-based stress reduction for health care professionals. *International Journal of Stress Management, 12*(2), 164–176.

Tang, Y.-Y., Ma, Y., Wang, J., Fan, Y., Feng, S., Lu, Q., … Posner, M. I. (2007). Short-term meditation training improves attention and self-regulation. *Proceedings of the National Academy of Sciences, 104*(43), 17152–17156.

Thayer, J. F., Åhs, F., Fredrikson, M., Sollers, J. J., III, & Wager, T. D. (2012). A meta-analysis of heart rate variability and neuroimaging studies: Implications for heart rate variability as a marker of stress and health. *Neuroscience & Biobehavioural Reviews, 36*(2), 747–756.

Thayer, J. F., & Lane, R. D. (2009). Claude Bernard and the heart–brain connection: Further elaboration of a model of neurovisceral integration. *Neuroscience & Biobehavioural Reviews, 33*(2), 81–88.

Ulrich, R. S. (1984). View through a window may influence recovery from surgery. *Science, 224*(4647), 420–421.

van der Kolk, B. A. (2014). *The body keeps the score: Brain, mind, and body in the healing of trauma.* Viking.

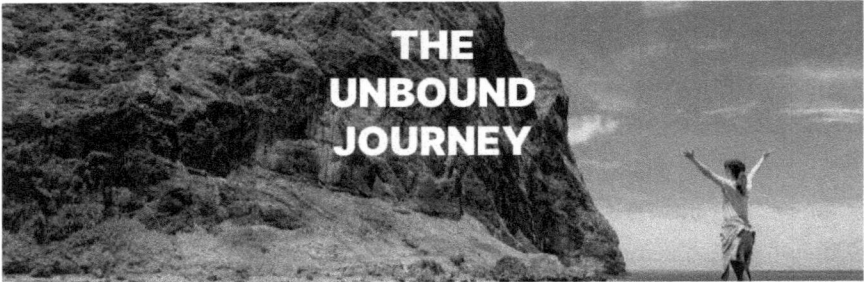

THE
UNBOUND
JOURNEY

12 - "Kindness" as Gentle Strength: Psychophysiological and Leadership Foundations for Kindness

Rationale for the Article

Kindness is the integrative hinge of the program: it operationalises self-love (inward), forgiveness (releasing harm), grounding (autonomic stability), and effective leadership (outward). By embedding brief, repeatable practices that modify stress biology and social climate, the chapter ensures that "heart-led" is not aspirational language but a measurable shift in regulation, relationships, and results.

Abstract

Kindness, defined as the intentional expression of care for oneself and others, functions as a core competency of emotional intelligence and a catalyst for resilient, ethical leadership. This article synthesises evidence from affective science, psychophysiology, and organisational behaviour to validate the focus of *Heart Unbound 2.0 - Chapter 12: Kindness*. We review mechanisms linking kind intention and behaviour to neuroendocrine and autonomic responses (e.g., oxytocin signaling, serotonergic modulation, vagally mediated heart-rate variability), and show how these pathways down-regulate threat, broaden cognitive bandwidth, and strengthen social bonds. Convergent findings from randomised and quasi-experimental studies indicate that compassion and loving-kindness trainings increase prosocial behaviour, well-being, and vagal tone while reducing stress reactivity and depressive symptoms. At the collective level, leader kindness predicts psychological safety, learning behaviour, and performance via norms of care and prosocial motivation. We distinguish mature kindness from permissiveness by emphasising boundaries and accountability as integral to compassionate practice. The paper concludes with brief, evidence-aligned practices and a targeted "Application in *Heart Unbound 2.0*" section that translate the science into accessible micro-rituals for individuals and teams.

Keywords: kindness; compassion; oxytocin; heart-rate variability; psychological safety; prosocial leadership; self-compassion

Introduction

Kindness is often framed as a moral ideal; current science also treats it as a trainable capacity with measurable effects on health, cognition, and collaboration. Within *Heart Unbound 2.0*, kindness is positioned as "gentle strength", a stance that softens harsh self-judgment while sustaining clear boundaries in relationships and work. This article integrates psychological, physiological, and leadership literatures to establish why kindness belongs in a rigorous personal-development and leadership curriculum.

Conceptualising Kindness: From Emotion to Competency

The construct sits at the intersection of compassion (sensitivity to suffering with a commitment to alleviate it) and prosocial behaviour (actions intended to benefit others). Evolutionary and affective accounts describe compassion/kindness as an adaptive caregiving response that coordinates affiliation and cooperation (Goetz et al., 2010). At the intrapersonal level, self-kindness overlaps with self-compassion, treating oneself with warmth, common humanity, and mindful awareness (Neff, 2003). As a competency, kindness involves intention, attention, and skillful action, not mere agreeableness or conflict avoidance.

Psychophysiological Mechanisms

Neuroendocrine pathways

Acts of care and trustworthy contact increase oxytocin, which supports social approach, trust, and reduced threat reactivity (Kosfeld et al., 2005; Zak et al., 2007). Serotonergic modulation further biases choices toward harm-aversion and prosociality (Crockett et al., 2010).

Autonomic regulation

Kindness practices (e.g., loving-kindness meditation; compassion training) are associated with higher vagally mediated heart-rate variability (HRV), an index of flexible parasympathetic regulation linked to emotion regulation and executive function (Kok et al., 2013; Porges, 2007). Through this lens, kindness is not "soft"; it is neuroregulation in action.

Broaden-and-build dynamics

Positive, other-oriented emotions broaden attentional scope and cognitive repertoires, building durable social and psychological resources that buffer future stress (Fredrickson, 2001). These upward spirals help explain sustained gains from brief kindness interventions (Kok et al., 2013).

Evidence From Interventions

Randomised trials show that compassion and loving-kindness training increase altruism and alter neural responses to others' suffering (Weng et al., 2013). A meta-analysis of "acts of kindness" demonstrates reliable improvements in the actor's well-being (Curry et al., 2018). Mindful Self-Compassion training improves affect, reduces distress, and strengthens self-regulation relative to controls (Neff & Germer, 2013).

Kindness in Leadership and Teams

Kindness operationalises as caring norms, high-quality connection, and compassionate responding to difficulty. In organisations, such practices predict psychological safety, the shared belief that interpersonal risk-taking is safe, which, in turn, predicts learning behaviour and performance (Edmondson, 1999). Field studies show that compassion episodes at work are frequent and consequential for commitment and effectiveness (Lilius et al., 2008). Prosocial motivation, the desire to have a positive impact on others, amplifies persistence and performance when work is interdependent (Grant, 2007). These findings align with servant and compassionate leadership models that anchor authority in care and stewardship (Worline & Dutton, 2017).

Boundaries, Accountability, and Misconceptions

Kindness is often misconstrued as niceness or permissiveness. Mature kindness includes clarity about limits and consequences; it communicates truth without humiliation. In self-kindness, boundaries protect rest and recovery (a hedge against burnout) and enable sustained contribution. In teams, "clear is kind" operationalises as timely feedback, fair process, and restorative responses to harm.

Practice: Brief, Evidence-Aligned Micro-Rituals

- **60-second vagal reset:** 4-6 breathing with a longer exhale before difficult conversations (Porges, 2007).

- **Compassionate imagery:** Two minutes of loving-kindness phrases ("May I/you be safe...") to prime prosocial mindset (Weng et al., 2013).

- **Three good hands:** Each day record one self-kind act, one kind act received, and one given; this sustains the kindness–well-being feedback loop (Curry et al., 2018).

- **Clear-and-care feedback:** Begin with impact and shared goals, offer behavioural specifics, and end with support and next steps (Edmondson, 1999; Worline & Dutton, 2017).

Application in *Heart Unbound 2.0*

The **Kindness** chapter translates theory into accessible, heart-led practice:

- **Self-Kindness Micro-Rituals:** 60-second breath + brief self-talk scripts to replace harsh inner commentary.

- **Kindness Labs (Daily Acts):** Small, intentional prosocial behaviours tracked for seven days to build the kindness–well-being loop.

- **Compassionate Communication Drills:** "Clear-is-kind" feedback practice with role-plays that pair candor with care.

- **Boundary Agreements:** Personal "non-negotiables" that safeguard rest and values, kindness to self as the basis for sustainable kindness to others.

> - **Leadership Alignment:** Team norms for psychological safety (check-ins, debriefs, repair rituals) that convert care into collective performance.
>
> These practices are personally healing and professionally transformative for emerging and senior leaders, and for anyone cultivating authentic self-leadership.

Conclusion

Across levels, from molecules to meetings, kindness functions as gentle strength. It calms the body, widens the mind, and binds groups together. Implemented with boundaries and accountability, kindness becomes a high-leverage intervention for individual resilience and collective excellence. These properties justify its centrality in *Heart Unbound 2.0* and recommend it as a core habit for contemporary leadership.

References

Crockett, M. J., Clark, L., Hauser, M. D., & Robbins, T. W. (2010). Serotonin selectively influences moral judgment and behaviour through harm aversion. *Proceedings of the National Academy of Sciences*, 107(40), 17433–17438.

Curry, O. S., Rowland, L. A., Van Lissa, C. J., Zlotowitz, S., McAlaney, J., & Whitehouse, H. (2018). Happy to help? A systematic review and meta-analysis of the effects of performing acts of kindness on the well-being of the actor. *Journal of Experimental Social Psychology*, 76, 320–329.

Edmondson, A. C. (1999). Psychological safety and learning behaviour in work teams. *Administrative Science Quarterly*, 44(2), 350–383.

Fredrickson, B. L. (2001). The role of positive emotions in positive psychology: The broaden-and-build theory of positive emotions. *American Psychologist*, 56(3), 218–226.

Goetz, J. L., Keltner, D., & Simon-Thomas, E. (2010). Compassion: An evolutionary analysis and empirical review. *Psychological Bulletin*, 136(3), 351–374.

Grant, A. M. (2007). Relational job design and the motivation to make a prosocial difference. *Academy of Management Review*, 32(2), 393–417.

Kok, B. E., Coffey, K. A., Cohn, M. A., Catalino, L. I., Vacharkulksemsuk,

T., Algoe, S. B., Brantley, M., & Fredrickson, B. L. (2013). How positive emotions build physical health: Perceived positive social connections account for the upward spiral between positive emotions and vagal tone. *Psychological Science*, 24(7), 1123–1132.

Kosfeld, M., Heinrichs, M., Zak, P. J., Fischbacher, U., & Fehr, E. (2005). Oxytocin increases trust in humans. *Nature*, 435, 673–676.

Lilius, J. M., Worline, M. C., Maitlis, S., Kanov, J., Dutton, J. E., & Frost, P. (2008). The contours and consequences of compassion at work. *Journal of Organisational Behaviour*, 29(2), 193–218.

Neff, K. D. (2003). Self-compassion: An alternative conceptualisation of a healthy attitude toward oneself. *Self and Identity*, 2(2), 85–101.

Neff, K. D., & Germer, C. K. (2013). A pilot study and randomised controlled trial of the Mindful Self-Compassion program. *Journal of Clinical Psychology*, 69(1), 28–44.

Porges, S. W. (2007). The polyvagal perspective. *Biological Psychology*, 74(2), 116–143.

Weng, H. Y., Fox, A. S., Shackman, A. J., Stodola, D. E., Caldwell, J. Z. K., Olson, M. C., Rogers, G. M., & Davidson, R. J. (2013). Compassion training alters altruism and neural responses to suffering. *Psychological Science*, 24(7), 1171–1180.

Zak, P. J., Stanton, A. A., & Ahmadi, S. (2007). Oxytocin increases generosity in humans. *PLOS ONE*, 2(11), e1128.

Worline, M. C., & Dutton, J. E. (2017). *Awakening compassion at work: The quiet power that elevates people and organisations.* Berrett-Koehler.

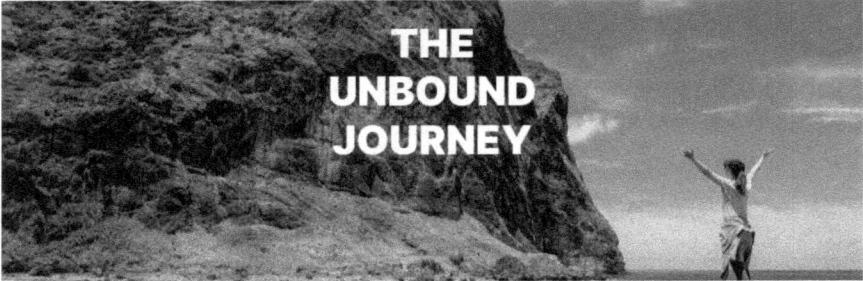

THE
UNBOUND
JOURNEY

13 - "God/The Divine": Psychological, Physiological, and Leadership Correlates of Sacred Connection

Rationale for the Article

This chapter anchors the curriculum's "heart-led" competencies in a rigorously defined construct of sacred connection. By linking everyday micro-rituals (gratitude, breath-prayer, service) to validated pathways, meaning, self-transcendence, and vagal regulation, it supplies the ethical and psychophysiological "spine" for the whole program. Leaders and participants gain language that is inclusive (spiritual but not necessarily religious) yet empirically grounded, enabling respectful dialogue across worldviews while safeguarding psychological safety and cultural humility (APA, 2017).

Abstract

God/The Divine, conceived broadly as felt relationship with a sacred, ultimate, or transcendent reality, appears to support mental health, stress regulation, prosocial motivation, and ethically grounded leadership. This article synthesises research in psychology of religion/spirituality, psychophysiology, and organisational science to validate Chapter 13 ("God/The Divine") of *Heart Unbound 2.0*. We outline mechanisms linking sacred connection to wellbeing, meaning-making, self-transcendence, positive religious coping, and emotion regulation, then review evidence that contemplative and devotional practices modulate autonomic balance, inflammation, and neural networks for attention and socio-affect. We translate these findings into leader behaviours (purpose, humility, compassion, service) consistent with servant, authentic, and spiritual leadership frameworks. The review highlights boundary conditions (spiritual struggle, cultural humility) and provides brief, evidence-aligned practices for personal and programmatic use.

Keywords: spirituality, religion, transcendence, meaning, autonomic nervous system, heart-rate variability, servant leadership, compassion, self-transcendent emotions

Introduction

Across cultures, humans report encounters with a sacred presence, named *God, the Divine, Spirit,* or *ultimate reality,* that confer purpose, comfort, and moral direction (Koenig et al., 2012; Pargament, 2007). Contemporary science now clarifies *how* such connection can enhance wellbeing and leadership: by organising meaning systems (Park, 2010), broadening emotional repertoires (Fredrickson, 2001), evoking self-transcendent emotions (Keltner & Haidt, 2003), and scaffolding prosocial self-regulation (McCullough & Willoughby, 2009). Physiologically, contemplative practices associated with the sacred shift autonomic balance toward parasympathetic dominance and build vagal flexibility, a biomarker of resilience (Kok & Fredrickson, 2010; Porges, 2011). Organisational research parallels these effects: purpose-centred, service-oriented leadership improves trust, commitment, and performance (Fry, 2003; Greenleaf, 2002/1977; Avolio & Gardner, 2005).

Conceptualising Sacred Connection

We adopt a broad, plural definition: **relationship with what one perceives as sacred** (Pargament, 2007). This includes theistic devotion, non-theistic transcendence (e.g., nature-based awe), and secular contemplative reverence. Two clarifications:

1. **Positive vs. negative religious coping.** Positive coping (e.g., benevolent religious reappraisals, collaborative problem-solving with the sacred) predicts better adjustment; negative coping (e.g., spiritual discontent, punishment appraisals) predicts distress (Pargament et al., 1998).

2. **Attachment to God.** Secure attachment representations of the divine associate with greater emotion regulation and wellbeing (Granqvist & Kirkpatrick, 2004).

Psychological Mechanisms

Meaning-Making and Purpose

Sacred worldviews offer coherent narratives and valued goals; meaning mediates associations between spirituality and wellbeing (Park, 2010; Steger, 2009). Purpose and gratitude practices further buffer stress and depression (Emmons & McCullough, 2003).

Self-Transcendence and Moral Emotion

Awe, elevation, and compassion broaden perspective ("small self"), increase prosociality, and orient behaviour toward common good (Keltner & Haidt, 2003; Piff et al., 2015). These emotions are frequently elicited in worship, ritual, and nature immersion.

Self-Regulation and Coping

Religious/spiritual frameworks support self-control and goal persistence, partly via internalised norms and ritual structure (McCullough & Willoughby, 2009). Forgiveness and benevolent reappraisal reduce rumination and anger, enhancing mental health (Worthington & Scherer, 2004; Koenig et al., 2012).

Psychophysiological Pathways

Autonomic Balance and HRV

Loving-kindness/compassion practices and repeated positive emotions predict increases in vagally mediated heart-rate variability (HRV), an index of flexible regulation (Kok & Fredrickson, 2010; Porges, 2011).

Stress Biology and Immune Markers

Mindfulness and related contemplative practices improve immune parameters and down-regulate stress markers (e.g., greater antibody response; Davidson et al., 2003) and may reduce inflammatory signaling (Tang et al., 2015).

Neural Networks

Long-term meditation associates with structural and functional alterations in attention and interoception networks (Lazar et al., 2005) and with training-related changes in empathy-related circuits (Weng et al., 2013). Group ritual also entrains physiology and fosters cohesion (Wiltermuth & Heath, 2009).

Population Health Signals

Frequent service attendance predicts lower mortality and better mental health, partly via social support and health behaviours (VanderWeele et al., 2016).

Leadership Implications

Frameworks

Servant (Greenleaf, 2002/1977), **authentic** (Avolio & Gardner, 2005), and **spiritual leadership** (Fry, 2003) models converge on transcendent purpose, humility, and care. These align with self-transcendent emotions and meaning processes reviewed above.

Mechanisms in Practice

- **Purpose & values clarity** → ethical decision-making under pressure (Fry, 2003).

- **Compassion at work** → stronger ties and recovery from strain (Dutton et al., 2002; Lilius et al., 2008).

- **Elevation & awe** in leaders → contagion of prosocial norms (Haidt, 2003; Piff et al., 2015).

Boundary Conditions and Cultural Humility

Spiritual struggle can exacerbate distress (Pargament et al., 1998). Programs must respect worldview diversity, avoid coercion, and use inclusive language; APA (2017) guidelines recommend culturally humble, consent-based integration of spirituality into care.

Application in *Heart Unbound 2.0*

God/The Divine - Accessible, heart-led practice (brief version).

- **Sacred Pause & Breath-Prayer:** two-minute exhale-lengthened breathing with a chosen sacred word/phrase to nudge parasympathetic tone and felt connection.

- **Contemplative Journaling:** "meaning-mapping" prompts (Where did I sense the sacred today? What value did I enact?) to consolidate purpose.

- **Micro-Rituals of Awe & Gratitude:** daily nature-awe minute and three gratitudes to cultivate self-transcendent emotion and broaden-and-build.

- **Service-as-Practice:** one intentional act of anonymous service weekly; debrief for moral elevation and team climate.

- **Leadership Alignment:** translate felt sacred values into two visible behaviours (e.g., humane scheduling; compassion debriefs) and a boundary that protects dignity. These practices are brief, repeatable, and evidence-congruent, suitable for emerging leaders through senior executives.

Conclusion

A plural, experiential relationship with the sacred engages robust psychological mechanisms (meaning, self-transcendence, adaptive coping) and measurable physiological shifts (vagal flexibility, immune benefits), while providing a moral–motivational architecture for compassionate, high-integrity leadership. Embedding concise, inclusive spiritual micro-practices within *Heart Unbound 2.0* is therefore both scientifically defensible and ethically prudent.

References

American Psychological Association. (2017). *Multicultural guidelines: An ecological approach to context, identity, and intersectionality.*

Avolio, B. J., & Gardner, W. L. (2005). Authentic leadership development: Getting to the root of positive forms of leadership. *The Leadership Quarterly,*

16(3), 315–338. https://doi.org/10.1016/j.leaqua.2005.03.001

Davidson, R. J., Kabat-Zinn, J., Schumacher, J., et al. (2003). Alterations in brain and immune function produced by mindfulness meditation. *Psychosomatic Medicine, 65*(4), 564–570. https://doi.org/10.1097/01.PSY.0000077505.67574.E3

Dutton, J. E., Frost, P., Worline, M., Lilius, J., & Kanov, J. (2002). Leading in times of trauma. *Harvard Business Review, 80*(1), 54–61.

Emmons, R. A., & McCullough, M. E. (2003). Counting blessings versus burdens. *Journal of Personality and Social Psychology, 84*(2), 377–389. https://doi.org/10.1037/0022-3514.84.2.377

Fredrickson, B. L. (2001). The role of positive emotions in positive psychology. *American Psychologist, 56*(3), 218–226. https://doi.org/10.1037/0003-066X.56.3.218

Fry, L. W. (2003). Toward a theory of spiritual leadership. *The Leadership Quarterly, 14*(6), 693–727. https://doi.org/10.1016/j.leaqua.2003.09.001

Granqvist, P., & Kirkpatrick, L. A. (2004). Religious conversion and perceived relationships with God. *Psychological Bulletin, 130*(4), 553–571. https://doi.org/10.1037/0033-2909.130.4.553

Greenleaf, R. K. (2002). *Servant leadership: A journey into the nature of legitimate power and greatness* (25th anniv. ed.). Paulist Press. (Original published 1977)

Haidt, J. (2003). Elevation and the positive psychology of morality. In C. L. M. Keyes & J. Haidt (Eds.), *Flourishing* (pp. 275–289). APA.

Keltner, D., & Haidt, J. (2003). Approaching awe. *Cognition and Emotion, 17*(2), 297–314. https://doi.org/10.1080/02699930302297

Koenig, H. G., King, D., & Carson, V. B. (2012). *Handbook of religion and health* (2nd ed.). Oxford University Press.

Kok, B. E., & Fredrickson, B. L. (2010). Upward spirals of the heart. *Biological Psychology, 85*(3), 432–436. https://doi.org/10.1016/j.biopsycho.2010.09.005

Lazar, S. W., Kerr, C. E., Wasserman, R. H., et al. (2005). Meditation experience is associated with increased cortical thickness. *NeuroReport, 16*(17), 1893–1897. https://doi.org/10.1097/01.wnr.0000186598.66243.19

Lilius, J. M., Worline, M. C., Maitlis, S., et al. (2008). The contours and consequences of compassion at work. *Journal of Organisational Behaviour, 29*(2), 193–218. https://doi.org/10.1002/job.508

McCullough, M. E., & Willoughby, B. L. B. (2009). Religion, self-regulation, and self-control. *Psychological Bulletin, 135*(1), 69–93. https://doi.org/10.1037/a0014213

Park, C. L. (2010). Making sense of the meaning literature. *Psychological Bulletin, 136*(2), 257–301. https://doi.org/10.1037/a0018301

Pargament, K. I. (2007). *Spiritually integrated psychotherapy: Understanding and addressing the sacred.* Guilford Press.

Pargament, K. I., Smith, B. W., Koenig, H. G., & Perez, L. (1998). Patterns of positive and negative religious coping. *Journal for the Scientific Study of Religion, 37*(4), 710–724. https://doi.org/10.2307/1388152

Piff, P. K., Dietze, P., Feinberg, M., Stancato, D., & Keltner, D. (2015). Awe, the small self, and prosocial behaviour. *Journal of Personality and Social Psychology, 108*(6), 883–899. https://doi.org/10.1037/pspi0000018

Porges, S. W. (2011). *The polyvagal theory.* Norton.

Steger, M. F. (2009). Meaning in life. *Psychological Inquiry, 20*(4), 381–385. https://doi.org/10.1080/10478400903333406

Tang, Y.-Y., Hölzel, B. K., & Posner, M. I. (2015). The neuroscience of mindfulness meditation. *Nature Reviews Neuroscience, 16*(4), 213–225. https://doi.org/10.1038/nrn3916

VanderWeele, T. J., Li, S., Tsai, A. C., & Kawachi, I. (2016). Association between religious service attendance and mortality. *JAMA Internal Medicine, 176*(6), 777–785. https://doi.org/10.1001/jamainternmed.2016.1615

Weng, H. Y., Fox, A. S., Shackman, A. J., et al. (2013). Compassion training alters altruism and neural responses. *Psychological Science, 24*(7), 1171–1180. https://doi.org/10.1177/0956797612469537

Wiltermuth, S. S., & Heath, C. (2009). Synchrony and cooperation. *Psychological Science, 20*(1), 1–5. https://doi.org/10.1111/j.1467-9280.2008.02253.x

Worthington, E. L., Jr., & Scherer, M. (2004). Forgiveness is an emotion-focused coping strategy. *Journal of Clinical Psychology, 60*(4), 493–505. https://doi.org/10.1002/jclp.10255

Author Note

This manuscript adopts inclusive language to honor diverse spiritual identities. Practitioners are encouraged to align exercises with participants' beliefs and to screen for spiritual struggle before recommending explicitly sacred practices.

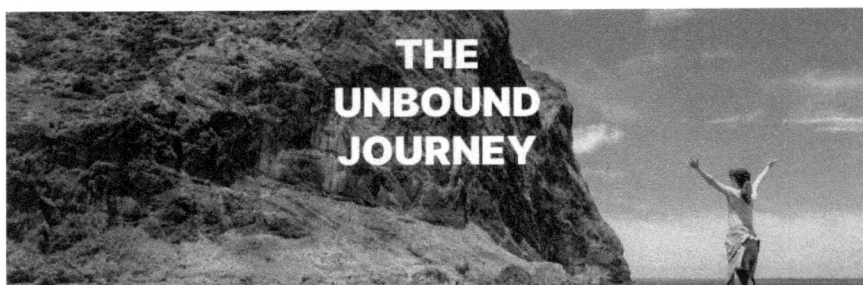

THE
UNBOUND
JOURNEY

14 - "Neurolinguistics" in Heart Unbound 2.0: How Language Rewires Emotion, Physiology, and Leadership

Rationale for this Article

Heart Unbound emphasises "heart-led" change; neurolinguistics provides the mechanistic spine. By linking micro-shifts in wording, metaphor, tone, and self-talk to specific neural and autonomic processes, and then to leader behaviours and team climate, this article gives the chapter empirical legitimacy and practical specificity. It shows participants **how** to translate compassion into circuits, circuits into states, and states into sustainable habits and cultures.

Abstract

Language does not merely describe inner life, it constructs, regulates, and reshapes it. This article validates Chapter 14 ("Neurolinguistics") of *Heart Unbound 2.0* by synthesising evidence from cognitive neuroscience, psychophysiology, and leadership communication. We review classic neurolinguistic foundations (Broca, Wernicke) and contemporary findings showing that self-talk, labeling, and reappraisal modulate limbic and prefrontal systems, alter autonomic activity, and change subsequent behaviour. Empirical literatures on affect labeling, cognitive reappraisal, self-affirmation, and motivating leader language demonstrate reliable effects on stress, problem-solving, prosociality, and team climate. We translate these mechanisms into brief, practicable tools, heart-aligned reframing, compassionate self-talk, affect labeling, implementation intentions, and voice-based practices, sized for coaching and leadership development contexts. We conclude with limitations and a research agenda for Heart Unbound's practice suite. Collectively, convergent data support the chapter's core claim: changing words changes neural processing, which changes state, which, through repetition and social reinforcement, changes trait and culture.

Keywords: neurolinguistics; self-talk; affect labeling; cognitive reappraisal; self-affirmation; polyvagal theory; motivating language; psychological safety; leadership communication

Introduction

Heart Unbound 2.0 positions language as a lever for emotion regulation and heart-led leadership. The promise is compelling: by curating inner and outer speech, participants can down-shift threat responses, up-shift executive control, and create climates of trust. This article integrates key psychological, physiological, and leadership literatures to (a) clarify mechanisms linking words to wellness and performance, and (b) translate those mechanisms into feasible practices for coaching, therapy-adjacent work, and leader development.

Theoretical and Neurological Foundations

From classic localisation to distributed language networks

Nineteenth-century lesion studies identified left-hemisphere regions crucial for speech production (Broca's area) and comprehension (Wernicke's area), inaugurating brain-based models of language (Broca, 1861/1960; Wernicke, 1874/1969). Contemporary neuroimaging has replaced strict modularity with distributed, dynamic networks spanning inferior frontal, superior temporal, and temporoparietal cortices that interact with affective and control systems (Hagoort, 2014).

Language as a constructor of thought and choice

Beyond production and parsing, language shapes attention, memory, and judgment. Framing and metaphor studies show that lexical choices guide inference and policy preferences (Tversky & Kahneman, 1981; Thibodeau & Boroditsky, 2011). Intrapersonally, self-talk scripts alter motivation and performance (Hatzigeorgiadis et al., 2011). These effects reflect a broader principle: repeated linguistic acts train neural pathways (Hebb, 1949) and can reorganise gray matter with practice (Draganski et al., 2004).

Words That Regulate: From Amygdala to Autonomic Balance

Affect labeling and naming emotions

Labeling feelings ("I feel anxious") reliably dampens amygdala activity and recruits right ventrolateral prefrontal cortex, improving regulation (Lieberman et al., 2007). The simple act of putting emotion into words therefore functions as an on-the-spot regulatory skill compatible with coaching and clinical settings.

Cognitive reappraisal and reframing

Reframing the meaning of a stressor engages prefrontal control networks and reduces limbic responses, with downstream benefits for mood and behaviour (Ochsner & Gross, 2005; Buhle et al., 2014). "Heart-aligned reframing" adapts this evidence: reinterpret challenge through values-consistent language ("This is hard *and* meaningful").

Self-affirmation and stress buffering

Self-affirmation theory shows that valuing core identities reduces defensiveness and improves executive functioning under pressure (Steele, 1988; Sherman & Cohen, 2006). Laboratory and field work demonstrate better problem-solving and health behaviour when participants complete brief value-affirmations (Creswell et al., 2013; Epton et al., 2015). Neuroimaging indicates engagement of reward and valuation circuits during affirmation (Cascio et al., 2016).

Voice, prosody, and the vagus

Prosodic features of speech interface with autonomic state. Polyvagal theory posits that warm vocal prosody co-regulates safety via the myelinated vagus, supporting social engagement and down-regulating sympathetic arousal (Porges, 2011). Compassionate self-talk and calm leader tone are therefore not cosmetic, they are physiological signals.

The Psychology of Self-Talk and Identity Language

Negative self-talk sustains shame and avoidance; compassionate self-talk predicts resilience and approach motivation (Beck, 1976; Neff, 2003). Studies contrasting self-criticism with self-reassurance show distinct neural signatures, with the latter linked to reduced threat processing (Longe et al., 2010). Subtle lexical shifts (e.g., adding *yet*; adopting growth-mindset language) sustain effort and learning (Dweck, 2006). Implementation intentions, if-then scripts stated in concrete language, improve follow-through on goals (Gollwitzer, 1999; Adriaanse et al., 2010).

Language and Leadership: From Individual State to Collective Climate

Leader talk shapes attention, meaning, and belonging. Motivating Language Theory (MLT) shows that direction-giving, empathetic, and meaning-making speech improves satisfaction, commitment, and performance (Mayfield & Mayfield, 2017). Charismatic leadership tactics that use metaphor, contrast, and moral conviction elevate perceived effectiveness (Antonakis et al., 2011). Psychological safety, a climate where interpersonal risk-taking feels safe, depends on consistent, respectful, non-punitive language (Edmondson, 1999, 2018). Inclusive, non-biased wording strengthens belonging and applicant diversity in talent pipelines (Madera et al., 2019).

Mechanistic bridge: The same micro-skills that calm an individual nervous system (labeling, reappraisal, affirming values, warm prosody) scale into conversational norms that regulate group affect and cognition, producing steadier decision-making and more ethical, prosocial cultures.

Evidence-Informed Practice: A Heart-Led Neurolinguistic Toolkit

1. **Affect Labeling (10–15 seconds) -** Name the present feeling ("anxious," "sad," "angry"). Pair with a slow exhale. Mechanism: R VLPFC ↑, amygdala ↓ (Lieberman et al., 2007).

2. **Heart-Aligned Reframing -** Convert catastrophic appraisals to values-consistent frames ("This challenge is an arena for courage"). Mechanism: prefrontal control and reappraisal (Buhle et al., 2014).

3. **Values Affirmation (2–3 min) -** Write about a core value and its enactment today. Mechanism: self-integrity, reward/valuation systems, stress buffering (Creswell et al., 2013; Cascio et al., 2016).

4. **Compassionate Self-Talk Script -** Replace self-criticism with supportive phrases ("This is tough; I can take the next wise step").

Mechanism: reduced threat reactivity; self-compassion outcomes (Neff, 2003; Longe et al., 2010).

5. **Implementation Intentions with Language Cues** - "If [trigger], then I will [specific behaviour]" (e.g., "If my heart rate spikes in a meeting, then I name the feeling and ask one clarifying question"). Mechanism: cue–response automatisation (Gollwitzer, 1999).

6. **Prosodic Grounding** - Before high-stakes interactions, lengthen exhale and speak 5–10% slower to signal safety. Mechanism: vagal engagement and social co-regulation (Porges, 2011).

7. **Leader Motivating Language Routines** - Open with purpose framing; give clear next actions; close by acknowledging effort and learning (Mayfield & Mayfield, 2017).

Application in Heart Unbound 2.0

Micro-Practices for Programs and Cohorts

- **Affect-Label Breaks:** At transition points, participants briefly name inner state + one breath.

- **Reframe Rounds:** In triads, one person shares a live stressor; peers offer two heart-aligned reframes each, grounded in values.

- **"Voice of the Heart" Recordings:** Participants record 60–90 seconds of compassionate self-talk to play morning/evening (self-compassion + prosody).

- **If-Then Cards:** Write and carry two implementation intentions that tie triggers to regulating language.

- **Leader Language Labs:** Practice MLT scripts (purpose → direction → empathy) with feedback on clarity, tone, and inclusion.

Limitations and Future Directions

Most lab studies use brief tasks with WEIRD samples; generalization to diverse identities and high-stakes leadership contexts warrants cautious adaptation. Some constructs (e.g., polyvagal interpretations) remain debated; program evaluation should incorporate mixed methods (HRV, experience sampling, behavioral coding). Future research within *Heart Unbound* could compare cohorts receiving standard training versus training plus neurolinguistic micro-practices on outcomes such as HRV, perceived psychological safety, and leader language audits.

Conclusion

Across levels, neuron, narrative, and network, language is leverage. Affect labeling, reappraisal, self-affirmation, compassionate prosody, and motivating leader language constitute a compact, evidence-aligned toolkit for the *Heart Unbound 2.0* journey. In practice, participants learn to speak differently so they can feel differently, decide differently, and lead differently.

References

Adriaanse, M. A., Gollwitzer, P. M., De Ridder, D. T. D., De Wit, J. B. F., & Kroese, F. (2010). Breaking habits with implementation intentions: A test of underlying processes. *Personality and Social Psychology Bulletin, 36*(4), 502–513. https://doi.org/10.1177/0146167210365053

Antonakis, J., Fenley, M., & Liechti, S. (2011). Can charisma be taught? Tests of two interventions. *Academy of Management Learning & Education, 10*(3), 374–396. https://doi.org/10.5465/amle.2010.0012

Beck, A. T. (1976). *Cognitive therapy and the emotional disorders.* International Universities Press.

Broca, P. (1960). Remarques sur le siège de la faculté du langage articulé. In *Mémoires d'anthropologie* (Vol. 1, pp. 165–196). (Original work published 1861)

Buhle, J. T., Silvers, J. A., Wager, T. D., Lopez, R., Onyemekwu, C., Kober, H., … Ochsner, K. N. (2014). Cognitive reappraisal of emotion: A meta-analysis of human neuroimaging studies. *Cerebral Cortex, 24*(11), 2981–2990. https://doi.org/10.1093/cercor/bht154

Cascio, C. N., O'Donnell, M. B., Tinney, F. J., Lieberman, M. D., Taylor, S. E., Strecher, V. J., & Falk, E. B. (2016). Self-affirmation activates brain systems associated with self-related processing and reward and is reinforced by future orientation. *Social Cognitive and Affective Neuroscience, 11*(4), 621–629. https://doi.org/10.1093/scan/nsv136

Creswell, J. D., Dutcher, J. M., Klein, W. M. P., Harris, P. R., & Levine, J. M. (2013). Self-affirmation improves problem-solving under stress. *PLoS ONE,*

8(5), e62593. https://doi.org/10.1371/journal.pone.0062593

Draganski, B., Gaser, C., Busch, V., Schuierer, G., Bogdahn, U., & May, A. (2004). Neuroplasticity: Changes in grey matter induced by training. *Nature, 427*(6972), 311–312. https://doi.org/10.1038/427311a

Dweck, C. S. (2006). *Mindset: The new psychology of success.* Random House.

Edmondson, A. C. (1999). Psychological safety and learning behaviour in work teams. *Administrative Science Quarterly, 44*(2), 350–383. https://doi.org/10.2307/2666999

Edmondson, A. C. (2018). *The fearless organisation: Creating psychological safety in the workplace for learning, innovation, and growth.* Wiley.

Epton, T., Harris, P. R., Kane, R., van Koningsbruggen, G. M., & Sheeran, P. (2015). The impact of self-affirmation on health-behaviour change: A meta-analysis. *Health Psychology, 34*(3), 187–196. https://doi.org/10.1037/hea0000116

Gollwitzer, P. M. (1999). Implementation intentions: Strong effects of simple plans. *American Psychologist, 54*(7), 493–503. https://doi.org/10.1037/0003-066X.54.7.493

Hagoort, P. (2014). Nodes and networks in the neural architecture for language: Broca's region and beyond. *Current Opinion in Neurobiology, 28*, 136–141. https://doi.org/10.1016/j.conb.2014.07.013

Hatzigeorgiadis, A., Zourbanos, N., Galanis, E., & Theodorakis, Y. (2011). Self-talk and sports performance: A meta-analysis. *Perspectives on Psychological Science, 6*(4), 348–356. https://doi.org/10.1177/1745691611413136

Hebb, D. O. (1949). *The organisation of behaviour: A neuropsychological theory.* Wiley.

Lieberman, M. D., Eisenberger, N. I., Crockett, M. J., Tom, S. M., Pfeifer, J. H., & Way, B. M. (2007). Putting feelings into words: Affect labeling disrupts amygdala activity in response to affective stimuli. *Psychological Science, 18*(5), 421–428. https://doi.org/10.1111/j.1467-9280.2007.01916.x

Longe, O., Maratos, F. A., Gilbert, P., Evans, G., Volker, F., Rockliff, H., & Rippon, G. (2010). Having a word with yourself: Neural correlates of self-criticism and self-reassurance. *NeuroImage, 49*(2), 1849–1856. https://doi.org/10.1016/j.neuroimage.2009.09.019

Madera, J. M., Hebl, M. R., Dial, H., Martin, R., & Valian, V. (2019). Raising doubt in letters of recommendation for academia: Gender differences and their impact. *Journal of Business and Psychology, 34*(3), 287–303. https://doi.org/10.1007/s10869-018-9541-1

Mayfield, J., & Mayfield, M. (2017). *Motivating language theory: Effective leader talk in the workplace*. Palgrave Macmillan.

Neff, K. D. (2003). Self-compassion: An alternative conceptualisation of a healthy attitude toward oneself. *Self and Identity, 2*(2), 85–101. https://doi.org/10.1080/15298860309032

Ochsner, K. N., & Gross, J. J. (2005). The cognitive control of emotion. *Trends in Cognitive Sciences, 9*(5), 242–249. https://doi.org/10.1016/j.tics.2005.03.010

Porges, S. W. (2011). *The polyvagal theory: Neurophysiological foundations of emotions, attachment, communication, and self-regulation*. Norton.

Sherman, D. K., & Cohen, G. L. (2006). The psychology of self-defense: Self-affirmation theory. *Advances in Experimental Social Psychology, 38*, 183–242. https://doi.org/10.1016/S0065-2601(06)38004-5

Steele, C. M. (1988). The psychology of self-affirmation: Sustaining the integrity of the self. *In* L. Berkowitz (Ed.), *Advances in experimental social psychology* (Vol. 21, pp. 261–302). Academic Press.

Thibodeau, P. H., & Boroditsky, L. (2011). Metaphors we think with: The role of metaphor in reasoning. *PLoS ONE, 6*(2), e16782. https://doi.org/10.1371/journal.pone.0016782

Tversky, A., & Kahneman, D. (1981). The framing of decisions and the psychology of choice. *Science, 211*(4481), 453–458. https://doi.org/10.1126/science.7455683

Wernicke, C. (1969). *The aphasic symptom complex*. In G. H. Eggert (Ed.), *Wernicke's works on aphasia* (pp. 91–145). Mouton. (Original work published 1874)

15 - "Compassion" as a Core Mechanism of Emotional Intelligence and Ethical Leadership: The Evidence for Compassion

Rationale for the Article

The chapter invites readers to treat compassion as a disciplined capability rather than sentiment. This article supplies the empirical scaffolding, mechanisms, controlled trials, and leadership outcomes, showing that compassionate states can be reliably induced, measured, and scaled. By connecting compassion to autonomic regulation, reward circuitry, and organisational performance, the paper ensures *Heart Unbound 2.0* rests on rigorous science while remaining profoundly practical for emerging and seasoned leaders.

Abstract

Compassion, the motivation to notice suffering and to act to alleviate it, has moved from moral ideal to measurable biopsychosocial capacity. This article synthesises psychological, physiological, and leadership science to examine compassion as the central mechanism envisioned in Chapter 15 ("Compassion") of *Heart Unbound 2.0*. We differentiate compassion from empathy, review neural and endocrine pathways (anterior insula, anterior cingulate cortex, ventral striatum, oxytocinergic signaling, and vagal regulation), and summarise randomised and quasi-experimental trials of compassion training (Mindful Self-Compassion, Compassion Cultivation

Training, loving-kindness meditation). Convergent findings link compassion with reduced distress and psychopathology, higher heart-rate variability, healthier cortisol dynamics, prosocial behaviour, psychological safety, and improved team effectiveness. We translate these data into implementable practices for individuals and leaders and propose measurement and boundary strategies that prevent empathic over-arousal while sustaining "wise, warm" action. The evidence base validates the chapter's claims that compassion is trainable, protective, and performance-relevant, an indispensable pillar for heart-led self-leadership and organisational life.

Keywords: compassion; self-compassion; empathy; oxytocin; heart-rate variability; psychological safety; leadership; loving-kindness; Compassion Cultivation Training; Mindful Self-Compassion

Opening reflection (practice inset)

Place a hand on your heart and take three slow breaths. Imagine warmth flowing first to yourself, then outward to others. Ask: *What would change if I met this moment with tenderness rather than judgment?* Let this question set the tone for reading.

Introduction

Across wisdom traditions and modern science, compassion is framed as a disciplined response to suffering that preserves dignity and catalyses repair (Goetz et al., 2010). In emotionally complex, high-stakes environments, compassion is not a luxury; it is a regulator of individual stress, a lubricant of coordination, and a predictor of ethical influence (Worline & Dutton, 2017). This review evaluates the empirical foundations for Chapter 15 of *Heart Unbound 2.0*, clarifying mechanisms, outcomes, and applications for personal practice and leadership.

Defining compassion and distinguishing it from empathy

Empathy refers to sharing or understanding another's state (affective or cognitive). Unbuffered, it can produce empathic distress and withdrawal. Compassion adds a prosocial intention to alleviate suffering and recruits distinct, more resilient neural systems (Singer & Klimecki, 2014). Experimental training that shifts people from pure empathy to compassion reduces negative affect while increasing helping behaviour and reward-circuit activation (Klimecki et al., 2014; Weng et al., 2013). In practice, *empathy connects; compassion mobilises.*

Psychological mechanisms: self-compassion as the internal basecamp

Self-compassion, ttreating oneself with kindness, common humanity, and mindful awareness, predicts less anxiety, depression, and shame and more adaptive motivation across cultures (MacBeth & Gumley, 2012; Neff, 2003, 2009). Self-compassionate people show reduced stress reactivity to negative events and healthier coping (Leary et al., 2007; Neff et al., 2007). Randomised trials of Mindful Self-Compassion (MSC) indicate medium-to-large improvements in self-compassion, mindfulness, and well-being, with decreases in stress and depression (Neff & Germer, 2013; Ferrari et al., 2019). Because compassion for others draws from the same regulatory systems, self-compassion functions as the foundation for sustainable caregiving and leadership presence (Gilbert, 2014).

Physiological and neural pathways of compassion

Autonomic regulation and heart-rate variability

Compassion practices reliably engage parasympathetic dominance indexed by vagally mediated heart-rate variability (HRV). Loving-kindness training increased daily positive emotions and, over time, vagal tone, a biomarker of flexible regulation and social approach (Kok et al., 2013). HRV findings are consistent with the neurovisceral integration model linking prefrontal control to cardiac vagal modulation (Thayer & Lane, 2000, 2009).

Endocrine and immune correlates

Compassion and affiliation states increase oxytocin release, which supports trust, social bonding, and cardiovascular down-regulation (Carter, 2014). In a randomised study, compassion meditation buffered inflammatory responses (IL-6) to psychosocial stress among high-practice participants (Pace et al., 2009).

Brain systems

Neuroimaging associates compassion with increased activity in the anterior insula and anterior cingulate (salience/feeling-for), ventromedial prefrontal cortex (valuation), and ventral striatum (caregiving reward), distinct from the pain-matrix predominance during empathic distress (Klimecki et al., 2014; Singer & Klimecki, 2014). Compassion meditation enhances empathic accuracy and modulates related neural activity (Mascaro et al., 2013).

Evidence for trainability

Multiple intervention families cultivate compassion:

- **Loving-kindness/compassion meditation (LKM/CM).** Longitudinal and randomised trials show gains in positive emotion, social connectedness, and resources (Fredrickson et al., 2008) and increased altruism alongside neural plasticity (Weng et al., 2013).

- **Compassion Cultivation Training (CCT).** An 8-week protocol increased compassion, mindfulness, and emotion regulation while reducing avoidance and distress (Jazaieri et al., 2013, 2016).

- **Compassion-Focused Therapy (CFT).** Targeting shame and threat-based self-systems, CFT improves self-reassurance and reduces psychopathology; meta-analyses support effectiveness across conditions (Gilbert, 2014; Kirby et al., 2017).

- **Mindful Self-Compassion (MSC).** RCTs demonstrate durable improvements in self-compassion and mental health with moderate effect sizes at follow-up (Neff & Germer, 2013; Ferrari et al., 2019).

Collectively, these studies validate the chapter's practice claims: compassion is a trainable, state-to-trait capacity with biopsychosocial dividends.

Compassion in leadership and teams

Compassion directly enables the relational conditions under which performance and learning flourish.

- **Psychological safety and learning.** Leaders who respond to fallibility with curiosity and care foster team psychological safety and adaptive learning (Edmondson, 1999).

- **Companionate emotional culture.** Field research in a hospital system found that norms of tenderness, care, and compassion predicted reduced burnout and improved performance and satisfaction (Barsade & O'Neill, 2014).

- **Organisational compassion.** Compassionate responses to pain, recognition, feeling, and action, create resilient, trustworthy systems (Worline & Dutton, 2017; Lilius et al., 2008).

- **Coaching with compassion.** Coaching that evokes personal vision and caring relationships activates neural networks linked to openness and renewal, improving engagement and development (Boyatzis et al., 2019).

- **Healthcare leadership.** Compassionate leadership models in health systems are associated with safer care and workforce well-being (West et al., 2017).

These literatures converge on a practical thesis: *compassion is an efficiency, not a cost*, because it reduces threat physiology, enables sense-making, and mobilises discretionary effort.

Boundaries and sustainability: from empathic distress to "wise warmth"

To avoid burnout, training emphasises (a) self-compassion and boundary clarity, (b) shifting from empathic sharing to compassionate care when arousal spikes, and (c) micro-recovery (breath, posture, gaze softening) that reinstates vagal tone (Klimecki et al., 2014; Neff, 2009). Recognising the distinction between *feeling with* and *acting for* protects helpers and sustains responsiveness over time (Figley, 1995; Singer & Klimecki, 2014).

Application in *Heart Unbound 2.0*: brief protocol suite

Practice stack (10–15 minutes/day).

1. **Compassion breath & posture (2 min).** Lengthen exhale (4–6s), soften jaw/shoulders; silently label: *"Suffering is here; warmth is possible."*

2. **Self-compassion break (3 min).** Mindfulness ("this is hard"), common humanity ("others struggle too"), kindness phrase (Neff & Germer, 2013).

3. **Loving-kindness micro-sequence (3–5 min).** *May I be safe… May you be safe… May we be at ease.*

4. **Compassionate micro-action (daily).** One concrete behaviour that reduces someone's workload or emotional load.

5. **Team norming (monthly).** Five-minute "compassion check-in" at the start of key meetings: What support will help you contribute today?

Measurement. Use the Self-Compassion Scale–Short Form (Neff, 2003), state compassion ratings, and brief HRV snapshots (if available) to visualise progress.

Conclusion

Compassion is not an optional virtue; it is a core technology of human regulation and collective effectiveness. Through self-compassion and outward compassion, individuals down-shift threat physiology, up-shift prosocial motivation, and create climates where truth and learning are safe. The cumulative evidence validates Chapter 15's central claim: practicing compassion is both personally healing and professionally transformative. In a volatile world, "wise warmth" is a competitive and humane advantage.

References

Barsade, S. G., & O'Neill, O. A. (2014). What's love got to do with it? A longitudinal study of the culture of companionate love and employee and client outcomes in a long-term care setting. *Administrative Science Quarterly, 59*(4), 551–598. https://doi.org/10.1177/0001839214538636

Boyatzis, R. E., Smith, M. L., & Van Oosten, E. (2019). *Helping people change: Coaching with compassion for lifelong learning and growth.* Harvard Business Review Press.

Carter, C. S. (2014). Oxytocin pathways and the evolution of human behaviour. *Annual Review of Psychology, 65*, 17–39. https://doi.org/10.1146/annurev-psych-010213-115110

Edmondson, A. (1999). Psychological safety and learning behaviour in work teams. *Administrative Science Quarterly, 44*(2), 350–383. https://doi.org/10.2307/2666999

Ferrari, M., Hunt, C., Harrysunker, A., Abbott, M. J., Beath, A. P., & Einstein, D. A. (2019). Self-compassion interventions and psychosocial outcomes: A meta-analysis of RCTs. *Mindfulness, 10*(8), 1455–1473.

https://doi.org/10.1007/s12671-019-01134-6

Figley, C. R. (1995). Compassion fatigue as secondary traumatic stress disorder: An overview. In C. R. Figley (Ed.), *Compassion fatigue* (pp. 1–20). Brunner/Mazel.

Fredrickson, B. L., Cohn, M. A., Coffey, K. A., Pek, J., & Finkel, S. M. (2008). Open hearts build lives: Positive emotions, induced through loving-kindness meditation, build consequential personal resources. *Journal of Personality and Social Psychology, 95*(5), 1045–1062. https://doi.org/10.1037/a0013262

Gilbert, P. (2014). *The compassionate mind* (Updated ed.). Constable. (See also Compassion-Focused Therapy corpus.)

Goetz, J. L., Keltner, D., & Simon-Thomas, E. (2010). Compassion: An evolutionary analysis and empirical review. *Psychological Bulletin, 136*(3), 351–374. https://doi.org/10.1037/a0018807

Jazaieri, H., McGonigal, K., Jinpa, T., Doty, J. R., Gross, J. J., & Goldin, P. R. (2013). A randomised controlled trial of compassion cultivation training: Effects on mindfulness, affect, and emotion regulation. *Motivation and Emotion, 37*(1), 21–35. https://doi.org/10.1007/s11031-012-9368-z

Jazaieri, H., Jinpa, T., McGonigal, K., Rosenberg, E., Finkelstein, J., Simon-Thomas, E., Cullen, M., Doty, J. R., Gross, J. J., & Goldin, P. R. (2016). Enhancing compassion: A randomized controlled trial of a compassion cultivation training program. *Journal of Happiness Studies, 17*(1), 89–105. https://doi.org/10.1007/s10902-014-9552-9

Kirby, J. N., Tellegen, C. L., & Steindl, S. R. (2017). A meta-analysis of compassion-focused therapy. *Clinical Psychology Review, 54*, 1–14. https://doi.org/10.1016/j.cpr.2017.04.003

Klimecki, O. M., Leiberg, S., Lamm, C., & Singer, T. (2014). Functional neural plasticity and associated changes in positive affect after compassion training. *Cerebral Cortex, 24*(7), 166–173. https://doi.org/10.1093/cercor/bhs142

Kok, B. E., Coffey, K. A., Cohn, M. A., Catalino, L. I., Vacharkulksemsuk, T., Algoe, S. B., Brantley, M., & Fredrickson, B. L. (2013). How positive emotions build physical health: Perceived positive social connections account for the upward spiral between positive emotions and vagal tone. *Proceedings of the National Academy of Sciences, 110*(48), 19119–19124. https://doi.org/10.1073/pnas.1308246110

Leary, M. R., Tate, E. B., Adams, C. E., Allen, A. B., & Hancock, J. (2007). Self-compassion and reactions to unpleasant self-relevant events. *Journal of Personality and Social Psychology, 92*(5), 887–904. https://doi.org/10.1037/0022-3514.92.5.887

Lilius, J. M., Worline, M. C., Maitlis, S., Kanov, J., Dutton, J. E., & Frost, P. (2008). The contours and consequences of compassion at work. *Journal of Organisational Behaviour, 29*(2), 193–218. https://doi.org/10.1002/job.508

MacBeth, A., & Gumley, A. (2012). Exploring compassion: A meta-analysis of the association between self-compassion and psychopathology. *Clinical Psychology Review, 32*(6), 545–552. https://doi.org/10.1016/j.cpr.2012.06.003

Mascaro, J. S., Rilling, J. K., Tenzin Negi, L., & Raison, C. L. (2013). Compassion meditation enhances empathic accuracy and related neural activity. *Social Cognitive and Affective Neuroscience, 8*(1), 48–55. https://doi.org/10.1093/scan/nss095

Neff, K. D. (2003). The development and validation of a scale to measure self-compassion. *Self and Identity, 2*(3), 223–250. https://doi.org/10.1080/15298860309027

Neff, K. D. (2009). Self-compassion. In M. R. Leary & R. H. Hoyle (Eds.), *Handbook of individual differences in social behaviour* (pp. 561–573). Guilford Press.

Neff, K. D., & Germer, C. K. (2013). A pilot study and randomised controlled trial of the Mindful Self-Compassion program. *Journal of Clinical Psychology, 69*(1), 28–44. https://doi.org/10.1002/jclp.21923

Neff, K. D., Kirkpatrick, K. L., & Rude, S. S. (2007). Self-compassion and adaptive psychological functioning. *Journal of Research in Personality, 41*(1), 139–154. https://doi.org/10.1016/j.jrp.2006.03.004

Pace, T. W. W., Negi, L. T., Adame, D. D., Cole, S. P., Sivilli, T. I., Brown, T. D., Issa, M. J., & Raison, C. L. (2009). Effect of compassion meditation on neuroendocrine, innate immune and behavioural responses to psychosocial stress. *Psychoneuroendocrinology, 34*(1), 87–98. https://doi.org/10.1016/j.psyneuen.2008.08.011

Singer, T., & Klimecki, O. M. (2014). Empathy and compassion. *Current Biology, 24*(18), R875–R878. https://doi.org/10.1016/j.cub.2014.06.054

Thayer, J. F., & Lane, R. D. (2000). A model of neurovisceral integration in emotion regulation and dysregulation. *Journal of Affective Disorders, 61*(3), 201–216. https://doi.org/10.1016/S0165-0327(00)00338-4

Thayer, J. F., & Lane, R. D. (2009). Claude Bernard and the heart–brain connection: Further elaboration of a model of neurovisceral integration. *Neuroscience & Biobehavioural Reviews, 33*(2), 81–88. https://doi.org/10.1016/j.neubiorev.2008.08.004

Weng, H. Y., Fox, A. S., Shackman, A. J., Stodola, D. E., Caldwell, J. Z. K., Olson, M. C., Rogers, G. M., & Davidson, R. J. (2013). Compassion training alters altruism and neural responses to suffering. *Proceedings of the National Academy of Sciences, 110*(15), 5738–5743. https://doi.org/10.1073/pnas.1218522110

West, M., Eckert, R., Collins, B., & Chowla, R. (2017). *Caring to change: How compassionate leadership can stimulate innovation in health care.* The King's Fund.

Worline, M. C., & Dutton, J. E. (2017). *Awakening compassion at work: The quiet power that elevates people and organisations.* Berrett-Koehler.

THE
UNBOUND
JOURNEY

16 - "Photographs": Seeing the Heart, Leading With Presence

Rationale for the Article

The *Happy Place* chapter invites participants to visualise and embody safe, restorative spaces. Validating the *Photographs* chapter ensures theoretical and empirical integrity for this next step. Photography strengthens the sensory memory and affective vividness needed for constructing a reliable "inner sanctuary." By grounding safe-space visualisation in neurobiology, narrative identity, and leadership research, this article provides the scholarly scaffolding that Chapter 17 builds upon, helping participants convert images of safety and joy into lasting emotional intelligence resources.

Abstract

Photographs are more than visual records; they are potent psychological and physiological anchors that influence memory, emotional regulation, and identity construction. This article validates the sixteenth chapter of *Heart Unbound 2.0 – Photographs*, through an integrative review of neuroscience, positive psychology, narrative identity, and contemporary leadership research. Photographic reflection activates autobiographical memory networks, down-regulates stress responses, and strengthens emotional intelligence capacities essential for authentic leadership. Drawing from polyvagal theory, self-compassion research, and reflective practice models, the paper argues that intentional photographic engagement, both taking and contemplatively viewing images, serves as a tool for self-awareness, resilience, and heart-centred leadership development. The article also demonstrates how this chapter's practices translate theory into accessible transformation for individuals and leaders.

Keywords: photographs, emotional intelligence, narrative identity, polyvagal theory, authentic leadership, Heart Unbound

Introduction

Images are foundational to human meaning-making. Long before written language, humans used visual symbols to transmit values and identity (Arnheim, 1974). In the digital era, photographs saturate daily life, yet their potential as deliberate tools for self-reflection and leadership development remains under-examined. The *Heart Unbound 2.0* program positions photography not as aesthetic hobby but as a heart-centred practice, helping participants see their own worth, surface tacit emotional narratives, and lead authentically.

Photographs and Psychological Well-Being

Memory consolidation and identity: Autobiographical memory integrates sensory, affective, and narrative elements (Conway & Pleydell-Pearce, 2000). Taking or curating photographs activates the hippocampus and medial prefrontal cortex, reinforcing personal identity coherence (Cabeza & St Jacques, 2007). Reflective photo practices can disrupt negative self-schemas and strengthen positive self-concept (Neimeyer et al., 2020).

Emotion regulation: Viewing personally meaningful images engages the brain's reward circuitry and dampens amygdala reactivity, promoting calm and positive affect (Bradley et al., 2015). Positive reminiscence via photographs correlates with reduced depressive rumination (Specht & King, 2022) and enhanced self-compassion (Gilbert & Choden, 2013).

Polyvagal perspective: According to Porges (2011), visual cues of safety, familiar faces, nurturing landscapes, activate the parasympathetic (ventral vagal) system, supporting social engagement and emotional regulation. Photo-elicitation can therefore serve as an accessible neurobiological "safety signal."

Photographs in Leadership and Emotional Intelligence

Authentic and heart-centred leadership: Leadership literature emphasises self-awareness, relational transparency, and values congruence (Avolio & Gardner, 2005; George, 2015). Reflecting on photographs, of personal milestones, mentors, or courageous moments, helps leaders clarify identity and purpose, aligning with emotionally intelligent leadership models (Goleman, Boyatzis, & McKee, 2013).

Narrative leadership: Storytelling strengthens leader-follower trust (Denning, 2011). Photographs function as narrative catalysts, allowing leaders to share origin stories and lived values visually. Integrating visual autobiography into coaching or development programs increases empathy and relational capacity (Shamir & Eilam, 2005).

Wellbeing and resilience in high-pressure contexts: Leaders in volatile environments benefit from resilience tools. Visual reminiscence can reduce burnout and restore meaning (West et al., 2020). For healthcare and corporate executives, curated photo reflection has been shown to increase mindfulness and compassion satisfaction (Potash et al., 2014).

Application in *Heart Unbound 2.0*

Mirroring the accessible practice design of the "I Am" chapter, *Photographs* integrates rigorous theory into **heart-led exercises** that are simultaneously healing and leadership-enhancing:

- **Photo-Journaling & Narrative Mapping:** Participants select or capture five images daily, then write short reflections linking each image to emotion, value, or moment of aliveness. This practice supports autobiographical coherence and gratitude.

- **Compassionate Gaze Practice:** Viewing self-portraits with curiosity and kindness to reduce self-criticism and build self-acceptance.

- **Memory-Based Safe Anchoring:** Using images of safe places or loved ones to down-regulate stress (polyvagal cueing) before challenging conversations or leadership tasks.

- **Leadership Story Curation:** Participants identify photographs that embody purpose, courage, or service, then craft visual narratives to share with teams, enhancing authenticity and connection.

These practices extend beyond personal healing into professional transformation, equipping emerging leaders and seasoned executives to lead with presence, empathy, and resilience.

Implications for Practice and Research

- **Therapeutic and coaching contexts:** Photographic reflection complements mindfulness-based stress reduction and narrative coaching.

- **Organisational wellbeing:** Visual storytelling workshops can reduce burnout and foster values alignment.

- **Future research:** Longitudinal studies could measure changes in heart-rate variability, self-compassion, and leadership 360-feedback scores after structured photographic interventions.

Conclusion

Photographs are not mere artefacts; they are neurobiological and narrative portals into the heart. By intentionally engaging with personal imagery, individuals access safety, regulate emotions, and re-author their leadership story. *Heart Unbound 2.0* leverages this ancient yet modern medium to cultivate authentic, resilient, and compassionate leaders.

References

Arnheim, R. (1974). *Art and visual perception: A psychology of the creative eye* (Rev. ed.). University of California Press.

Avolio, B. J., & Gardner, W. L. (2005). Authentic leadership development: Getting to the root of positive forms of leadership. *The Leadership Quarterly, 16*(3), 315–338. https://doi.org/10.1016/j.leaqua.2005.03.001

Bradley, M. M., Miccoli, L. M., Escrig, M. A., & Lang, P. J. (2015). The pupil as a measure of emotional arousal and autonomic activation. *Psychophysiology, 52*(10), 1386–1398. https://doi.org/10.1111/psyp.12471

Cabeza, R., & St Jacques, P. L. (2007). Functional neuroimaging of autobiographical memory. *Trends in Cognitive Sciences, 11*(5), 219–227. https://doi.org/10.1016/j.tics.2007.02.005

Conway, M. A., & Pleydell-Pearce, C. W. (2000). The construction of autobiographical memories in the self-memory system. *Psychological Review, 107*(2), 261–288. https://doi.org/10.1037/0033-295X.107.2.261

Denning, S. (2011). *The leader's guide to storytelling: Mastering the art and discipline of business narrative* (Rev. ed.). Jossey-Bass.

George, B. (2015). *Discover your true north* (2nd ed.). Wiley.

Gilbert, P., & Choden. (2013). *Mindful compassion: How the science of compassion can help you understand your emotions, live in the present, and connect deeply with others.* Constable & Robinson.

Goleman, D., Boyatzis, R., & McKee, A. (2013). *Primal leadership: Unleashing the power of emotional intelligence* (10th anniversary ed.). Harvard Business Review Press.

Neimeyer, R. A., Torres, C., & Smith, D. C. (2020). Narrative resonance and the reconstruction of identity. *Death Studies, 44*(9), 567–577. https://doi.org/10.1080/07481187.2018.1522385

Porges, S. W. (2011). *The polyvagal theory: Neurophysiological foundations of emotions, attachment, communication, and self-regulation.* Norton.

Potash, J. S., Ho, R. T. H., Chan, F., Wang, X. L., & Cheng, C. (2014). Can art therapy reduce death anxiety and burnout in end-of-life care workers? A quasi-experimental study. *International Journal of Palliative Nursing, 20*(5), 233–240. https://doi.org/10.12968/ijpn.2014.20.5.233

Shamir, B., & Eilam, G. (2005). "What's your story?" A life-stories approach to authentic leadership development. *The Leadership Quarterly, 16*(3), 395–417. https://doi.org/10.1016/j.leaqua.2005.03.005

Specht, J., & King, L. A. (2022). Reminiscence and well-being: A meta-analytic review. *Journal of Positive Psychology, 17*(6), 823–839. https://doi.org/10.1080/17439760.2021.1890068

West, C. P., Dyrbye, L. N., & Shanafelt, T. D. (2020). Physician burnout: Contributors, consequences, and solutions. *Journal of Internal Medicine, 288*(6), 606–618. https://doi.org/10.1111/joim.13101

THE
UNBOUND
JOURNEY

17 - "Happy Place": Building an Inner Sanctuary for Regulation, Meaning, and Authentic Leadership

---

Rationale for the Article

Chapter 17 is a hinge in the curriculum: it converts earlier foundations (breath, gratitude, affirmation, photographs) into a **state-regulation toolkit** participants can deploy under pressure. By grounding "happy place" practices in autonomic physiology, attention science, and leadership evidence, this article provides the scholarly backbone necessary for accreditation, evaluation, and organisational adoption. It also specifies measurable outcomes (HRV, psychological safety, compassion indices), strengthening translational rigour for universities, corporates, and public sector programs.

Abstract

The seventeenth chapter of *Heart Unbound 2.0* - **Happy Place** - proposes that intentionally cultivating an inner (and often imaginal) sanctuary enhances emotional regulation, resilience, and values-aligned leadership. This article validates that claim by integrating evidence from affective neuroscience, psychophysiology, environmental and clinical psychology, and leadership science. We synthesise mechanisms through which "safe-place" imagery and preferred restorative environments influence autonomic balance (vagal activity and heart-rate variability), attentional restoration, autobiographical coherence, and broaden-and-build effects on prosocial functioning. We also translate these mechanisms into practicable protocols for coaching, therapy, and leadership development and connect them to *Heart Unbound 2.0* pedagogy. A brief "Application in *Heart Unbound 2.0*" section (modelled on Chapter 3, **I Am**) operationalises mirror/voice work, identity journaling, daily rituals, and leadership alignment for the **Happy Place** module. We conclude with implications for measurement (e.g., HRV), organisational deployment, and future research.

Keywords: safe-place imagery; heart-rate variability; polyvagal theory; attentional restoration; positive emotions; self-compassion; authentic leadership; *Heart Unbound 2.0*

Introduction

Across spiritual traditions, therapeutic modalities, and everyday self-care, people return, mentally or physically, to a personal refuge of calm. Contemporary science provides converging support: imagery of safety and preferred places down-regulates limbic arousal, increases parasympathetic tone, restores directed attention, and broadens social cognition (Fredrickson, 2013; Kaplan, 1995; Porges, 2011; Thayer & Lane, 2000). For leaders, those states underpin presence, perspective taking, and values-congruent action (Avolio & Gardner, 2005; Boyatzis & McKee, 2005; Edmondson, 2019). This paper reviews the evidence base and translates it into an applied framework that validates *Heart Unbound 2.0* Chapter 17- **Happy Place**.

Conceptualising "Happy Place"

We define a **happy place** as a personally salient environmental memory or imaginal scene reliably associated with safety, contentment, and meaning. It may be physical (e.g., ocean shoreline), relational (the presence of a loved one), or purely imaginal. Three traditions inform this construct:

1. **Environmental psychology:** "restorative environments" (natural settings, favourite places) replenish depleted attention and reduce psychophysiological stress (Kaplan, 1995; Korpela et al., 2001; Ulrich et al., 1991).

2. **Clinical imagery and compassion-focused work:** "safe/safeness imagery" is used to regulate affect and cultivate self-soothing (Gilbert, 2014; Holmes & Mathews, 2010; Shapiro, 2018).

3. **Contemplative science:** mindfulness and loving-kindness practices alter interoception and autonomic balance, improving emotion regulation and prosociality (Kabat-Zinn, 2013; Tang, Hölzel, & Posner, 2015; Neff, 2011).

Psychological and Physiological Mechanisms

1. Autonomic regulation and the vagal system

Safety cues, familiar faces, soothing landscapes, predictable sensory inputs, activate the ventral vagal complex, shifting state from defensive mobilisation to social engagement (Porges, 2011). Heart-rate variability (HRV), a proxy for vagal flexibility, increases with imagery-based relaxation and compassion cultivations (Chalmers et al., 2014; Kok et al., 2013). Higher resting HRV predicts superior executive functioning and adaptive emotion regulation (Thayer & Lane, 2000).

2. Attentional restoration and stress recovery

Attention Restoration Theory posits that "soft fascination" in nature replenishes top-down attentional resources (Kaplan, 1995). Complementary Stress Recovery Theory shows rapid reductions in blood pressure and negative affect after exposure to natural scenes (Ulrich et al., 1991). Internalised "place imagery" appears to mimic these effects (Berto, 2005).

3. Positive emotion and broaden-and-build

Positive affect widens momentary thought–action repertoires and incrementally builds psychological and social resources (Fredrickson, 2013). Happy-place practice reliably elicits calm contentment and gratitude, catalysing upward spirals linked to resilience and social connectedness (Garland et al., 2010; Emmons & McCullough, 2003).

4. Narrative identity and memory reconsolidation

Autobiographical memory is reconstructed with each retrieval (Conway & Pleydell-Pearce, 2000). Repeatedly visiting a place of safeness during reflection or journaling supports identity coherence, counterweights threat-based schemas, and promotes self-continuity under stress (Singer, 2004; Neimeyer, 2004).

5. Interoception, imagery, and emotion generation

Mental imagery recruits sensory cortices and autonomic responses similarly to perception (Kosslyn et al., 2001). Interoceptive awareness practices (e.g., breath to heart area) paired with imagery strengthen body-based predictors of emotion regulation (Craig, 2002; Critchley et al., 2004). This predicts reduced allostatic load over time (McEwen, 1998; Sapolsky, 2004).

6. Digital distraction and the erosion of presence

Chronic interruptions worsen affect and memory, while heavy media multitasking correlates with reduced sustained attention and socio-emotional outcomes (Mark et al., 2014; Ophir, Nass, & Wagner, 2009). Happy-place rituals function as "micro-breaks" that restore attentional control and mood (Sianoja et al., 2018) and counter the well-documented link between mind-wandering and lower momentary happiness (Killingsworth & Gilbert, 2010).

Evidence-Informed Practice Model for Happy Place

Protocol (10–12 minutes; clinical, coaching, or leadership contexts)

1. **Grounding (1–2 min):** diaphragmatic breathing, hand to sternum; set intention (Tang et al., 2015).

2. **Cueing safeness (2–3 min):** evoke sensory details (sight/sound/temperature/texture) of the chosen place; include a compassionate other if helpful (Gilbert, 2014).

3. **Somatic anchoring (2–3 min):** notice interoceptive signals of calm; pair with a phrase/mantra (e.g., "Here I am home").

4. **Integration (2–4 min):** brief journaling on values/next best action; optionally rehearse an upcoming challenge while maintaining safeness.

5. **Transfer:** identify environmental micro-cues (photo, scent, nature exposure) to reactivate the state in daily life.

Measurement and evaluation

- **Physiology:** pre/post HRV (RMSSD), respiration rate.

- **Self-report:** Self-Compassion Scale (Neff, 2003), Positive and Negative Affect Schedule, Perceived Stress Scale, state mindfulness.

- **Leadership outcomes:** psychological safety climate (Edmondson, 2019), compassion at work indices, 360-feedback on presence and regulation.

Applications to Leadership and Teams

Leaders who reliably access calm and perspective demonstrate better emotion regulation and ethical clarity (Avolio & Gardner, 2005; George, 2015). Team-level practices, 90-second safe-place resets before high-stakes meetings; "pause zones" with natural elements; gratitude and micro-moment rituals, improve wellbeing and reduce burnout risk (Maslach & Leiter, 2016; West et al., 2020). Psychological safety is strengthened when leaders disclose their own restoration strategies and invite others to craft personal sanctuaries (Edmondson, 2019; Boyatzis & McKee, 2005).

Application in Heart Unbound 2.0

Grounding turns the chapter's theory into simple, heart-led habits you can use anywhere:

- **Coherent Breath Reset (60–120s):** Breathe at ~5–6 breaths/min with a *longer exhale* to settle the nervous system and lift HRV. Use before hard conversations, role changes, or when you feel keyed up.

- **5–4–3–2–1 Presence Scan (eyes-open, trauma-sensitive):** Name 5 things you see, 4 you hear, 3 you feel, 2 you smell, 1 you taste, or swap senses as needed. Add a grounding object (stone, pen) for touch anchoring.

- **Nature Micro-Rituals (5–10 min):** Step outside for an "attention reset." Notice sky/air/ground, optionally stand barefoot, and take three slow breaths while naming one thing you appreciate about the place you're in.

- **Embodied Leadership Check:** "Feet–Seat–Breath" scan before decisions: feel your feet, feel your seat, soften jaw/shoulders, take three coherent breaths, then choose. Leaders may add a brief HRV/biofeedback read to reinforce regulation.

- **Team Grounding Minute (opt-in):** Open meetings with 60 seconds of shared breath or quiet noticing to invite psychological safety and clearer dialogue.

Why it works: These practices are **personally restorative** and **professionally transferable**, giving emerging and senior leaders a

---

> repeatable way to return to presence, act from values, and model calm, authentic self-leadership.

Case Vignette (Emmanuel)

The Emmanuel narrative, moving from chronic busyness to barefoot recovery in grass, illustrates classic restorative pathways: rapid down-regulation (Ulrich et al., 1991), attentional restoration (Kaplan, 1995), and broaden-and-build accrual (Fredrickson, 2013). As load decreased, sense-making and values clarity increased, enabling more deliberate, human-centred leadership choices.

Limitations and Future Directions

Randomised field trials comparing happy-place protocols with standard mindfulness would clarify incremental benefits. Dose–response curves (frequency × duration) and boundary conditions (e.g., trauma histories; van der Kolk, 2014) warrant study. Multimodal outcomes (HRV + behavioural metrics) in leadership populations remain sparse and are recommended.

Conclusion

A well-crafted **happy place** is not escapism; it is a neurobiological resource and a moral technology. By stabilising physiology, restoring attention, and broadening perspective, it enables people, and leaders, to act with clarity and care. *Heart Unbound 2.0* operationalises this science in accessible practices that scale from the inner life to team culture.

References

Avolio, B. J., & Gardner, W. L. (2005). Authentic leadership development: Getting to the root of positive forms of leadership. *The Leadership Quarterly, 16*(3), 315–338. https://doi.org/10.1016/j.leaqua.2005.03.001

Berto, R. (2005). Exposure to restorative environments helps restore attentional capacity. *Journal of Environmental Psychology, 25*(3), 249–259. https://doi.org/10.1016/j.jenvp.2005.07.001

Boyatzis, R., & McKee, A. (2005). *Resonant leadership*. Harvard Business

School Press.

Chalmers, J. A., Quintana, D. S., Abbott, M. J. A., & Kemp, A. H. (2014). Anxiety disorders are associated with reduced heart rate variability: A meta-analysis. *Frontiers in Psychiatry, 5,* 80. https://doi.org/10.3389/fpsyt.2014.00080

Conway, M. A., & Pleydell-Pearce, C. W. (2000). The construction of autobiographical memories in the self-memory system. *Psychological Review, 107*(2), 261–288. https://doi.org/10.1037/0033-295X.107.2.261

Craig, A. D. (2002). How do you feel? Interoception: The sense of the physiological condition of the body. *Nature Reviews Neuroscience, 3*(8), 655–666. https://doi.org/10.1038/nrn894

Critchley, H. D., Wiens, S., Rotshtein, P., Ohman, A., & Dolan, R. J. (2004). Neural systems supporting interoceptive awareness. *Nature Neuroscience, 7*(2), 189–195. https://doi.org/10.1038/nn1176

Edmondson, A. C. (2019). *The fearless organisation: Creating psychological safety in the workplace for learning, innovation, and growth.* Wiley.

Emmons, R. A., & McCullough, M. E. (2003). Counting blessings versus burdens. *Journal of Personality and Social Psychology, 84*(2), 377–389. https://doi.org/10.1037/0022-3514.84.2.377

Fredrickson, B. L. (2013). Positive emotions broaden and build. In P. Devine & A. Plant (Eds.), *Advances in experimental social psychology* (Vol. 47, pp. 1–53). Academic Press.

Garland, E. L., Fredrickson, B. L., Kring, A. M., Johnson, D. P., Meyer, P. S., & Penn, D. L. (2010). Upward spirals of positive emotions counter depression. *Clinical Psychological Science, 1*(3), 256–270. https://doi.org/10.1177/2167702613486607

George, B. (2015). *Discover your true north* (2nd ed.). Wiley.

Gilbert, P. (2014). *The compassionate mind approach to recovering from trauma.* Constable & Robinson.

Holmes, E. A., & Mathews, A. (2010). Mental imagery in emotion and emotional disorders. *Clinical Psychology Review, 30*(3), 349–362. https://doi.org/10.1016/j.cpr.2010.01.001

Kabat-Zinn, J. (2013). *Full catastrophe living* (Rev. ed.). Bantam.

Kaplan, S. (1995). The restorative benefits of nature. *Journal of Environmental*

Psychology, 15(3), 169–182. https://doi.org/10.1016/0272-4944(95)90001-2

Killingsworth, M. A., & Gilbert, D. T. (2010). A wandering mind is an unhappy mind. *Science, 330*(6006), 932. https://doi.org/10.1126/science.1192439

Kok, B. E., Coffey, K. A., Cohn, M. A., Catalino, L. I., Vacharkulksemsuk, T., Algoe, S. B., … Fredrickson, B. L. (2013). High vagal tone is associated with social connectedness. *Emotion, 13*(4), 656–668. https://doi.org/10.1037/a0032720

Korpela, K. M., Ylén, M., Tyrväinen, L., & Silvennoinen, H. (2001). Favorite places and restorative experiences. *Environment and Behaviour, 33*(5), 572–589. https://doi.org/10.1177/00139160121973133

Kosslyn, S. M., Ganis, G., & Thompson, W. L. (2001). Neural foundations of imagery. *Nature Reviews Neuroscience, 2*(9), 635–642. https://doi.org/10.1038/35090055

Mark, G., Iqbal, S. T., Czerwinski, M., Johns, P., & Sano, A. (2014). Bored Mondays and focused afternoons. *Proceedings of CHI*, 3025–3034. https://doi.org/10.1145/2556288.2557204

Maslach, C., & Leiter, M. P. (2016). Understanding the burnout experience. *World Psychiatry, 15*(2), 103–111. https://doi.org/10.1002/wps.20311

McEwen, B. S. (1998). Protective and damaging effects of stress mediators. *New England Journal of Medicine, 338*(3), 171–179. https://doi.org/10.1056/NEJM199801153380307

Neff, K. D. (2011). Self-compassion, self-esteem, and well-being. *Social and Personality Psychology Compass, 5*(1), 1–12. https://doi.org/10.1111/j.1751-9004.2010.00330.x

Neimeyer, R. A. (2004). Fostering posttraumatic growth. *Psychological Inquiry, 15*(1), 53–59. https://doi.org/10.1207/s15327965pli1501_03

Ophir, E., Nass, C., & Wagner, A. D. (2009). Cognitive control in media multitaskers. *Proceedings of the National Academy of Sciences, 106*(37), 15583–15587. https://doi.org/10.1073/pnas.0903620106

Porges, S. W. (2011). *The polyvagal theory*. Norton.

Sapolsky, R. M. (2004). *Why zebras don't get ulcers* (3rd ed.). Holt.

Shapiro, F. (2018). *Eye movement desensitisation and reprocessing (EMDR) therapy* (3rd ed.). Guilford.

Sianoja, M., Syrek, C. J., de Bloom, J., Korpela, K. M., & Kinnunen, U. (2018). Enhancing daily well-being at work through lunchtime park walks. *Scandinavian Journal of Work, Environment & Health, 44*(3), 262–270. https://doi.org/10.5271/sjweh.3703

Singer, J. A. (2004). Narrative identity and meaning making. *Journal of Personality, 72*(3), 437–459. https://doi.org/10.1111/j.0022-3506.2004.00268.x

Tang, Y.-Y., Hölzel, B. K., & Posner, M. I. (2015). The neuroscience of mindfulness meditation. *Nature Reviews Neuroscience, 16*(4), 213–225. https://doi.org/10.1038/nrn3916

Thayer, J. F., & Lane, R. D. (2000). A model of neurovisceral integration. *Biological Psychology, 74*(2), 242–264. https://doi.org/10.1016/S0301-0511(01)00105-6

Ulrich, R. S., Simons, R. F., Losito, B. D., Fiorito, E., Miles, M. A., & Zelson, M. (1991). Stress recovery during exposure to natural and urban environments. *Journal of Environmental Psychology, 11*(3), 201–230. https://doi.org/10.1016/S0272-4944(05)80184-7

van der Kolk, B. A. (2014). *The body keeps the score*. Viking.

West, C. P., Dyrbye, L. N., & Shanafelt, T. D. (2020). Physician burnout: Contributors, consequences, and solutions. *Journal of Internal Medicine, 288*(6), 606–618. https://doi.org/10.1111/joim.13101

THE
UNBOUND
JOURNEY

18 - "Drawing and Painting": Visual Art as a Mechanism for Regulation, Meaning-Making, and Ethical Leadership

Rationale for the Article

For accreditation, institutional adoption, and research partnerships, the program requires a **scholarly backbone** that links creative exercises to measurable outcomes. This article supplies that foundation by (a) synthesising peer-reviewed evidence for art-making's effects on stress biology, attention, and identity; (b) specifying a replicable protocol and metrics (e.g., HRV, self-compassion, psychological safety); and (c) demonstrating clear **leadership relevance** through arts-based development literature. The result is a chapter that is pedagogically elegant **and** evaluable across universities, corporations, and public-sector agencies.

Abstract

Chapter 18 of *Heart Unbound 2.0* - **Drawing and Painting** - posits that visual art is not a matter of artistic proficiency but an evidence-based pathway to emotional regulation, self-awareness, and values-aligned leadership. This article integrates findings from affective neuroscience, psychophysiology, environmental and clinical psychology, and leadership development to validate those claims. Research demonstrates that brief art-making reduces stress biomarkers, enhances parasympathetic tone, engages neural circuits supporting self-referential integration, and facilitates emotion regulation and autobiographical coherence. Arts-based pedagogies also strengthen leadership capabilities including perspective taking, presence, and reflective judgment. We translate these mechanisms into a structured practice model, include an "Application in *Heart Unbound 2.0*" section modelled on Chapter 3 (*I Am*), and propose measurement strategies suitable for education, corporate, and public-sector settings.

Keywords: art-making; drawing; painting; emotion regulation; heart-rate variability; self-compassion; trauma-informed practice; authentic leadership; *Heart Unbound 2.0*

Introduction

From Paleolithic handprints to contemporary sketchbooks, humans have long used images to externalise feeling and consolidate identity. While popular culture often treats drawing and painting as aesthetic pursuits, convergent evidence shows that **deliberate art-making** functions as a psychophysiological regulator, a meaning-making tool, and a catalyst for leadership growth (Bolwerk et al., 2014; Kaimal, Ray, & Muniz, 2016; Taylor & Ladkin, 2009; WHO, 2019). *Heart Unbound 2.0* operationalises these insights in an accessible pedagogy. This article reviews the relevant science and derives practice principles that validate Chapter 18.

Theoretical Foundations

Emotion regulation and neurovisceral integration

Emotion regulation depends on flexible coordination between cortical control networks and autonomic physiology (Gross, 2015; Thayer & Lane, 2000). Practices that increase **vagal tone**, indexed by heart-rate variability (HRV), improve executive control, social engagement, and stress recovery (Chalmers et al., 2014; Porges, 2011). Rhythmic, sensorimotor activities such as drawing and brushwork are well-suited to this task: they impose a paced, predictable motor pattern, recruit interoceptive awareness, and reliably down-shift arousal (Critchley et al., 2004; Kaimal et al., 2016).

Mental imagery, meaning, and memory

Creating visual images recruits perceptual cortices and midline "self" systems (Kosslyn, Ganis, & Thompson, 2001; Singer, 2004). Art-making therefore supports **autobiographical coherence**, the organisation of personal experience into narratives that make sense of change, loss, and aspiration (Conway & Pleydell-Pearce, 2000; Neimeyer, 2004). Such coherence underpins ethical discernment and leadership authenticity (Avolio & Gardner, 2005; George, 2015).

Positive emotion and broaden-and-build

Even brief creative activity elicits interest, calm, and gratitude, emotions that broaden attention and build durable psychological and social resources (Fredrickson, 2013). These upward spirals predict resilience and prosocial behaviour at work (Garland et al., 2010; Boyatzis & McKee, 2005).

Empirical Evidence for Drawing and Painting

Psychophysiological studies

In mixed-methods laboratory work, **45 minutes of free art-making** produced **significant reductions in salivary cortisol** across ages and experience levels (Kaimal et al., 2016). Neuroimaging shows that **producing art** (not merely viewing it) increases functional connectivity in the default-mode network, implicated in self-referential processing and emotion integration (Bolwerk, Mack-Andrick, Lang, Dörfler, & Maihöfner, 2014). Coloring structured forms (e.g., mandalas) reduces state anxiety (Curry & Kasser, 2005; van der Vennet & Serice, 2012). A WHO scoping review synthesising over 900 publications concludes that visual-arts participation improves mental health outcomes, reduces stress, and supports social inclusion across the lifespan (WHO, 2019).

Clinical and community outcomes

Art therapy demonstrates utility in trauma, grief, and mood disturbance, providing exposure-titrated, nonverbal access to affect with improved symptoms and functioning (Hass-Cohen & Carr, 2008; Slayton, D'Archer, & Kaplan, 2010; Uttley et al., 2015). Compassion-focused imagery and arts approaches reduce shame and enhance self-soothing, critical for self-compassion and recovery (Gilbert, 2014).

Leadership and organisations

Arts-based methods sharpen attention, sense-making, and ethical imagination in leaders and teams (Taylor & Ladkin, 2009; Schiuma, 2011). Reflective drawing and visual narrative help executives externalise dilemmas, surface tacit assumptions, and align action with values, core features of authentic leadership and resonant leadership (Avolio & Gardner, 2005; Boyatzis & McKee, 2005). Field studies show that short, nature- or art-based micro-breaks also restore attentional control and mood during demanding workdays (Sianoja et al., 2018).

Mechanisms of Action in Drawing and Painting

1. **Bottom-up soothing:** repetitive fine-motor activity and controlled breathing during mark-making cue safety via the ventral vagal complex (Porges, 2011).

2. **Interoceptive attunement:** attention to somatic sensation while creating increases insula-mediated awareness linked to self-regulation (Critchley et al., 2004).

3. **Flow states:** moderate challenge with clear feedback supports flow, reducing rumination and improving affect (Csikszentmihalyi, 2008).

4. **Symbolic distance:** images provide tolerable distance from intense feelings, allowing graded exposure and cognitive reappraisal (Holmes & Mathews, 2010; Malchiodi, 2015).

5. **Narrative externalisation:** pages and canvases serve as "transitional spaces" for identity work and values clarification (Singer, 2004; Neimeyer, 2004).

Evidence-Informed Practice Model (Drawing & Painting)

Session arc (12–15 minutes; adaptable):

1. **Grounding:** hand to heart, four slow breaths (interoceptive cue).

2. **Prompt:** "Draw what you feel" or "Map the safe place that steadies you."

3. **Create:** 8–10 minutes of uninterrupted mark-making; invite rhythm and breath pacing.

4. **Title & two words:** name the piece; write two feeling words to aid meta-awareness.

5. **Meaning-making:** brief reflection: What value is present? What action does this image invite?

6. **Transfer:** photograph as a cue; identify a micro-ritual (e.g., 90-second drawing reset before hard meetings).

Measurement:

- **Physiology:** HRV (RMSSD) or pulse/respiratory rate pre/post where feasible (Chalmers et al., 2014).

- **Self-report:** Self-Compassion Scale (Neff, 2003), PANAS, Perceived Stress Scale, Emotion Regulation Questionnaire (Gross & John).

- **Leadership outcomes:** psychological safety (Edmondson, 2019), 360-degree ratings for presence/listening.

Application in Heart Unbound 2.0

The Drawing & Painting chapter translates theory into accessible, heart-led practice:

- **Breath-to-Brush Arrival:** Hand-to-heart, three slow breaths, then breath-paced mark-making to settle the nervous system and cue presence.

- **Draw-What-You-Feel:** 10-minute non-verbal emotional mapping (color/line/space) that names and regulates feeling; close with a one-word title.

- **Inner Landscape & Values Palette:** Map inner states (calm bay, worry ridge, hope meadow) and encode 3–5 values as colors; identify one aligned action for the week.

- **Grief–Joy Diptych / Memory-Honouring Portrait:** Paired images to hold loss and vitality, or a symbol/portrait that honours a person, season, or value; optional ritual witnessing.

- **Release–Renew Layering:** First layer externalises tension; second layer washes/covers/adds forms for what you are inviting next; end with a compassionate self-statement.

- **Daily Micro-Rituals:** One-line day, color-breath square, non-dominant scribble, or threshold sketch (2–5 minutes) to build consistency and emotional steadiness.

- **Meaning-Making & Safe Sharing:** Two-sentence artist statement ("This is about… It wants me to remember…") and consent-led appreciative witnessing ("I see/I sense…").

- **Leadership Alignment:** Team "weather maps," values palettes, and visual retrospectives (Keep/Stop/Start canvases) that convert personal insight into collective action and psychological safety.

These practices are personally healing and professionally transformative for emerging and senior leaders, and for anyone cultivating authentic self-leadership.

Programmatic Alignment: Learning Objectives and EI Domains

Chapter 18's objectives (emotional awareness, regulation, self-compassion, and confidence in daily creative ritual) align with established emotional-intelligence models: accurate self-appraisal, self-management, empathy, and relationship management (Goleman, Boyatzis, & McKee, 2013; Mayer, Salovey, & Caruso). Drawing and painting provide **nonverbal channels** for each domain, making internal states visible (self-awareness), stabilising physiology (self-regulation), deepening perspective taking (empathy), and enabling **creative communication** within teams.

Conclusion

Drawing and painting are not ancillary "nice-to-haves"; they are **regulatory technologies** that quiet threat, integrate experience, and invite courageous, values-aligned action. By embedding visual art into daily practice, *Heart Unbound 2.0* equips individuals and leaders to convert inner steadiness into outer service, one breath, one line, one choice at a time.

References

Avolio, B. J., & Gardner, W. L. (2005). Authentic leadership development: Getting to the root of positive forms of leadership. *The Leadership Quarterly, 16*(3), 315–338. https://doi.org/10.1016/j.leaqua.2005.03.001

Bolwerk, A., Mack-Andrick, J., Lang, F. R., Dörfler, A., & Maihöfner, C. (2014). How art changes your brain: Differential effects of visual art production and cognitive art evaluation on functional brain connectivity. *PLOS ONE, 9*(7), e101035. https://doi.org/10.1371/journal.pone.0101035

Boyatzis, R., & McKee, A. (2005). *Resonant leadership*. Harvard Business School Press.

Chalmers, J. A., Quintana, D. S., Abbott, M. J. A., & Kemp, A. H. (2014). Anxiety disorders are associated with reduced heart rate variability: A meta-analysis. *Frontiers in Psychiatry, 5,* 80. https://doi.org/10.3389/fpsyt.2014.00080

Conway, M. A., & Pleydell-Pearce, C. W. (2000). The construction of autobiographical memories in the self-memory system. *Psychological Review, 107*(2), 261–288. https://doi.org/10.1037/0033-295X.107.2.261

Critchley, H. D., Wiens, S., Rotshtein, P., Ohman, A., & Dolan, R. J. (2004). Neural systems supporting interoceptive awareness. *Nature Neuroscience, 7*(2), 189–195. https://doi.org/10.1038/nn1176

Csikszentmihalyi, M. (2008). *Flow: The psychology of optimal experience* (2nd ed.). Harper Perennial.

Edmondson, A. C. (2019). *The fearless organisation.* Wiley.

Fredrickson, B. L. (2013). Positive emotions broaden and build. In P. Devine & A. Plant (Eds.), *Advances in experimental social psychology* (Vol. 47, pp. 1–53). Academic Press.

Garland, E. L., Fredrickson, B. L., Kring, A. M., Johnson, D. P., Meyer, P. S., & Penn, D. L. (2010). Upward spirals of positive emotions counter depression. *Clinical Psychological Science, 1*(3), 256–270. https://doi.org/10.1177/2167702613486607

George, B. (2015). *Discover your true north* (2nd ed.). Wiley.

Gilbert, P. (2014). *The compassionate mind approach to recovering from trauma.* Constable & Robinson.

Goleman, D., Boyatzis, R., & McKee, A. (2013). *Primal leadership: Unleashing the power of emotional intelligence* (10th anniversary ed.). Harvard Business Review Press.

Gross, J. J. (2015). Emotion regulation: Current status and future prospects. *Psychological Inquiry, 26*(1), 1–26. https://doi.org/10.1080/1047840X.2014.940781

Hass-Cohen, N., & Carr, R. (Eds.). (2008). *Art therapy and clinical neuroscience.* Jessica Kingsley.

Holmes, E. A., & Mathews, A. (2010). Mental imagery in emotion and emotional disorders. *Clinical Psychology Review, 30*(3), 349–362. https://doi.org/10.1016/j.cpr.2010.01.001

Kabat-Zinn, J. (2013). *Full catastrophe living* (Rev. ed.). Bantam.

Kaimal, G., Ray, K., & Muniz, J. (2016). Reduction of cortisol levels and participants' responses following art making. *Art Therapy, 33*(2), 74–80. https://doi.org/10.1080/07421656.2016.1166832

Kosslyn, S. M., Ganis, G., & Thompson, W. L. (2001). Neural foundations of imagery. *Nature Reviews Neuroscience, 2*(9), 635–642. https://doi.org/10.1038/35090055

Malchiodi, C. A. (2015). *Creative interventions with traumatised children* (2nd ed.). Guilford.

Neff, K. D. (2003). The development and validation of a scale to measure self-compassion. *Self and Identity, 2*(3), 223–250. https://doi.org/10.1080/15298860309027

Neimeyer, R. A. (2004). Fostering posttraumatic growth. *Psychological Inquiry, 15*(1), 53–59. https://doi.org/10.1207/s15327965pli1501_03

Porges, S. W. (2011). *The polyvagal theory*. Norton.

Schiuma, G. (2011). *The value of arts for business*. Cambridge University Press.

Sianoja, M., Syrek, C. J., de Bloom, J., Korpela, K. M., & Kinnunen, U. (2018). Enhancing daily well-being at work through lunchtime park walks. *Scandinavian Journal of Work, Environment & Health, 44*(3), 262–270. https://doi.org/10.5271/sjweh.3703

Singer, J. A. (2004). Narrative identity and meaning making. *Journal of Personality, 72*(3), 437–459. https://doi.org/10.1111/j.0022-3506.2004.00268.x

Slayton, S. C., D'Archer, J., & Kaplan, F. (2010). Outcome studies on the efficacy of art therapy: A review of findings. *Art Therapy, 27*(3), 108–118. https://doi.org/10.1080/07421656.2010.10129660

Taylor, S. S., & Ladkin, D. (2009). Understanding arts-based methods in managerial development. *Journal of Management Development, 28*(6), 558–572. https://doi.org/10.1108/02621710910959608

Thayer, J. F., & Lane, R. D. (2000). A model of neurovisceral integration. *Biological Psychology, 74*(2), 242–264. https://doi.org/10.1016/S0301-0511(01)00105-6

Uttley, L., Stevenson, M., Scope, A., Rawdin, A., & Sutton, A. (2015). The clinical and cost effectiveness of art therapy for non-psychotic mental health disorders: A systematic review. *Health Technology Assessment, 19*(18), 1–120. https://doi.org/10.3310/hta19180

van der Kolk, B. A. (2014). *The body keeps the score*. Viking.

van der Vennet, R., & Serice, S. (2012). Can coloring mandalas reduce anxiety? A replication. *Art Therapy, 29*(2), 87–92. https://doi.org/10.1080/07421656.2012.680047

World Health Organisation. (2019). *What is the evidence on the role of the arts in improving health and well-being?* WHO Regional Office for Europe.

19 - "Sunrise and Sunset": Daily Thresholds for Regulation, Meaning, and Heart-Led Leadership

Rationale for the Article

Program partners (universities, corporates, public sector) increasingly require *evidence-linked* protocols with measurable outcomes. This article provides the scientific scaffolding for Chapter 19 by: (a) grounding dawn/dusk rituals in circadian and autonomic physiology; (b) linking nature-based micro-practices to validated psychological processes (attention restoration, broaden-and-build, gratitude); and (c) specifying leadership-relevant metrics (HRV, psychological safety). The result is a module that is spiritually resonant **and** academically defensible.

Abstract

Chapter 19 of *Heart Unbound 2.0* - **Sunrise and Sunset** - invites participants to treat dawn and dusk as restorative rituals that recalibrate physiology, clarify meaning, and strengthen values-aligned leadership. This article integrates evidence from circadian neuroscience, psychophysiology, environmental and positive psychology, and leadership research to validate those claims. Morning and evening light entrain circadian rhythms, optimise melatonin-serotonin dynamics, improve sleep and mood, and support executive control. Nature-based micro-rituals around sunrise and sunset enhance attention restoration, vagal regulation, and broaden-and-build effects on prosocial functioning, capacities central to authentic leadership and psychological safety in teams. We translate the science into brief, scalable practices and specify outcomes suitable for evaluation.

Keywords: sunrise; sunset; circadian rhythms; heart-rate variability; attentional restoration; positive emotions; authentic leadership; psychological safety; *Heart Unbound 2.0*

Introduction

Across cultures, the daily arc of the sun has served as a temporal compass and spiritual teacher. Contemporary science now shows that *how* we meet dawn and dusk matters for health, cognition, and leadership. Early-day natural light sets the phase of the circadian system; pre-sleep darkness and sunset ritual prepare the organism for recovery (Czeisler et al., 1999; Wright et al., 2013). These transitions are therefore ideal "choice points" for cultivating self-awareness, regulation, and values alignment, the core aims of *Heart Unbound 2.0*. This paper synthesises relevant mechanisms and translates them into practices that validate Chapter 19.

Theoretical Foundations

Circadian entrainment and light as a biological signal

Specialised intrinsically photosensitive retinal ganglion cells (ipRGCs) transmit environmental light to the suprachiasmatic nucleus (SCN), entraining circadian rhythms that regulate sleep-wake cycles, endocrine function, mood, and performance (Berson et al., 2002; Hattar et al., 2002). Blue-enriched light in the morning advances circadian phase and promotes alertness; evening light delays melatonin onset and impairs sleep (Brainard et al., 2001; Chang et al., 2015; Thapan et al., 2001). Real-world studies show that several days of natural light–dark exposure quickly resets circadian timing and improves sleep and mood (Wright et al., 2013; Stothard et al., 2017).

Neurochemistry, affect, and cognition

Morning light is associated with higher central serotonin turnover, a substrate for mood stability and impulse control, and supports next-night melatonin synthesis (Lambert et al., 2002). Adequate circadian alignment improves executive function and emotion regulation through neurovisceral integration of prefrontal and autonomic systems (Thayer & Lane, 2000). Consistent dawn/dusk rituals thus provide reliable "windows" to train calm focus and intentionality.

Attention restoration and positive emotion

Natural settings and soft-fascination stimuli (e.g., sky color gradients) replenish directed attention and accelerate stress recovery (Kaplan, 1995; Ulrich et al., 1991). Positive emotions arising in awe-evoking vistas at sunrise or sunset broaden thought–action repertoires and build resources for resilience and cooperation (Fredrickson, 2013).

Digital era misalignment

Evening device light suppresses melatonin, reduces REM sleep, and diminishes next-day alertness (Chang et al., 2015). "Social jetlag", a mismatch between biological and social clocks, predicts poorer health and mood (Roenneberg et al., 2012). Structured dusk routines that protect darkness counter these effects.

Psychophysiological Mechanisms Relevant to Chapter 19

1. **Vagal regulation and heart-rate variability (HRV).** Slow breathing and parasympathetic activation during reflective sunrise/sunset practices increase HRV, a marker of flexible self-regulation and social engagement (Chalmers et al., 2014; Porges, 2011).

2. **State–trait carryover.** Morning intention setting improves self-regulatory capacity and goal alignment across the day; evening reflection and gratitude reduce rumination and aid sleep (Emmons & McCullough, 2003; Gross, 2015).

3. **Meaning and narrative coherence.** Ritualised beginnings and endings scaffold autobiographical coherence and moral clarity, key components of authentic leadership (Avolio & Gardner, 2005; Singer, 2004).

Implications for Leadership and Teams

Authentic and resonant leadership

Self-regulation, presence, and values congruence underpin trust and ethical behaviour (Avolio & Gardner, 2005; Boyatzis & McKee, 2005). Leaders who anchor their day with dawn intention and dusk reflection report greater perspective taking and steadier emotional tone, conditions that create

psychological safety (Edmondson, 2019).

<u>Temporal leadership and team rituals</u>

Temporal structuring around shared micro-practices (e.g., 60-second "sunrise check-in" at morning brief; "sunset gratitude" at end of shift) aligns attention, reduces decision fatigue, and supports recovery (Mohammed & Nadkarni, 2014; Sonnentag & Fritz, 2015). Brief nature-exposed breaks (outdoors at dusk) improve mood and restore attention (Sianoja et al., 2018).

Evidence-Informed Practice Model: Rise & Release

Aim: Leverage dawn/dusk as low-friction anchors for self-awareness, autonomic balance, and values-aligned action.

Morning - Rise (5–8 min).

1. **Light before scroll:** Step outside or to a bright window for 2–5 minutes of natural light exposure.
2. **Coherent breathing:** ~6 breaths/min for 60–120 seconds (HRV upregulation).
3. **Intention prompt:** "What will I bring into the light today?" Write one sentence; select one values-consistent behaviour.
4. **Micro-commitment:** Identify the smallest action (e.g., "open the meeting by appreciating one contribution").

Evening - Release (7–10 min).

1. **Sunset cue or artificial lights dimmed:** Reduce blue light ≥1 hour before bed.
2. **Breathe & feel:** Hand to heart, slow exhale pacing.
3. **Gratitude + letting-go:** Note three gains; name one burden to set down.
4. **Closure phrase:** "This day is complete; I can rest." (Supports pre-sleep de-arousal.)

Measurement suggestions.

- **Physiology:** resting HRV (RMSSD) weekly; sleep onset latency and efficiency.

- **Self-report:** PANAS, Perceived Stress Scale, Self-Compassion Scale (Neff, 2003).

- **Leadership outcomes:** team psychological safety (Edmondson, 2019), 360-ratings for presence/listening.

Application in Heart Unbound 2.0

The *Sunrise and Sunset* chapter translates theory into accessible, heart-led practice:

- **Dawn Intention & Light:** 90-second sky-gazing with a hand-over-heart check-in, one "I am …" intention, and brief outdoor light exposure to anchor circadian rhythm and mood.

- **Sunset Release & Gratitude:** Three lengthened exhales, a two-column note ("Carry ↔ Let Go"), and three gratitudes to close the day with kindness and enoughness.

- **Sky-Breath Coherence:** 5 minutes of paced breathing synced to the horizon (e.g., inhale 4, exhale 6) to settle the nervous system and restore emotional balance.

- **Threshold Journaling / Sketching:** One page (or a simple colour wash) at dawn or dusk to name feelings, draw the sky's colours, and translate experience into insight.

- **Nature Micro-Exposures:** 10–15 minutes of phone-free walking at first or last light (barefoot grounding when possible) to steady attention and lift affect.

- **Digital Sundown:** A device "sunset" 60–90 minutes before sleep; swap screens for window-viewing, candlelight, or stargazing to honour the body's night protocol.

- **30/30 Commitment (Relational Practice):** Watch 30 consecutive sunrises or sunsets—solo, with a partner, or a peer circle with a short shared reflection to deepen connection.

- **Leadership Alignment:**
  o *Rise stand-ups* (2 minutes): name purpose, one courageous act, one support ask.

> o *Set debriefs* (5 minutes): what worked, what we release, one repair or appreciation, team rhythms that convert care into performance.
>
> These practices are personally healing and professionally transformative, supporting emerging leaders, seasoned executives, and anyone cultivating authentic self-leadership through daily renewal and gentle closure.

Limitations and Future Directions

Randomised trials should compare dawn/dusk routines with generic mindfulness to test incremental benefits. Chronotype differences and shift-work contexts require tailored protocols. Combining wearables (light, HRV, sleep) with behavioral outcomes would strengthen causal inference.

Conclusion

Sunrise and sunset are daily thresholds where biology, psychology, and meaning naturally converge. Meeting them with intention entrains the clock, steadies the heart, and clarifies the next right action. In *Heart Unbound 2.0*, these thresholds become accessible leadership technologies: begin with light and purpose; end with gratitude and release.

References

Avolio, B. J., & Gardner, W. L. (2005). Authentic leadership development: Getting to the root of positive forms of leadership. *The Leadership Quarterly, 16*(3), 315–338. https://doi.org/10.1016/j.leaqua.2005.03.001

Berson, D. M., Dunn, F. A., & Takao, M. (2002). Phototransduction by retinal ganglion cells that set the circadian clock. *Science, 295*(5557), 1070–1073. https://doi.org/10.1126/science.1067262

Boyatzis, R., & McKee, A. (2005). *Resonant leadership: Renewing yourself and connecting with others through mindfulness, hope, and compassion.* Harvard Business School Press.

Brainard, G. C., et al. (2001). Action spectrum for melatonin regulation in humans: Evidence for a novel circadian photoreceptor. *The Journal of Neuroscience, 21*(16), 6405–6412. https://doi.org/10.1523/JNEUROSCI.21-16-06405.2001

Chalmers, J. A., Quintana, D. S., Abbott, M. J.-A., & Kemp, A. H. (2014). Anxiety disorders are associated with reduced heart rate variability: A meta-analysis. *Frontiers in Psychiatry, 5,* 80. https://doi.org/10.3389/fpsyt.2014.00080

Chang, A.-M., Aeschbach, D., Duffy, J. F., & Czeisler, C. A. (2015). Evening use of light-emitting eReaders negatively affects sleep, circadian timing, and next-morning alertness. *Proceedings of the National Academy of Sciences, 112*(4), 1232–1237. https://doi.org/10.1073/pnas.1418490112

Czeisler, C. A., et al. (1999). Stability, precision, and near-24-hour period of the human circadian pacemaker. *Science, 284*(5423), 2177–2181. https://doi.org/10.1126/science.284.5423.2177

Edmondson, A. C. (2019). *The fearless organisation: Creating psychological safety in the workplace for learning, innovation, and growth.* Wiley.

Emmons, R. A., & McCullough, M. E. (2003). Counting blessings versus burdens. *Journal of Personality and Social Psychology, 84*(2), 377–389. https://doi.org/10.1037/0022-3514.84.2.377

Fredrickson, B. L. (2013). Positive emotions broaden and build. In P. G. Devine & A. Plant (Eds.), *Advances in experimental social psychology* (Vol. 47, pp. 1–53). Academic Press.

Gross, J. J. (2015). Emotion regulation: Current status and future prospects. *Psychological Inquiry, 26*(1), 1–26. https://doi.org/10.1080/1047840X.2014.940781

Hattar, S., Liao, H.-W., Takao, M., Berson, D. M., & Yau, K.-W. (2002). Melanopsin-containing retinal ganglion cells: Architecture, projections, and intrinsic photosensitivity. *Science, 295*(5557), 1065–1070. https://doi.org/10.1126/science.1069609

Kaplan, S. (1995). The restorative benefits of nature. *Journal of Environmental Psychology, 15*(3), 169–182. https://doi.org/10.1016/0272-4944(95)90001-2

Lambert, G. W., Reid, C., Kaye, D. M., Jennings, G. L., & Esler, M. D. (2002). Effect of sunlight and season on serotonin turnover in the brain. *The Lancet, 360*(9348), 1840–1842. https://doi.org/10.1016/S0140-6736(02)11737-5

Mohammed, S., & Nadkarni, S. (2014). Are we all on the same temporal page? The moderating effects of temporal leadership and team temporal processes. *Journal of Applied Psychology, 99*(3), 404–422. https://doi.org/10.1037/a0035640

Neff, K. D. (2003). The development and validation of a scale to measure self-compassion. *Self and Identity, 2*(3), 223–250. https://doi.org/10.1080/15298860309027

Porges, S. W. (2011). *The polyvagal theory: Neurophysiological foundations of emotions, attachment, communication, and self-regulation.* Norton.

Roenneberg, T., Allebrandt, K. V., Merrow, M., & Vetter, C. (2012). Social jetlag and obesity. *Current Biology, 22*(10), 939–943. https://doi.org/10.1016/j.cub.2012.03.038

Singer, J. A. (2004). Narrative identity and meaning making. *Journal of Personality, 72*(3), 437–459. https://doi.org/10.1111/j.0022-3506.2004.00268.x

Sianoja, M., Syrek, C. J., de Bloom, J., Korpela, K. M., & Kinnunen, U. (2018). Enhancing daily well-being at work through lunchtime park walks. *Scandinavian Journal of Work, Environment & Health, 44*(3), 262–270. https://doi.org/10.5271/sjweh.3703

Sonnentag, S., & Fritz, C. (2015). Recovery from job stress: The stressor-detachment model as an integrative framework. *Journal of Organisational Behaviour, 36*(S1), S72–S103. https://doi.org/10.1002/job.1924

Stothard, E. R., et al. (2017). Circadian entrainment to the natural light–dark cycle across seasons and the weekend. *Current Biology, 27*(4), 508–513. https://doi.org/10.1016/j.cub.2016.12.041

Thapan, K., Arendt, J., & Skene, D. J. (2001). An action spectrum for melatonin suppression. *The Journal of Physiology, 535*(1), 261–267. https://doi.org/10.1111/j.1469-7793.2001.t01-1-00261.x

Thayer, J. F., & Lane, R. D. (2000). A model of neurovisceral integration in emotion regulation and dysregulation. *Journal of Affective Disorders, 61*(3), 201–216. https://doi.org/10.1016/S0165-0327(00)00338-4

Ulrich, R. S., Simons, R. F., Losito, B. D., Fiorito, E., Miles, M. A., & Zelson, M. (1991). Stress recovery during exposure to natural and urban environments. *Journal of Environmental Psychology, 11*(3), 201–230. https://doi.org/10.1016/S0272-4944(05)80184-7

Wright, K. P., Jr., et al. (2013). Entrainment of the human circadian clock to the natural light–dark cycle. *Current Biology, 23*(16), 1554–1558. https://doi.org/10.1016/j.cub.2013.06.039

THE
UNBOUND
JOURNEY

20 - "Heart Whispers": Expressive Writing as a Mechanism for Regulation, Meaning-Making, and Heart-Led Leadership

Rationale for the Article

Program partners increasingly request scientifically anchored practices with measurable outcomes. This article grounds Chapter 20 in robust research on expressive writing, affect labeling, autonomic regulation, and authentic leadership, translating evidence into a brief, low-cost protocol and evaluation plan. It thus safeguards fidelity, supports institutional adoption, and preserves the chapter's contemplative spirit while meeting professional standards.

Abstract

Heart Whispers (Chapter 20 of **Heart Unbound 2.0**) invites participants to write directly "from the heart," translating felt experience into language. This article integrates psychological, physiological, and leadership literature to evaluate and validate that practice. Evidence from expressive-writing research shows small-to-moderate improvements in mental and physical health, sleep, immune indices, and working memory following brief, structured writing (Baikie & Wilhelm, 2005; Frattaroli, 2006; Smyth, 1998). Neurobiological findings indicate that affect labeling and narrative formation down-regulate limbic reactivity and engage prefrontal regulatory networks (Lieberman et al., 2007; Thayer & Lane, 2000). Slow, embodied journaling practices likely augment parasympathetic activation and heart-rate variability

(HRV), a marker of adaptive self-regulation (Chalmers et al., 2014; Shaffer & Ginsberg, 2017). In leadership contexts, identity-work and authentic self-disclosure strengthen trust, psychological safety, and values-aligned action (Avolio & Gardner, 2005; Collins & Miller, 1994; Edmondson, 2019; Walumbwa et al., 2008). We translate this evidence into a brief protocol, measurement plan, and implementation guidance for programs and organisations.

Keywords: expressive writing; affect labeling; interoception; heart-rate variability; emotion regulation; narrative identity; psychological safety; authentic leadership; *Heart Unbound 2.0*

Introduction

"Heart whisper" writing is a structured form of expressive journaling that privileges immediacy, honesty, and embodiment over polish. The practice aligns with long histories of reflective writing as a method of spiritual and psychological inquiry, and with contemporary evidence that translating affect into words promotes regulation, insight, and health (Pennebaker & Chung, 2011; McAdams, 2001). This paper reviews core mechanisms and outcomes and proposes an evidence-informed protocol suitable for Chapter 20.

Psychological Mechanisms

Expressive writing and narrative coherence

Experimental disclosure paradigms, 15–20 minutes of writing across several days about one's deepest thoughts and feelings, reliably yield improvements in health and well-being (Smyth, 1998; Frattaroli, 2006). Benefits are partly mediated by the movement from raw experience to coherent story, integrating emotion with autobiographical meaning (Pennebaker & King, 1999; McAdams, 2001).

Affect labeling and emotion regulation

Neuroimaging shows that labeling feelings with words reduces amygdala activity and increases right ventrolateral prefrontal engagement, a plausible mechanism for the calming effect of "writing from" emotion rather than only "about" it (Lieberman et al., 2007). Within Gross's process model, heart-led writing functions as cognitive change and response modulation, lowering reactivity while preserving contact with felt experience (Gross, 2015).

Self-compassion and motivation

Approaching inner material with warmth rather than self-criticism predicts resilience and adaptive striving (Neff, 2003; Deci & Ryan, 2000). Heart-whisper prompts that normalise vulnerability foster compassionate goal pursuit rather than defensive avoidance.

Physiological Mechanisms

Autonomic balance and HRV

Slow, attentive writing naturally couples with paced breathing and interoceptive awareness. Parasympathetic dominance and higher resting HRV are associated with better emotion regulation and executive control (Thayer & Lane, 2000; Shaffer & Ginsberg, 2017). Meta-analytic data link anxiety and dysregulation to reduced HRV, underscoring the value of practices that nudge vagal tone upward (Chalmers et al., 2014).

Interoception and embodiment

Interoceptive accuracy, sensing internal states, is central to adaptive decision-making and self-regulation (Craig, 2002; Critchley et al., 2004; Khalsa & Lapidus, 2016). Hand-to-heart orientation plus reflective writing recruits these channels, reinforcing a bottom-up sense of safety while the narrative system integrates meaning.

Health correlates of writing

Expressive writing has been associated with improved immune functioning and disease outcomes in some populations (Baikie & Wilhelm, 2005; Smyth, Stone, Hurewitz, & Kaell, 1999) and with gains in working memory that may support self-control in daily life (Klein & Boals, 2001).

Leadership Relevance

Authentic leadership, trust, and psychological safety

Leadership development research emphasises self-awareness, relational transparency, and internalised moral perspective (Avolio & Gardner, 2005; Walumbwa et al., 2008). Self-disclosure, when skillful and context-appropriate, predicts liking, closeness, and trust (Collins & Miller, 1994) and is a precursor to **psychological safety**, the belief that interpersonal risk-taking will not be punished (Edmondson, 2019). Written self-reflection provides a private space to surface values and prepare transparent, values-consistent action.

Voice and inclusion

Leaders who metabolise emotion and clarify intention are better positioned to invite dissenting views and learning behaviours. Journaling routines can be paired with inclusive practices to strengthen a "speak-up" climate.

Evidence-Informed Practice: The Heart Whispers Protocol

Set (1–2 min). Posture upright; one hand over the heart; three slow breaths (~6/min). State intention: *I will listen with kindness.*

Write (7–12 min). Prompt examples: "If my heart could speak, it would say…," "What truth have I not yet written?" Write continuously, without editing.

Name (1 min). Circle one word or sentence that carries energy; label the predominant feeling (affect labeling).

Close (1–2 min). Two lines of compassionate response to self; one value-aligned micro-commitment for the next 24 hours.

Dosage. 10–15 minutes, 3–4 days/week for 2–4 weeks, then as needed, consistent with expressive-writing trials (Pennebaker & Chung, 2011; Baikie & Wilhelm, 2005).

Safeguards. Offer titration guidance; cue participants to pause if arousal spikes; signpost to clinical supports for trauma histories.

Application in Heart Unbound 2.0

The *Heart Whispers* chapter translates theory into accessible, heart-led practice:

- **Heart–Breath Drop-In:** 60–90 seconds hand-over-heart with coherent breathing (e.g., inhale 4, exhale 6) to signal safety and shift from thinking to feeling.

- **7-Minute Free-Write:** Unedited, continuous writing to the prompt *"If my heart could speak, it would say…"* no stopping, no correcting, just truth on the page.

- **Write FROM, not ABOUT:** Two-pass exercise, (1) describe the event, (2) let the emotion speak in first-person ("I am grief...") then notice the shift in clarity and relief.

- **Prompt Ladder:** Rotating cues to deepen access. *What I'm not saying is... / The need beneath my anger is... / The forgiveness I'm ready to explore is... / One small courageous step is...*

- **Carry / Release Page:** End each entry with two columns ("Keep with me" ↔ "Lay down tonight") to turn insight into gentle action and closure.

- **Sensation Lexicon:** Quick body scan and three words for felt sense (e.g., *tight / warm / fluttering*) to build emotional granularity and self-regulation.

- **Ritualise the Container:** Name your practice (e.g., *Morning Heart Notes*), choose time and place, light a candle, and close with a gratitude line, small ceremony, big coherence.

- **Safety & Boundaries:** "For-my-eyes-only" permission, optional single-line share, and tear/shred option, trauma-sensitive, choice-based expression that protects the nervous system.

- **Review & Codes:** Weekly look-back to extract three "heart codes" (themes, needs, values) and one micro-commitment for the week ahead.

- **21-Day Track:** Simple streak and mood check-in (0–10) to notice dose–response between practice, calm, and clarity.

- **Leadership Alignment:**
  - *One-Line Transparency* at stand-ups ("What my heart is asking of me today is...")
  - *Five-Minute After-Action Reflection* (what mattered, what to repair, one appreciation) to convert inner honesty into values-aligned behaviour and team trust.

These practices are personally healing and professionally transformative, supporting emerging leaders, seasoned executives, and anyone cultivating authentic self-leadership through a daily conversation with the heart.

Evaluation and Implementation

- **Physiology:** Weekly resting HRV (RMSSD or HF-HRV), sleep latency/quality.

- **Psychological:** Perceived Stress Scale; Positive and Negative Affect Schedule; Self-Compassion Scale (Neff, 2003).

- **Leadership/Team:** Psychological Safety Scale (Edmondson, 2019) and 360 ratings for authenticity and listening.

- **Process markers:** Linguistic indicators of insight and agency (Pennebaker & King, 1999).

Limitations and Future Directions

Effects of expressive writing vary by population and topic; not all health outcomes replicate across contexts (Baikie & Wilhelm, 2005; Frattaroli, 2006). Trials comparing "from-emotion" versus "about-emotion" writing with physiological endpoints (HRV, sleep) and leadership outcomes are warranted. Trauma-informed adaptations and culturally responsive prompts should be developed.

Conclusion

Heart-whisper journaling is more than a reflective exercise: it is a compact, evidence-consistent intervention that links language, body, and value. By converting felt sense into words within a compassionate frame, practitioners down-regulate threat, build coherence, and choose wiser action. In organisations and communities, those capacities mature into trust, voice, and humane leadership, the heart of *Heart Unbound 2.0*.

References

Avolio, B. J., & Gardner, W. L. (2005). Authentic leadership development: Getting to the root of positive forms of leadership. *The Leadership Quarterly, 16*(3), 315–338. https://doi.org/10.1016/j.leaqua.2005.03.001

Baikie, K. A., & Wilhelm, K. (2005). Emotional and physical health benefits of expressive writing. *Advances in Psychiatric Treatment, 11*(5), 338–346. https://doi.org/10.1192/apt.11.5.338

Chalmers, J. A., Quintana, D. S., Abbott, M. J.-A., & Kemp, A. H. (2014). Anxiety disorders are associated with reduced heart rate variability: A meta-analysis. *Frontiers in Psychiatry, 5,* 80. https://doi.org/10.3389/fpsyt.2014.00080

Collins, N. L., & Miller, L. C. (1994). Self-disclosure and liking: A meta-analytic review. *Psychological Bulletin, 116*(3), 457–475. https://doi.org/10.1037/0033-2909.116.3.457

Craig, A. D. (2002). How do you feel? Interoception: The sense of the physiological condition of the body. *Nature Reviews Neuroscience, 3*(8), 655–666. https://doi.org/10.1038/nrn894

Critchley, H. D., Wiens, S., Rotshtein, P., Öhman, A., & Dolan, R. J. (2004). Neural systems supporting interoceptive awareness. *Nature Neuroscience, 7*(2), 189–195. https://doi.org/10.1038/nn1176

Deci, E. L., & Ryan, R. M. (2000). The "what" and "why" of goal pursuits: Human needs and the self-determination of behaviour. *Psychological Inquiry, 11*(4), 227–268. https://doi.org/10.1207/S15327965PLI1104_01

Edmondson, A. C. (2019). *The fearless organisation: Creating psychological safety in the workplace for learning, innovation, and growth.* Wiley.

Frattaroli, J. (2006). Experimental disclosure and its moderators: A meta-analysis. *Psychological Bulletin, 132*(6), 823–865. https://doi.org/10.1037/0033-2909.132.6.823

Gross, J. J. (2015). Emotion regulation: Current status and future prospects. *Psychological Inquiry, 26*(1), 1–26. https://doi.org/10.1080/1047840X.2014.940781

Khalsa, S. S., & Lapidus, R. C. (2016). Can interoception improve the pragmatic search for biomarkers in psychiatry? *Frontiers in Psychiatry, 7,* 121. https://doi.org/10.3389/fpsyt.2016.00121

Klein, K., & Boals, A. (2001). Expressive writing can increase working memory capacity. *Journal of Experimental Psychology: General, 130*(3), 520–533. https://doi.org/10.1037/0096-3445.130.3.520

Lieberman, M. D., Eisenberger, N. I., Crockett, M. J., Tom, S. M., Pfeifer, J. H., & Way, B. M. (2007). Putting feelings into words. *Psychological Science, 18*(5), 421–428. https://doi.org/10.1111/j.1467-9280.2007.01916.x

McAdams, D. P. (2001). The psychology of life stories. *Review of General*

Psychology, 5(2), 100–122. https://doi.org/10.1037/1089-2680.5.2.100

Neff, K. D. (2003). The development and validation of a scale to measure self-compassion. *Self and Identity, 2*(3), 223–250. https://doi.org/10.1080/15298860309027

Pennebaker, J. W., & Beall, S. K. (1986). Confronting a traumatic event: Toward an understanding of inhibition and disease. *Journal of Abnormal Psychology, 95*(3), 274–281. https://doi.org/10.1037/0021-843X.95.3.274

Pennebaker, J. W., & Chung, C. K. (2011). Expressive writing: Connections to physical and mental health. In H. S. Friedman (Ed.), *The Oxford handbook of health psychology* (pp. 417–437). Oxford University Press.

Pennebaker, J. W., & King, L. A. (1999). Linguistic styles: Language use as an individual difference. *Journal of Personality and Social Psychology, 77*(6), 1296–1312. https://doi.org/10.1037/0022-3514.77.6.1296

Shaffer, F., & Ginsberg, J. P. (2017). An overview of heart rate variability metrics and norms. *Frontiers in Public Health, 5,* 258. https://doi.org/10.3389/fpubh.2017.00258

Smyth, J. M. (1998). Written emotional expression: Effect sizes, outcome types, and moderating variables. *Psychological Science, 9*(1), 66–69. https://doi.org/10.1111/1467-9280.00014

Smyth, J. M., Stone, A. A., Hurewitz, A., & Kaell, A. (1999). Effects of writing about stressful experiences on symptom reduction in patients with asthma or rheumatoid arthritis. *JAMA, 281*(14), 1304–1309. https://doi.org/10.1001/jama.281.14.1304

Thayer, J. F., & Lane, R. D. (2000). A model of neurovisceral integration in emotion regulation and dysregulation. *Journal of Affective Disorders, 61*(3), 201–216. https://doi.org/10.1016/S0165-0327(00)00338-4

Walumbwa, F. O., Avolio, B. J., Gardner, W. L., Wernsing, T. S., & Peterson, S. J. (2008). Authentic leadership: Development and validation of a theory-based measure. *Journal of Management, 34*(1), 89–126. https://doi.org/10.1177/0149206307308913

THE
UNBOUND
JOURNEY

21 - "Relaxation" as a Core Method in *Heart Unbound 2.0*: Psychophysiological Evidence, Leadership Relevance, and Practice

Rationale

Chapter 21 asks participants to replace the cultural myth of "busy" with the evidence-based reality that recovery builds capacity. This article provides the scientific scaffolding for that shift: (a) a clear mechanism (parasympathetic activation/HRV), (b) validated methods (breathing, PMR, mindfulness, nature, micro-breaks), and (c) leadership relevance (recovery → self-control, compassion, and psychological safety). The synthesis equips facilitators and participants to justify the time invested in relaxation as a strategic intervention for well-being, relationships, and high-quality leadership.

Abstract

Relaxation is framed in Chapter 21 of *Heart Unbound 2.0* as a foundational competency for emotional intelligence and self-leadership. This article integrates psychological, psychophysiological, and leadership research to examine the mechanisms and outcomes of structured relaxation practices (e.g., slow breathing, progressive muscle relaxation, mindfulness-based protocols, nature exposure, micro-breaks). Evidence converges on autonomic rebalancing, particularly parasympathetic activation indexed by heart-rate variability (HRV), as a principal pathway linking relaxation to improved self-regulation, mood, executive functioning, and interpersonal effectiveness. We further synthesise organisational scholarship showing that recovery experiences and compassionate, authentic leadership depend on rest, detachment from demands, and reflective practices. A practice framework aligned to *Heart Unbound 2.0* is offered ("Body–Breath–Balance"), together with a brief case illustration, implementation guidance, and an evaluation agenda. The article concludes with a rationale for Chapter 21's centrality within the curriculum.

Keywords: relaxation response; parasympathetic activation; heart-rate variability; emotional intelligence; recovery experiences; authentic leadership; mindfulness

Introduction

Relaxation is not merely the absence of effort; it is a learnable psychophysiological skill that underwrites emotion regulation, clarity of attention, and ethical action. Across clinical, health, and organisational sciences, relaxation practices reliably reduce stress reactivity and build adaptive capacity (Benson & Proctor, 2000; Manzoni et al., 2008; Zaccaro et al., 2018). Chapter 21 of *Heart Unbound 2.0* positions relaxation as "the art of letting go," advancing the program's aims of heart-led presence and values-aligned leadership. This article reviews the strongest available evidence and translates it into a practitioner-ready protocol consistent with the program's pedagogy.

Theoretical and Historical Background

Early behavioural medicine established a counter-stress "relaxation response" characterised by reduced oxygen consumption, slower heart rate, and lower blood pressure (Benson & Proctor, 2000). Behavioural techniques such as progressive muscle relaxation (PMR) emerged from Jacobson's (1938) work and subsequent manuals (Bernstein & Borkovec, 1973). Contemporary affective neuroscience and polyvagal theory extend these ideas, emphasising the vagus nerve's role in cueing safety, social engagement, and flexible self-regulation (Porges, 2011). In organisational research, recovery theory argues that detachment from job demands, relaxation, mastery, and control during non-work time restore energetic and self-regulatory resources (Sonnentag & Fritz, 2007; Sonnentag, 2018).

Psychophysiology of Relaxation

Autonomic balance and HRV

Relaxation practices reliably shift autonomic activity from sympathetic dominance toward parasympathetic activation. HRV, a time-domain and frequency-domain measure of beat-to-beat variability, indexes this shift and predicts cognitive control, emotion regulation, and resilience (Laborde et al., 2017; Thayer et al., 2012). HRV-biofeedback protocols that train slow diaphragmatic breathing near resonance frequency ($\approx$0.1 Hz) produce medium-to-large improvements in anxiety, depression, and stress (Lehrer et al., 2020).

Breathing and interoception

Slow, paced breathing (with elongated exhalation) increases vagal efferent activity and baroreflex gain, dampening HPA-axis output and subjective arousal (Zaccaro et al., 2018). Yogic breathing reviews report benefits for mood and autonomic stability (Brown & Gerbarg, 2005).

Mindfulness and the default mode

Mindfulness practices cultivate non-reactive awareness, down-regulate self-referential default-mode network activity, and alter stress physiology (Brewer et al., 2011; Kabat-Zinn, 2003). Genomic studies suggest the relaxation response modulates expression of inflammatory and energy-metabolism pathways (Bhasin et al., 2013; Dusek et al., 2008).

Nature exposure and sensory rest

Exposure to natural environments reduces physiological arousal and rumination while improving cognition (Ulrich, 1984; Berman et al., 2008; Bratman et al., 2015). Such effects align with Chapter 21's guidance to include "walking outside" and "digital sabbaths" as routine recovery tools.

Evidence for Specific Relaxation Methods

- **Progressive muscle relaxation (PMR).** Ten-year meta-analysis shows PMR reduces anxiety with effects comparable to cognitive techniques in non-clinical and clinical samples (Manzoni et al., 2008).

- **Mindfulness-based protocols.** MBSR yields moderate reductions in stress and improvements in mood and quality of life across populations (Kabat-Zinn, 2003).

- **Slow-breathing / HRV-biofeedback.** Randomized and quasi-experimental studies report improvements in HRV, sleep, mood, and executive function (Lehrer et al., 2020).

- **Micro-breaks and detachment.** Meta-analytic evidence indicates that short rest breaks restore vigor and reduce fatigue; psychological detachment predicts end-of-day well-being (Wendsche & Lohmann-Haislah, 2017; Sonnentag & Fritz, 2007).

- **Sleep and circadian alignment.** Adequate sleep supports memory consolidation, emotion regulation, and moral self-control (Diekelmann & Born, 2010; Barnes et al., 2015). Chronic stress without recovery elevates allostatic load (McEwen, 2007).

Leadership and Organisational Relevance

Leader effectiveness rests on the ability to regulate attention and affect under pressure while creating psychologically safe, values-consistent climates (Avolio & Gardner, 2005; Edmondson, 1999). Recovery experiences predict proactive behaviour and reduce burnout, a syndrome of exhaustion, cynicism, and inefficacy with substantial organisational costs (Maslach & Leiter, 2016; Sonnentag, 2018). Positive emotion and vagal tone co-evolve in "upward spirals," supporting empathic connection and ethical decision-making (Fredrickson, 2001; Kok & Fredrickson, 2010). In short, relaxation practices are not peripheral wellness perks; they are enabling conditions for sustained, human-centered leadership.

Practice Framework Aligned to *Heart Unbound 2.0*

The Body–Breath–Balance Protocol (10–15 minutes)

1. **Set safety cues (1 minute).** Posture of ease; one palm over the heart; soften gaze.

---

2. **Balanced heart breathing (3–5 minutes).** Inhale 4 s, exhale 6 s, nasal breathing; silent note "in/soften." Target a calm, regular rhythm rather than maximal depth (Lehrer et al., 2020; Zaccaro et al., 2018).

3. **Micro-PMR scan (3–4 minutes).** Tense–release sequence (jaw, shoulders, hands, abdomen) at ~30–40% effort (Bernstein & Borkovec, 1973).

4. **Open monitoring (2–4 minutes).** Non-judgmental awareness of sensations; label thoughts "thinking," return to breath (Kabat-Zinn, 2003).

5. **Intention & closure (1 minute).** Identify one boundary or micro-break to protect recovery before the next task (Sonnentag & Fritz, 2007).

Adaptations. For high arousal, extend exhalation (e.g., 4–8). For hypo-arousal, add gentle movement (shoulder rolls, standing sway) before breathing.

Building a Sustainable Relaxation Routine

- **Daily micro-moments** (1–2 minutes) between meetings to maintain HRV and attentional control.

- **Weekly detachment windows** (technology-free "Sabbath" hours).

- **Nature contact** (15–20 minutes outside when possible).

- **Sleep-protective boundaries** (consistent shut-down rituals; Diekelmann & Born, 2010).

Case Illustration (Glen-Condensed)

A small-business owner presenting with chronic overwork integrated two micro-practices: (a) three daily 5-minute Body–Breath–Balance sessions; (b) a 90-minute weekly tech-free nature walk. Within eight weeks he reported improved sleep, calmer reactivity in family interactions, and steadier decision-making. These changes align with evidence that short, regular recovery improves affect, cognitive flexibility, and social presence (Lehrer et al., 2020; Wendsche & Lohmann-Haislah, 2017; Fredrickson, 2001).

Implementation and Measurement

Programs can track multi-level outcomes:

- **Physiological:** resting HRV (RMSSD), sleep duration.

- **Psychological:** Perceived Stress Scale; Recovery Experience Questionnaire; Self-Compassion Scale.

- **Leadership/Team:** psychological safety (Edmondson, 1999); burnout (Maslach & Leiter, 2016).

Brief A/B week designs allow leaders to see within-person effects of recovery scheduling.

Limitations and Future Directions

Most relaxation studies show medium effects with heterogeneity in protocols and measurement. More randomised, mechanism-focused trials in leadership populations are warranted (e.g., HRV-mediated pathways to ethical behavior and team climate). Culturally sensitive adaptations and accessibility (e.g., low-stimulus practices for trauma-exposed participants) should be standard.

Conclusion

Relaxation is a first-order capability for emotional intelligence and leadership. By restoring autonomic balance, it enlarges the space between stimulus and response, enabling presence, compassion, and values-driven action. Chapter 21 of *Heart Unbound 2.0* is therefore not ancillary self-care, it is core curriculum for sustainable, heart-led performance.

References

Avolio, B. J., & Gardner, W. L. (2005). Authentic leadership development: Getting to the root of positive forms of leadership. *The Leadership Quarterly, 16*(3), 315–338. https://doi.org/10.1016/j.leaqua.2005.03.001

Barnes, C. M., Gunia, B. C., & Wagner, D. T. (2015). Sleep and moral awareness. *Journal of Sleep Research, 24*(2), 181–188. https://doi.org/10.1111/jsr.12231

Benson, H., & Proctor, W. (2000). *The relaxation response.* HarperCollins. (Original work published 1975)

Bernstein, D. A., & Borkovec, T. D. (1973). *Progressive relaxation training: A manual for the helping professions.* Research Press.

Berman, M. G., Jonides, J., & Kaplan, S. (2008). The cognitive benefits of interacting with nature. *Psychological Science, 19*(12), 1207–1212. https://doi.org/10.1111/j.1467-9280.2008.02225.x

Bhasin, M. K., Dusek, J. A., Chang, B.-H., Joseph, M. G., Denninger, J. W., Fricchione, G. L., & Benson, H. (2013). Relaxation response induces temporal transcriptome changes in energy metabolism, insulin secretion and inflammatory pathways. *PLOS ONE, 8*(5), e62817. https://doi.org/10.1371/journal.pone.0062817

Bratman, G. N., Hamilton, J. P., Hahn, K. S., Daily, G. C., & Gross, J. J. (2015). Nature experience reduces rumination and subgenual prefrontal cortex activation. *Proceedings of the National Academy of Sciences, 112*(28), 8567–8572. https://doi.org/10.1073/pnas.1510459112

Brewer, J. A., Worhunsky, P. D., Gray, J. R., Tang, Y.-Y., Weber, J., & Kober, H. (2011). Meditation experience is associated with differences in default mode network activity and connectivity. *Proceedings of the National Academy of Sciences, 108*(50), 20254–20259. https://doi.org/10.1073/pnas.1112029108

Brown, R. P., & Gerbarg, P. L. (2005). Sudarshan Kriya yogic breathing in the treatment of stress, anxiety, and depression: Part II, Clinical applications and guidelines. *Journal of Alternative and Complementary Medicine, 11*(4), 711–717. https://doi.org/10.1089/acm.2005.11.711

Diekelmann, S., & Born, J. (2010). The memory function of sleep. *Nature Reviews Neuroscience, 11*(2), 114–126. https://doi.org/10.1038/nrn2762

Dusek, J. A., Otu, H. H., Wohlhueter, A. L., Bhasin, M., Zerbini, L. F., Joseph, M. G., Benson, H., & Libermann, T. A. (2008). Genomic counter-stress changes induced by the relaxation response. *PLOS ONE, 3*(7), e2576. https://doi.org/10.1371/journal.pone.0002576

Edmondson, A. C. (1999). Psychological safety and learning behaviour in work teams. *Administrative Science Quarterly, 44*(2), 350–383. https://doi.org/10.2307/2666999

Fredrickson, B. L. (2001). The role of positive emotions in positive psychology: The broaden-and-build theory of positive emotions. *American Psychologist, 56*(3), 218–226. https://doi.org/10.1037/0003-066X.56.3.218

Jacobson, E. (1938). *Progressive relaxation* (2nd ed.). University of Chicago

Press.

Kabat-Zinn, J. (2003). Mindfulness-based interventions in context: Past, present, and future. *Clinical Psychology: Science and Practice, 10*(2), 144–156. https://doi.org/10.1093/clipsy.bpg016

Kok, B. E., & Fredrickson, B. L. (2010). Upward spirals of the heart: Autonomic flexibility, as indexed by vagal tone, reciprocally and prospectively predicts positive emotions. *Biological Psychology, 85*(3), 432–436. https://doi.org/10.1016/j.biopsycho.2010.09.005

Laborde, S., Mosley, E., & Thayer, J. F. (2017). Heart rate variability and performance: A systematic review and meta-analysis of HRV training and associations with self-control. *Frontiers in Psychology, 8,* 301. https://doi.org/10.3389/fpsyg.2017.00301

Lehrer, P. M., Kaur, K., Sharma, A., Shah, K., Huseby, R., Bhavsar, J., Zhang, Y., & Sharma, V. (2020). Heart rate variability biofeedback improves emotional and physical health and performance: A systematic review and meta analysis. *Applied Psychophysiology and Biofeedback, 45*(3), 109–129. https://doi.org/10.1007/s10484-020-09466-z

Manzoni, G. M., Pagnini, F., Castelnuovo, G., & Molinari, E. (2008). Relaxation training for anxiety: A ten-years systematic review with meta-analysis. *BMC Psychiatry, 8,* 41. https://doi.org/10.1186/1471-244X-8-41

Maslach, C., & Leiter, M. P. (2016). Understanding the burnout experience: Recent research and its implications for psychiatry. *World Psychiatry, 15*(2), 103–111. https://doi.org/10.1002/wps.20311

McEwen, B. S. (2007). Physiology and neurobiology of stress and adaptation: Central role of the brain. *Physiological Reviews, 87*(3), 873–904. https://doi.org/10.1152/physrev.00041.2006

Porges, S. W. (2011). *The polyvagal theory: Neurophysiological foundations of emotions, attachment, communication, and self-regulation.* W. W. Norton.

Sonnentag, S. (2018). The recovery paradox: Portraying the complex interplay between job stressors, lack of recovery, and poor well-being. *Research in Organisational Behaviour, 38,* 169–185. https://doi.org/10.1016/j.riob.2018.11.002

Sonnentag, S., & Fritz, C. (2007). The Recovery Experience Questionnaire: Development and validation of a measure for assessing recuperation and unwinding from work. *Journal of Occupational Health Psychology, 12*(3), 204–221.

https://doi.org/10.1037/1076-8998.12.3.204

Thayer, J. F., & Lane, R. D. (2000). A model of neurovisceral integration in emotion regulation and dysregulation. *Journal of Affective Disorders, 61*(3), 201–216. https://doi.org/10.1016/S0165-0327(00)00338-4

Thayer, J. F., Åhs, F., Fredrikson, M., Sollers, J. J., III, & Wager, T. D. (2012). A meta-analysis of heart rate variability and neuroimaging studies: Implications for heart–brain interactions. *NeuroImage, 59*(3), 2137–2147. https://doi.org/10.1016/j.neuroimage.2011.10.007

Ulrich, R. S. (1984). View through a window may influence recovery from surgery. *Science, 224*(4647), 420–421. https://doi.org/10.1126/science.6143402

Wendsche, J., & Lohmann-Haislah, A. (2017). A meta-analysis on the effects of rest breaks on performance, fatigue, and well-being. *Work & Stress, 31*(1), 1–22. https://doi.org/10.1080/02678373.2017.1317839

Zaccaro, A., Piarulli, A., Laurino, M., Garbella, E., Menicucci, D., Neri, B., & Gemignani, A. (2018). How breath-control can change your life: A systematic review on psychophysiological correlates of slow breathing. *Frontiers in Human Neuroscience, 12,* 353. https://doi.org/10.3389/fnhum.2018.00353

Note. This article translates established evidence into practice consistent with Chapter 21 ("Relaxation") of *Heart Unbound 2.0*, offering a rigorous foundation for facilitators and participants while preserving the program's heart-led orientation.

22 - Re-parenting the "Inner Child": Psychophysiological and Leadership Foundations

---

Rationale for the Article

Heart Unbound 2.0 seeks durable changes in emotion regulation, connection, and ethical leadership. Inner-child work directly addresses developmental gaps that drive dysregulation and relational reactivity, activates reliable psychophysiological levers (breath-mediated vagal tone), employs empirically supported methods (self-compassion, expressive writing, art processes), and transfers cleanly to leadership behaviours that foster authenticity and psychological safety (Avolio & Gardner, 2005; Edmondson, 1999; Neff & Germer, 2013; Pennebaker & Smyth, 2016; Porges, 2011).

Abstract

This article elaborates and evaluates "Inner Child," Chapter 22 of *Heart Unbound 2.0*, positioning inner-child work as a trauma-informed, developmentally coherent practice that integrates attachment theory, transactional analysis, depth psychology, and contemporary psychophysiology. We synthesise evidence for mechanisms of change, autonomic regulation (polyvagal theory; heart-rate variability), compassionate self-relating, expressive writing, and arts-based symbolisation, and map these mechanisms onto a practical, staged protocol (Body–Breath–Balance, compassionate re-parenting dialogue, creative play, boundary setting, reflective journaling). Leadership implications include increased authenticity, psychological safety, and values-aligned action. A brief evaluation framework and case vignette illustrate feasibility and outcomes. We conclude that Chapter 22 provides a rigorous, scalable bridge between personal healing and professional effectiveness.

Keywords: inner child; attachment; polyvagal theory; self-compassion; expressive writing; leadership; psychological safety

Introduction

Across clinical, coaching, and organisational settings, recurrent adult patterns, perfectionism, people-pleasing, emotional distancing, are increasingly understood as protective adaptations shaped by early attachment experiences and retained in autonomic memory (Ainsworth et al., 1978; Bowlby, 1969/1982; Schore, 2012). Depth psychology names the **Divine Child** as a symbol of creativity and renewal (Jung, 1959/1968), while transactional analysis places the **Child** ego state, both Natural and Adapted, alongside **Parent** and **Adult** to explain moment-to-moment interpersonal dynamics (Berne, 1961). Interpersonal neurobiology and polyvagal theory specify the underlying physiology: cues of safety recruit ventral vagal pathways and enable social engagement and executive functions; cues of danger bias sympathetic defense or dorsal withdrawal (Porges, 2011; Thayer & Lane, 2000).

Chapter 22 of *Heart Unbound 2.0* operationalises these convergent traditions into a structured, trauma-informed sequence that is accessible to lay participants and professionals. Here we (a) articulate the theoretical foundations, (b) summarise empirical support for each method, (c) translate the science into program components, (d) link outcomes to leadership practice, and (e) propose an evaluation plan.

Conceptual Foundations

Attachment and developmental learning

Secure early caregiving calibrates internal working models and stress physiology; insecurity forecasts difficulties with regulation and intimacy (Ainsworth et al., 1978; Bowlby, 1969/1982; Siegel, 2012). Inner-child framing renders these legacies *approachable*: younger parts are engaged with curiosity, validation, and new corrective experiences.

Depth psychology and symbolic integration

Jung's Child archetype represents vitality and transformation; reclaiming it supports individuation and meaning (Jung, 1959/1968). Expressive, imaginal methods permit symbolic processing when explicit language is insufficient (Malchiodi, 2012).

Transactional analysis (TA)

Berne's Parent–Adult–Child model provides a practical map for state recognition and repair, strengthening Adult mediation, soothing the Adapted Child, and protecting the Natural Child (Berne, 1961).

Psychophysiology of safety

Polyvagal theory and neurovisceral integration explain how slow, coherent breathing, prosody, and warm touch increase vagal tone and prefrontal flexibility (Lehrer & Gevirtz, 2014; Porges, 2011; Thayer & Lane, 2000).

Evidence-Informed Methods

1. **Self-compassion and re-parenting.** Compassion-based protocols reliably reduce shame, anxiety, and dysregulation while increasing resilience (Gilbert, 2009; Neff & Germer, 2013). In inner-child language, the Adult self becomes a consistent, protective caregiver.

2. **Expressive writing.** Brief, structured writing on deepest thoughts and feelings improves health, sleep, and narrative coherence (Pennebaker & Smyth, 2016).

3. **Arts-based symbolisation and play.** Drawing, music, movement, and play safely externalise affect, broaden positive emotion, and support integration (Fredrickson, 2001; Malchiodi, 2012).

4. **Breath-based regulation.** Resonance-frequency breathing ($\approx$5–6 breaths/min) increases HRV and emotion regulation capacity, creating conditions for reflective work (Lehrer & Gevirtz, 2014).

Program Translation: Chapter 22 Protocol

Stage 1 - Body–Breath–Balance (Somatic Safety). Three minutes of 4–6 breathing with hand-on-heart; brief body scan; optional soothing soundscape. *Mechanism:* vagal up-regulation; state shift to safety (Porges, 2011; Thayer & Lane, 2000).

Stage 2 - Compassionate Re-parenting Dialogue. Short scripts from Adult to Child (e.g., "You are safe with me; your feelings matter"), coupled with boundary statements. *Mechanism:* corrective attachment experience; reduced self-criticism (Gilbert, 2009).

Stage 3 - Creative Play Windows. 10–15 minutes of low-stakes drawing, singing, movement, or nature play. *Mechanism:* broaden-and-build, implicit emotion processing (Fredrickson, 2001; Malchiodi, 2012).

Stage 4 - Reflective Writing (Heart-Whisper). Seven-minute free-write beginning: *"If my younger self could speak now, it would say…"* *Mechanism:* narrative integration and health benefits (Pennebaker & Smyth, 2016).

Stage 5 - Values and Boundaries. Translate insights to one concrete boundary and one joy ritual for the week. *Mechanism:* autonomy and internalisation (Deci & Ryan, 2000).

Brief case vignette (composite)

A mid-career professional with anxious attachment and perfectionism completed four weekly cycles. Outcomes included decreased self-criticism, improved sleep onset, and easier boundary setting with a supervisor; resting RMSSD increased from 22 ms to 34 ms (clinically modest but meaningful), and Self-Compassion Scale scores improved from low to average range.

Leadership Implications

Unmet child-state needs often manifest as controlling, avoidant, or approval-seeking leadership. Practicing Chapter 22 skills increases **authenticity** and **self-regulation** (Avolio & Gardner, 2005), supports **resonant leadership** climates (Boyatzis & McKee, 2005), and contributes to **psychological safety**, the strongest predictor of team learning (Edmondson, 1999). Linking rituals of play and reflection to team practices (e.g., check-ins, gratitude rounds, protected focus time) aligns with self-determination theory's needs for autonomy, competence, and relatedness (Deci & Ryan, 2000).

Application in *Heart Unbound 2.0* - Inner Child

The Inner Child chapter translates theory into accessible, heart-led practice:

- **Safety & Soothing Micro-Rituals:** 60-second "hand-on-heart + longer exhale" sequences (with gentle self-talk: *I see you. You're safe with me.*) to down-shift the nervous system when younger parts are activated.

- **Reparenting Dialogues:** Brief, written or spoken scripts that validate feelings, ask needs (*What do you need right now?*), and make a specific caring promise (*I'll protect your time/boundary today*).

- **Then/Now Journaling:** Two-column reflections ("What child-me learned" → "What adult-me knows and chooses now") to update old beliefs and create corrective emotional experiences.

- **Play Prescriptions:** 10–15 minute, scheduled micro-play (drawing, music, nature, silliness) and a weekly "Joy Appointment" to restore spontaneity and delight.

- **Parts Mapping Check-ins:** Quick TA-informed scan (Parent–Adult–Child) to notice who's "driving," followed by an Adult re-centering step and a compassionate next action.

- **Boundary Rehearsals:** "Big NO / Little YES" practice, one protective boundary for the inner child paired with a small, nurturing permission each day.

- **Repair & Self-Compassion Rituals:** Three-step RAIN-style flow (Recognize–Allow–Inquire–Nurture) after triggers; optional letter to younger self to close the loop with kindness.

- **Co-regulation Containers:** Identify one trusted person; practise 3 minutes of shared slow breathing, warm eye contact, and a grounding phrase to restore felt safety together.

- **Creative Comfort Toolkit:** Sensory resources (soft object, scent, music, weighted wrap) plus "feel-it, draw-it, move-it" prompts to express what words can't.

> • **Leadership Alignment:** Translate inner-child care into outer-adult action, values-based decisions, humane pacing, playfully energizing team moments, and psychological-safety check-ins.
>
> These practices are personally healing and professionally transformative for emerging and senior leaders, and for anyone cultivating courageous, authentic self-leadership.

Implementation and Evaluation

Format. Four 75-minute sessions or a one-day intensive with follow-up practice prompts.

Outcomes and measures.

- Emotion regulation: DERS-SF.
- Self-compassion: Self-Compassion Scale–Short Form.
- Perceived stress: PSS-10.
- Attachment security: ECR-S (baseline, optional).
- Leadership climate: Edmondson Team Psychological Safety (for intact teams).
- Physiology: resting HRV (RMSSD) pre/post where feasible.

Design. Pragmatic pre–post with 4–8-week follow-up; for organisations, cluster wait-list or stepped-wedge designs are realistic. Mixed-methods (quantitative scales + short reflective interviews) capture both mechanisms and meaning.

Safeguards. Clear opt-out, titration of trauma content, referral pathways, and facilitator training in trauma-informed care (van der Kolk, 2014; Levine, 2010).

Limitations and Future Directions

Evidence for each component is strong; rigorous tests of the *integrated* protocol are needed. Future research should compare Chapter 22 against active controls (e.g., generic stress-management), examine team-level spillover (psychological safety, retention), and explore dose–response and digital delivery.

Conclusion

Inner-child work is neither nostalgic nor regressive; it is a developmentally precise, physiologically grounded pathway to integration. By pairing autonomic safety with compassionate re-parenting, playful symbolisation, and coherent narrative, Chapter 22 of *Heart Unbound 2.0* offers a scalable intervention that advances personal healing and ethical, resonant leadership.

References

Ainsworth, M. D. S., Blehar, M., Waters, E., & Wall, S. (1978). *Patterns of attachment: A psychological study of the strange situation.* Lawrence Erlbaum.

Avolio, B. J., & Gardner, W. L. (2005). Authentic leadership development: Getting to the root of positive forms of leadership. *The Leadership Quarterly, 16*(3), 315–338. https://doi.org/10.1016/j.leaqua.2005.03.001

Berne, E. (1961). *Transactional analysis in psychotherapy.* Grove Press.

Bowlby, J. (1969/1982). *Attachment and loss: Vol. 1. Attachment* (2nd ed.). Basic Books.

Boyatzis, R. E., & McKee, A. (2005). *Resonant leadership: Renewing yourself and connecting with others through mindfulness, hope, and compassion.* Harvard Business School Press.

Deci, E. L., & Ryan, R. M. (2000). The "what" and "why" of goal pursuits: Human needs and the self-determination of behaviour. *Psychological Inquiry, 11*(4), 227–268. https://doi.org/10.1207/S15327965PLI1104_01

Edmondson, A. C. (1999). Psychological safety and learning behaviour in work teams. *Administrative Science Quarterly, 44*(2), 350–383. https://doi.org/10.2307/2666999

Fredrickson, B. L. (2001). The broaden-and-build theory of positive emotions. *American Psychologist, 56*(3), 218–226. https://doi.org/10.1037/0003-066X.56.3.218

Gilbert, P. (2009). *The compassionate mind.* Constable.

Jung, C. G. (1959/1968). *The archetypes and the collective unconscious* (2nd ed., R. F. C. Hull, Trans.). Princeton University Press.

Lehrer, P. M., & Gevirtz, R. (2014). Heart rate variability biofeedback: How and why does it work? *Frontiers in Psychology, 5,* 756. https://doi.org/10.3389/fpsyg.2014.00756

Levine, P. A. (2010). *In an unspoken voice: How the body releases trauma and restores goodness.* North Atlantic Books.

Malchiodi, C. A. (Ed.). (2012). *Handbook of art therapy* (2nd ed.). Guilford Press.

Neff, K. D., & Germer, C. K. (2013). A pilot study and randomised controlled trial of the Mindful Self-Compassion program. *Journal of Clinical Psychology, 69*(1), 28–44. https://doi.org/10.1002/jclp.21923

Pennebaker, J. W., & Smyth, J. M. (2016). *Opening up by writing it down* (3rd ed.). Guilford Press.

Porges, S. W. (2011). *The polyvagal theory: Neurophysiological foundations of emotions, attachment, communication, and self-regulation.* W. W. Norton.

Schore, A. N. (2012). *The science of the art of psychotherapy.* W. W. Norton.

Siegel, D. J. (2012). *The developing mind: How relationships and the brain interact to shape who we are* (2nd ed.). Guilford Press.

Thayer, J. F., & Lane, R. D. (2000). A model of neurovisceral integration in emotion regulation and dysregulation. *Annals of the New York Academy of Sciences, 998,* 125–145. https://doi.org/10.1111/j.1749-6632.2000.tb05461.x

van der Kolk, B. A. (2014). *The body keeps the score: Brain, mind, and body in the healing of trauma.* Viking.

THE
UNBOUND
JOURNEY

23 - "Declutter": Creating Cognitive, Physiological, and Leadership Space for Heart-Led Change

Rationale for the Article

The Declutter chapter operationalises a simple truth: space is a psychological and physiological intervention. Reducing external and internal clutter lowers stress biomarkers, restores executive bandwidth for emotion regulation, and creates conditions for values-aligned action, core outcomes across *Heart Unbound 2.0* (Saxbe & Repetti, 2010; Thayer & Lane, 2000). This article validates the chapter's practices with cross-disciplinary evidence and offers measurement-ready protocols for practitioners.

Abstract

This article contends that decluttering, of rooms, devices, calendars, and inner narratives, is not cosmetic housekeeping but a psychologically and physiologically meaningful intervention that advances the aims of *Heart Unbound 2.0*. Integrating research from environmental and cognitive psychology, affective neuroscience, and leadership studies, we describe how visual and temporal clutter drains attentional resources, elevates stress biology, and degrades judgment through choice overload. We show that simplifying contexts and commitments reliably strengthens emotion regulation, restores executive bandwidth, and supports values-aligned, ethical decision-making by enhancing vagal tone and working memory. Evidence is translated into practice through the HEART-SPACE protocol for individuals and a team playbook (e.g., 5S, meeting hygiene, digital-quiet norms), alongside pragmatic outcome metrics for evaluation. We conclude that creating space is a low-cost, high-leverage pathway to compassionate self-leadership and culture change, empirically validating Chapter 23 ("Declutter") as a core mechanism of heart-led transformation.

Introduction

"Declutter" is often framed as aesthetic tidying. In behavioural science, it is better understood as the purposeful reduction of *stimulus load* (what the eyes, brain, and calendar must process) and *constraint load* (the number of micro-decisions required to navigate a day). Load taxes working memory, increases sympathetic arousal, and degrades judgment (Lavie, 2005; Mullainathan & Shafir, 2013). By contrast, ordered, light-filled, and simplified contexts facilitate autonomy, competence, and relatedness, the psychological nutrients of well-being and motivation (Deci & Ryan, 2000). We synthesise evidence for four, mutually reinforcing domains of declutter, physical space, digital attention, time, and inner narrative, and translate findings into practical tools for individuals and leaders.

Conceptualising Declutter

We define declutter as a **systematic reduction of non-value stimuli, possessions, tasks, and scripts** so that attention, physiology, and behaviour can align with personally endorsed values.

- **Physical declutter**: removal or re-ordering of objects to reduce visual clutter and signal affordances (Rosenholtz et al., 2007).

- **Digital declutter**: batch processing and boundarying of notifications/inputs (Mark et al., 2008; Kushlev & Dunn, 2015).

- **Temporal declutter**: pruning commitments and designing default rhythms (Mullainathan & Shafir, 2013).

- **Narrative/emotional declutter**: surfacing and releasing unhelpful beliefs via mindfulness and acceptance-based skills (Kabat-Zinn, 1990; Hayes et al., 1999).

Psychological Mechanisms

Attention and Working Memory

Visual clutter competes for finite attentional resources, increasing search time and error (Rosenholtz et al., 2007). Naturalistic studies link cluttered homes with more depressed mood and disrupted diurnal cortisol (Saxbe & Repetti, 2010). Conversely, orderly spaces bias people toward healthier choices and prosociality, while disordered spaces can transiently boost creativity, illustrating context-dependent effects (Vohs et al., 2013).

Choice Overload and Decision Quality

Too many options reduce satisfaction and follow-through (Iyengar & Lepper, 2000). Scarcity of cognitive bandwidth (from cluttered tasks and timelines) narrows focus to the urgent at the expense of the important (Mullainathan & Shafir, 2013). Decluttering reduces decision points and restores prospective memory via clear cues and defaults (Gollwitzer, 1999; Lally et al., 2010).

Values, Materiality, and Well-Being

Accumulation is not neutral. Meta-analytic work shows that materialistic goal orientation correlates with lower well-being and higher distress (Dittmar et al., 2014). Minimal, intentional environments can support self-determination via autonomy (choosing what matters), competence (clear affordances), and relatedness (space for connection) (Deci & Ryan, 2000).

Physiological Mechanisms

Stress Biology and Autonomic Regulation

Cluttered, chaotic environments are associated with flatter diurnal cortisol slopes, an index of chronic stress (Saxbe & Repetti, 2010). The *neurovisceral integration model* explains how prefrontal regulation (executive attention) and cardiac vagal control covary; higher vagally mediated HRV is linked to better emotion regulation (Thayer & Lane, 2000). Simplifying inputs, practicing slow exhalation, and creating restorative spaces increase parasympathetic tone (Porges, 2011). Environmental quality (ventilation, air quality, daylight) also improves perceived health and performance (Wargocki et al., 2000) and attention restoration (Berman et al., 2008).

Declutter for Leadership and Teams

Cognitive and Ethical Bandwidth

Leaders operate under heavy "decision load." Reducing unnecessary artifacts, handoffs, and inbox interruptions improves working memory, reduces time-pressure bias, and supports ethical reflection (Dane, 2011; Mark et al., 2008). Organisational 5S (Sort, Set in order, Shine, Standardize, Sustain) offers a repeatable method to remove waste and make the "right action" the easy action (Hirano, 1995).

Compassionate, Heart-Led Cultures

Coaching and leadership styles that evoke the *positive emotional attractor* (vision, compassion, hope) elicit parasympathetic activation and broaden thinking (Boyatzis et al., 2013). Decluttered meeting structures (shorter agendas, single-tasking, device norms) and values-aligned calendars create the conditions for compassionate presence and better decisions.

Evidence-Aligned Practices for *Heart Unbound 2.0*

The HEART-SPACE Protocol (individual practice)

1. **H**one one locus (single drawer, one folder, or one belief).

2. **E**liminate by rule: *useful, beautiful, or values-aligned*, else release (Deci & Ryan, 2000; Dittmar et al., 2014).

3. **A**rrange for action: place the next visible cue where behaviour happens (Gollwitzer, 1999).

4. **R**estore physiology: 5 minutes of 4–6 breathing to raise HRV (Thayer & Lane, 2000; Porges, 2011).

5. **T**rack a *minimum viable habit* until automaticity (~66 days on average; Lally et al., 2010).

6. **S**eal boundaries: batch email/notifications twice daily (Kushlev & Dunn, 2015).

7. **P**ractice attention restoration: 10–20 minutes in nature (Berman et al., 2008).

8. **A**udit calendar weekly: subtract before you add (Mullainathan & Shafir, 2013).

9. **C**ompassion check: release with gratitude; keep without guilt (Hayes et al., 1999).

10. **E**valuate with simple metrics (see below).

Suggested measures. Perceived Stress Scale (PSS-10), WHO-5 Well-Being Index, weekly HRV snapshot (if available), and two behaviour counts: number of notifications/day and *decisions deferred*.

Team/Organisation Playbook

- **5S one process per quarter** (Hirano, 1995).

- **Meeting hygiene**: single decision per meeting; devices face-down; default 25/50-minute blocks.

- **Digital quiet hours** and *email batching* norms (Kushlev & Dunn, 2015).

- **Space for nature**: biophilic cues, daylight, plants (Berman et al., 2008; Wargocki et al., 2000).

Application in Heart Unbound 2.0

The Declutter chapter translates theory into accessible, heart-led practice:

- **Space & Self Audits (10-minute sprints):** One drawer/desk/bag at a time with the heart question, *"What is this supporting in me now?"* Keep what nourishes; bless & release what does not.

- **Heart-Breath Release Ritual:** 3 slow rounds of balanced heart breathing, hand to chest, then let go of one object/thought/story while saying, *"Thank you for what you gave. I release you."*

- **Decluttering Map (Physical • Mental • Emotional):** Weekly three-line plan: *I release → Action.* Journal the shift to anchor new clarity.

- **Digital Quiet & Calendar Boundaries:** A protected weekly "unplug" block, notifications off after sunset, and a simple "yes/no" rule: if it drains, it's redesigned, delegated, or declined.

- **Joy-Forward Curation (Feng Shui micro-zones):** Create small, intentional zones (rest, create, focus). Use the energy test: *"Does this lift my breath or tighten it?"* Keep only what lifts.

- **Inner Narrative Cleanse:** Identify one limiting belief or looping worry, thank it, rewrite a compassionate truth, then pair with a regulating practice (breath, brief walk, gentle shake).

- **Closing & Intention Ritual:** After each clear-out, visualize the new space, choose one word (e.g., *Peace, Focus, Light*), and place a simple "anchor" object that represents it.

- **Maintenance in Minutes:** Daily three: surface reset (60 seconds), one-in/one-out rule, and a micro-pause of mindful breathing between tasks. Monthly: a 30-minute whole-home/whole-heart reset.

These practices create spaciousness in rooms, calendars, and nervous systems, personally healing and professionally clarifying for emerging and senior leaders, and for anyone ready to live by intention rather than accumulation.

Cultural Lineages that Anticipate the Science

Feng Shui's attention to flow mirrors load reduction and affordance design; Zen-informed minimalism privileges essence over excess; mindfulness reframes decluttering as compassionate presence (Kabat-Zinn, 1990). These traditions converge with contemporary evidence on attention, cortisol, and HRV.

Special Considerations

Decluttering can surface grief or compulsive saving. Screen for hoarding-spectrum presentations and trauma history; refer to evidence-based care when indicated (American Psychiatric Association, 2013; Hayes et al., 1999).

Conclusion

Decluttering is a high-leverage lever for heart-led change. By reducing non-value stimuli and decisions, individuals and leaders free attentional and physiological bandwidth for compassion, creativity, and values-aligned action. The practices above translate robust science into the lived experience of *Heart Unbound 2.0*: more space, more coherence, more heart.

References

American Psychiatric Association. (2013). *Diagnostic and statistical manual of mental disorders* (5th ed.).

Berman, M. G., Jonides, J., & Kaplan, S. (2008). The cognitive benefits of interacting with nature. *Psychological Science, 19*(12), 1207–1212. https://doi.org/10.1111/j.1467-9280.2008.02225.x

Boyatzis, R. E., Rochford, K., & Jack, A. I. (2013). Antagonistic neural networks underlying differentiated leadership styles. *Frontiers in Human Neuroscience, 7*, 919. https://doi.org/10.3389/fnhum.2013.00919

Deci, E. L., & Ryan, R. M. (2000). The "what" and "why" of goal pursuits. *Psychological Inquiry, 11*(4), 227–268. https://doi.org/10.1207/S15327965PLI1104_01

Dane, E. (2011). Paying attention to mindfulness and its effects on task performance. *Journal of Management, 37*(4), 997–1018. https://doi.org/10.1177/0149206310367948

Dittmar, H., Bond, R., Hurst, M., & Kasser, T. (2014). The relationship between materialism and personal well-being: A meta-analysis. *Journal of Personality and Social Psychology, 107*(5), 879–924. https://doi.org/10.1037/a0037409

Gollwitzer, P. M. (1999). Implementation intentions. *American Psychologist, 54*(7), 493–503. https://doi.org/10.1037/0003-066X.54.7.493

Grossman, P., Niemann, L., Schmidt, S., & Walach, H. (2004). Mindfulness-based stress reduction and health benefits: A meta-analysis. *Journal of Psychosomatic Research, 57*(1), 35–43. https://doi.org/10.1016/S0022-3999(03)00573-7

Hayes, S. C., Strosahl, K. D., & Wilson, K. G. (1999). *Acceptance and commitment therapy: An experiential approach to behaviour change.* Guilford.

Hirano, H. (1995). *5 Pillars of the visual workplace: The sourcebook for 5S implementation.* Productivity Press.

Iyengar, S. S., & Lepper, M. R. (2000). When choice is demotivating. *Journal of Personality and Social Psychology, 79*(6), 995–1006. https://doi.org/10.1037/0022-3514.79.6.995

Kabat-Zinn, J. (1990). *Full catastrophe living.* Delacorte.

Kushlev, K., & Dunn, E. W. (2015). Checking email less frequently reduces stress. *Computers in Human Behaviour, 43*, 220–228. https://doi.org/10.1016/j.chb.2014.11.005

Lally, P., van Jaarsveld, C. H. M., Potts, H. W. W., & Wardle, J. (2010). How are habits formed? *European Journal of Social Psychology, 40*(6), 998–1009. https://doi.org/10.1002/ejsp.674

Lavie, N. (2005). Distracted and confused? *Trends in Cognitive Sciences, 9*(2), 75–82. https://doi.org/10.1016/j.tics.2004.12.004

Mark, G., Gudith, D., & Klocke, U. (2008). The cost of interrupted work: More speed and stress. In *CHI '08* (pp. 107–110). ACM. https://doi.org/10.1145/1357054.1357072

Mullainathan, S., & Shafir, E. (2013). *Scarcity: Why having too little means so much.* Times Books.

Porges, S. W. (2011). *The polyvagal theory.* Norton.

Rosenholtz, R., Li, Y., & Nakano, L. (2007). Measuring visual clutter. *Journal of Vision, 7*(2), 17. https://doi.org/10.1167/7.2.17

Saxbe, D. E., & Repetti, R. L. (2010). No place like home: Home tours correlate with daily patterns of mood and cortisol. *Personality and Social Psychology Bulletin, 36*(1), 71–81. https://doi.org/10.1177/0146167209352864

Thayer, J. F., & Lane, R. D. (2000). A model of neurovisceral integration. *Journal of Affective Disorders, 61*(3), 201–216. https://doi.org/10.1016/S0165-0327(00)00338-4

Vohs, K. D., Redden, J. P., & Rahinel, R. (2013). Physical order and disorder. *Psychological Science, 24*(9), 1860–1867. https://doi.org/10.1177/0956797613480186

Wargocki, P., Wyon, D. P., Sundell, J., Clausen, G., & Fanger, P. O. (2000). The effects of outdoor air supply rate… *Indoor Air, 10*(4), 222–236. https://doi.org/10.1034/j.1600-0668.2000.010004222.x

Kaplan, R., & Kaplan, S. (1989). *The experience of nature.* Cambridge University Press.

Berman, M. G., et al. already above.

24 - Laughter as Neurocardiac Regulator, Social Glue, and Leadership Resource

Rationale for the Article

Laughter is often relegated to "nice-to-have," yet evidence shows it is a *mechanism* for autonomic recovery, cognitive flexibility, and prosocial bonding, all central to the program's aims of authentic self-leadership and compassionate impact. Grounding Chapter 24's practices in peer-reviewed science clarifies that cultivating joy is not sentimentality; it is a strategic intervention that supports safety, learning, and ethical influence across personal and professional domains (Cameron, 2012; Porges, 2007).

Abstract

This article examines laughter as a rigorously evidenced pathway to emotional regulation, physiological repair, and relational cohesion, core aims of *Heart Unbound 2.0*. Integrating affective science, psychoneuroimmunology, and contemporary leadership research, we show that laughter reliably down-regulates stress physiology (e.g., cortisol), engages parasympathetic recovery via vagal mechanisms, elevates endogenous opioids, and strengthens immune activity. Psychologically, laughter broadens attention and coping options, accelerates resilience, and deepens empathy and perspective-taking. In teams, leader and group humor predict trust, psychological safety, and creativity when expressed inclusively and ethically. We translate these findings into a structured, heart-led practice sequence, micro-laughter breaks, dyadic "joy bids," leader cues, and measurement guidelines, positioning laughter as a daily, measurable competency rather than a discretionary extra. The result is a compact validation of Chapter 24's claim: joy is not a luxury; it is a scientifically supported regulator that restores clarity, connection, and courage in individuals and systems.

Keywords: laughter; emotion regulation; parasympathetic activation; resilience; psychological safety; leader humor; positive emotion; broaden-and-build

Introduction

Chapter 24 of *Heart Unbound 2.0* proposes that laughter is "medicine for the soul" and a practical means to restore balance in the nervous system, renew connection, and uplift collective morale. Contemporary science supports this proposition. Positive emotion theorists argue that joy and amusement broaden cognitive repertoires and build durable resources (Fredrickson, 2001; Tugade & Fredrickson, 2004). Psychoneuroimmunology demonstrates that humorous stimuli and spontaneous laughter moderate neuroendocrine stress markers and enhance immune parameters (Berk et al., 1989; Bennett & Lengacher, 2009). Social and organisational scholarship further shows that appropriately used leader humor predicts trust, engagement, and creativity through psychological safety (Cooper et al., 2018; Edmondson, 1999).

This article synthesises these literatures to validate and extend the chapter's practices. We (a) review mechanisms linking laughter with health and self-leadership; (b) examine its social and leadership effects; and (c) offer an implementation framework aligned with *Heart Unbound 2.0*'s heart-led pedagogy.

Conceptual Foundations: Positive Emotion as Capacity Builder

The broaden-and-build theory proposes that positive emotions expand momentary thought-action repertoires and, over time, build enduring resources (Fredrickson, 2001). In stressful contexts, amusement and light-heartedness counteract narrowed attention and threat vigilance, enabling reappraisal and flexible problem solving (Gross, 1998; Tugade & Fredrickson, 2004). These processes explain observed links between laughter and improved coping, optimism, and social connectedness (Pressman & Cohen, 2005).

Humor styles matter. Affiliative and self-enhancing humor correlate with well-being and relationship quality, whereas aggressive or self-defeating humor can undermine trust (Martin et al., 2003). Heart-led laughter is therefore mindful, aimed at inclusion, not superiority.

Physiological Mechanisms: From Cortisol Downshift to Vagal Up-Toning

Endorphin System and Analgesia

Laughter triggers endogenous opioid release, indexed by increased pain thresholds and social bonding effects (Dunbar et al., 2012). These opioids contribute to the "warm-afterglow" that sustains affiliative motivation.

Stress Hormones and Immune Function

Experimental and field studies show reductions in cortisol and catecholamines following humorous stimuli, alongside increases in natural killer cell activity, immunoglobulins, and T-cell counts (Berk et al., 1989; Bennett & Lengacher, 2009). These effects situate laughter within psychoneuroimmunology as a low-cost, behaviourally accessible immuno-modulator.

Autonomic Regulation and the Polyvagal Lens

Spontaneous and induced laughter stimulate rhythmic exhalation, abdominal movement, and facial/vocal prosody, all of which engage the myelinated vagus that supports social connection and recovery (Porges, 2007). The resulting increase in parasympathetic tone (reflected in heart-rate variability) aligns with the chapter's emphasis on "rest-and-restore" states.

Social and Leadership Effects: Humor as Prosocial Resource

Psychological Safety and Team Learning

Humor, when respectful and inclusive, signals approachability and reduces status distance, thereby supporting psychological safety, the shared belief that "this is a place where I can speak up" (Edmondson, 1999). Meta-analytic evidence associates leader humor with job satisfaction, creativity, and performance via relational resources (Cooper et al., 2018; Mesmer-Magnus et al., 2012).

Bonding and Prosociality

Evolutionary accounts view laughter as a vocal grooming mechanism that scales bonding beyond dyads (Gervais & Wilson, 2005). Oxytocin-related pathways likely interact with endorphin responses to increase trust and cooperative intent (Dunbar et al., 2012).

Ethical Boundaries

Humor is powerful and double-edged. Aggressive, sarcastic, or identity-based joking erodes dignity and safety (Martin et al., 2003). Heart-led programs must codify norms for inclusive, non-derogatory humor aligned with values-based leadership (Avolio & Gardner, 2005).

Evidence-Informed Practices Aligned to Chapter 24

1) Micro-Laughter Breaks (Self-Regulation)

- **Protocol:** Two to three 60–120-second intervals/day of "smile-to-laugh" induction (gentle breath, eye-softening, audible chuckle that escalates to natural laughter).

- **Mechanism:** Prolonged exhalation and thoraco-abdominal movement increase vagal engagement; positive affect broadens attention (Porges, 2007; Fredrickson, 2001).

2) Dyadic "Joy Bids" (Relational Hygiene)

- **Protocol:** Partners exchange brief, humorous appreciations or micro-stories; keep content affiliative, never at another's expense.

- **Outcomes:** Increased felt safety and bonding; buffers stress via social support pathways (Cohen & Wills, 1985).

3) Laughter Yoga and Induction (Group Recovery)

- **Evidence:** Small trials show improved mood and reduced depressive symptoms, especially in older adults (Shahidi et al., 2011).

- **Adaptation:** Pair with *Heart Unbound* breath practices to avoid hyperventilation and honor accessibility.

4) Leader Cues for Psychological Safety

- **Behaviours:** Self-deprecating (not self-diminishing) humor, warm storytelling, and explicit "no-punching-down" norms.

- **Outcomes:** Higher voice behaviour and creative engagement (Cooper et al., 2018; Edmondson, 1999).

5) Measurement and Learning Loops

- **Physiology:** Optional HRV snapshots pre/post micro-laughter.
- **Psychosocial:** Brief scales, Positive and Negative Affect Schedule (PANAS), Humor Styles Questionnaire, affiliative/self-enhancing subscales (Martin et al., 2003).
- **Team:** Psychological Safety Scale (Edmondson, 1999).

Application to *Heart Unbound 2.0*: Laughter in the Heart-Led Curriculum

Practice Stack for Daily Use

1. **Balanced Heart Breathing** → 60 seconds.
2. **Smile-to-Laughter Ladder** → 90 seconds (soft chuckle to natural laugh).
3. **Meaning-Making Prompt** → "What did this lighten or make possible?" (journaling 2–3 lines).
4. **Prosocial Extension** → Share one "joy bid" with a colleague or family member.

Facilitator Guidance

- Open with consent and accessibility cues (seating options, trauma-sensitive invitations).
- Debrief for *felt sense* (warmth, breath ease), not just funniness, to reinforce interoceptive learning.
- Track weekly practice frequency and brief reflections to consolidate habit memory.

Application in Heart Unbound 2.0

The Laughter chapter translates theory into accessible, heart-led practice:

- **60-Second Laugh Reset:** A micro-ritual of inhale–smile–exhale with a gentle "haaa" sound, loosening jaw/shoulders, to flip the nervous system from stress to ease, anytime, anywhere.

- **Daily "Joy Reps" (7-Day Sprint):** One deliberate laughter prompt per day (funny clip, call a witty friend, silly walk, gratitude-with-a-grin). Track mood before/after to wire the joy-resilience loop.

- **Laughter Meditation + Shake:** 5–10 minutes: breath, intentional chuckle → natural laughter → whole-body shake → quiet rest. Use after heavy meetings or when rumination spikes.

- **Empathic Humour Agreements:** Simple guardrails for home/teams: humour that includes (never punches down), opt-in play, a safe "pause word," and quick repair if a joke mislands.

- **Light-Hearted Communication Drills:** "Clear-and-kind with levity", state the issue, add a warm reframe or shared absurdity, then a concrete next step. Practise in pairs.

- **Joy Map → Calendar:** Build your Joy Map (people/places/activities that spark laughter). Schedule two micro-joys weekly; protect them with a "no-doom-scroll" boundary.

- **Levity-Led Leadership:** Meeting openers (one-word mood + emoji), micro-celebrations, "laugh & learn" debriefs, and a rotating "spark of the week" to convert connection into collective performance.

These practices are personally healing and professionally transformative for emerging and senior leaders, and for anyone cultivating authentic, heart-led self-leadership.

Ethical Considerations and Inclusion

- **Cultural sensibilities:** Humor content should be culturally humble and never identity-denigrating.

- **Trauma sensitivity:** Offer opt-in participation, seated options, and breath-anchoring; name that tears or quiet are welcome responses.

- **Boundaries:** Establish "laugh with, not at" as a core covenant.

Conclusion

Laughter is a low-cost, high-yield regulator that simultaneously restores the body, widens the mind, and binds communities. By aligning laughter practices with breath, reflective meaning-making, and leadership behaviours, *Heart Unbound 2.0* elevates joy from an outcome to a method, one that is physiologically grounded, psychologically sound, and organisationally wise.

References

Avolio, B. J., & Gardner, W. L. (2005). Authentic leadership development: Getting to the root of positive forms of leadership. *The Leadership Quarterly, 16*(3), 315–338. https://doi.org/10.1016/j.leaqua.2005.03.001

Bennett, M. P., & Lengacher, C. (2009). Humor and laughter may influence health: III. Laughter and health outcomes. *Evidence-Based Complementary and Alternative Medicine, 6*(2), 159–164. https://doi.org/10.1093/ecam/nem149

Berk, L. S., Tan, S. A., Fry, W. F., Napier, B. J., Lee, J. W., Hubbard, R. W., Lewis, J. E., & Eby, W. C. (1989). Neuroendocrine and stress hormone changes during mirthful laughter. *The American Journal of the Medical Sciences, 298*(6), 390–396. https://doi.org/10.1097/00000441-198912000-00006

Cameron, K. S. (2012). *Positive leadership* (2nd ed.). Berrett-Koehler.

Cohen, S., & Wills, T. A. (1985). Stress, social support, and the buffering hypothesis. *Psychological Bulletin, 98*(2), 310–357. https://doi.org/10.1037/0033-2909.98.2.310

Cooper, C. D., Kong, D. T., & Crossley, C. (2018). Leader humor as an interpersonal resource: Integrating three theoretical perspectives and meta-analysing the literature. *Academy of Management Journal, 61*(2), 769–796. https://doi.org/10.5465/amj.2016.0359

Dunbar, R. I. M., Baron, R., Frangou, A., Pearce, E., van Leeuwen, E. J. C., Stow, J., Partridge, G., MacDonald, I., Barra, V., & van Vugt, M. (2012). Social laughter is correlated with an elevated pain threshold. *Proceedings of the Royal Society B, 279*(1731), 1161–1167. https://doi.org/10.1098/rspb.2011.1373

Edmondson, A. (1999). Psychological safety and learning behaviour in work teams. *Administrative Science Quarterly, 44*(2), 350–383. https://doi.org/10.2307/2666999

Fredrickson, B. L. (2001). The role of positive emotions in positive psychology: The broaden-and-build theory of positive emotions. *American Psychologist, 56*(3), 218–226. https://doi.org/10.1037/0003-066X.56.3.218

Gross, J. J. (1998). The emerging field of emotion regulation: An integrative review. *Review of General Psychology, 2*(3), 271–299. https://doi.org/10.1037/1089-2680.2.3.271

Gervais, M., & Wilson, D. S. (2005). The evolution and functions of laughter and humor: A synthetic approach. *The Quarterly Review of Biology, 80*(4), 395–430. https://doi.org/10.1086/498281

Martin, R. A., Puhlik-Doris, P., Larsen, G., Gray, J., & Weir, K. (2003). Individual differences in uses of humor and their relation to psychological well-being: Development of the Humor Styles Questionnaire. *Journal of Research in Personality, 37*(1), 48–75. https://doi.org/10.1016/S0092-6566(02)00534-2

Mesmer-Magnus, J., Glew, D. J., & Viswesvaran, C. (2012). A meta-analysis of positive humor in the workplace. *Journal of Managerial Psychology, 27*(2), 155–190. https://doi.org/10.1108/02683941211199554

Porges, S. W. (2007). The polyvagal perspective. *Biological Psychology, 74*(2), 116–143. https://doi.org/10.1016/j.biopsycho.2006.06.009

Pressman, S. D., & Cohen, S. (2005). Does positive affect influence health? *Psychological Bulletin, 131*(6), 925–971. https://doi.org/10.1037/0033-2909.131.6.925

Shahidi, M., Mojtahed, A., Modabbernia, A., Mojtahed, M., Shafiabady, A., Delavar, A., & Honari, H. (2011). Laughter yoga versus group exercise program in elderly depressed women: A randomised controlled trial. *International Journal of Geriatric Psychiatry, 26*(3), 322–327. https://doi.org/10.1002/gps.2545

Tugade, M. M., & Fredrickson, B. L. (2004). Resilient individuals use positive emotions to bounce back from negative emotional experiences. *Journal of Personality and Social Psychology, 86*(2), 320–333. https://doi.org/10.1037/0022-3514.86.2.320

THE
UNBOUND
JOURNEY

25 - "Listening" as Heart-Led Practice: Psychological, Physiological, and Leadership Foundations for *Listening*

Rationale for the Article

Listening is the integrator of the entire curriculum. It is the mechanism by which identity work ("I Am") becomes lived behaviour, by which compassion becomes co-regulated safety, and by which values become collective practice. Without teachable, measurable listening behaviours, programs risk remaining inspirational but not transformational. Chapter 25 supplies the evidence base and the protocol.

Abstract

Listening is more than the absence of speaking; it is a biologically regulating, psychologically curative, and relationally transformative practice. This article synthesises evidence from counseling psychology, social neuroscience, and leadership studies to validate Chapter 25 (*Listening*) of *Heart Unbound 2.0*. High-quality listening, defined by presence, empathic attunement, reflective responding, and judicious silence, predicts speaker attitude clarity, reduced defensiveness, and perceived responsiveness (Itzchakov, Kluger, & Castro, 2017; Weger et al., 2014). Mechanistically, listening co-regulates the autonomic nervous system (polyvagal pathways), increases heart-rate variability, and supports social bonding through neurochemical mediators (Porges, 2011; Kok & Fredrickson, 2010; Kosfeld et al., 2005). In organisations, leader listening creates psychological safety, learning, and values-aligned action (Edmondson, 1999; Schein & Schein, 2018; Greenleaf, 1977). We translate these findings into a structured, heart-led skills protocol and show how Chapter 25 integrates with Chapter 3 ("I Am") to strengthen self-listening, identity coherence, and values-driven leadership.

Keywords: active listening; empathy; polyvagal theory; heart-rate variability; psychological safety; values-based leadership; *Heart Unbound 2.0*

Introduction

Heart Unbound 2.0 positions listening as an act of love and a method of transformation. Contemporary research concurs: when people feel deeply heard, they think more clearly, regulate affect more effectively, and trust more readily (Bodie, 2011; Itzchakov et al., 2017). This paper (a) clarifies what "heart-based listening" entails, (b) summarises psychological and physiological mechanisms, (c) links listening to leadership and collective performance, and (d) offers an evidence-informed practice framework that operationalises Chapter 25 for individuals and teams.

Conceptual foundations: From hearing to heart-based listening

Hearing is sensory; listening is relational. Person-centered psychotherapy defines the gold standard: unconditional positive regard, accurate empathy, and congruence (Rogers, 1957). In applied dialogue traditions (e.g., motivational interviewing), listening is enacted through open questions, affirmations, reflections, and summaries (OARS), which reliably increase autonomy and change talk (Miller & Rollnick, 2013). In nonviolent communication, empathic listening prioritises needs and feelings rather than judgments, strengthening mutual understanding (Rosenberg, 2015). Across traditions, the shared denominator is presence: attention to words, tone, pauses, and what remains unsaid.

Empirically, "high-quality listening" increases speakers' attitude clarity and reduces ambivalence and defensiveness (Itzchakov et al., 2017; Itzchakov, Kluger, & Castro, 2018). In first-time interactions, active listening outperforms advice-giving for felt understanding (Weger et al., 2014). Measurement tools such as the Active-Empathic Listening Scale enable reliable assessment for training and research (Drollinger et al., 2006).

Physiological mechanisms: Co-regulation, safety, and social bonding

Listening is embodied. Polyvagal theory proposes that cues of safety, soft prosody, facial expressivity, and receptive posture, recruit the myelinated vagus, down-regulating threat responses and enabling social engagement (Porges, 2011). Higher resting heart-rate variability (HRV), a proxy for vagal flexibility, covaries with positive emotions and social connectedness, forming "upward spirals" of well-being (Kok & Fredrickson, 2010). Neurovisceral integration models further link prefrontal regulation and cardiac vagal tone to adaptive emotion regulation (Thayer & Lane, 2009). Listening also intersects with social neurochemistry: oxytocin increases interpersonal trust, a substrate of disclosure and collaboration (Kosfeld et al., 2005). These mechanisms explain why the felt experience of being heard can calm arousal, expand perspective, and restore access to executive functioning.

Listening, emotional intelligence, and self-listening

Emotional intelligence (EI) frameworks identify self-awareness, self-management, social awareness, and relationship management as mutually reinforcing capacities (Goleman, Boyatzis, & McKee, 2013). Listening trains all four: monitoring reactivity (self-awareness), pausing before reply (self-management), attuning to others' affect (social awareness), and responding with empathic precision (relationship management). Mindfulness strengthens the attentional stability required for such listening (Kabat-Zinn, 2003), while self-compassion provides the intrapersonal stance needed for "listening inward" without harsh judgment (Neff, 2003). In Chapter 25, these literatures justify exercises that cultivate stillness, interoceptive awareness, and compassionate inner dialogue.

Leadership and teams: Psychological safety through listening

Leader listening is a lever for culture. Psychological safety, the shared belief that a team is safe for interpersonal risk taking, predicts learning behaviour and performance (Edmondson, 1999). Leaders enact safety through humble inquiry and "respectful questions," which invite voice instead of telling others what to do (Schein & Schein, 2018; van Quaquebeke & Felps, 2018). High-quality listening reduces speakers' defensiveness in polarised conversations, enabling attitude openness, vital for change leadership (Itzchakov et al., 2017). Servant leadership extends the logic: attending first to others' needs and growth builds trust and commitment (Greenleaf, 1977). Collectively, these findings validate Chapter 25's claim that listening is a strategic competency, not merely a soft skill.

An evidence-informed practice framework for Chapter 25

1. Micro-skills (individual)

- **Presence first.** One breath cycle before responding lowers reactivity (Kabat-Zinn, 2003; Thayer & Lane, 2009).

- **OARS sequence.** Use open questions, affirmations, reflections, and summaries to scaffold autonomy and precision (Miller & Rollnick, 2013).

- **Reflective accuracy.** Paraphrase content **and** name emotion; check for accuracy (Weger et al., 2014).

- **Judicious silence.** Allow meaning to emerge without rushing; silence can signal safety (Rogers, 1957).

- **Self-monitoring.** Notice judgment/"inner chatter"; return attention to the speaker (Bodie, 2011).

2. Co-regulation practices (dyads)

- **Signals of safety.** Soften facial muscles and voice; align posture; maintain kind eye contact (Porges, 2011).

- **HRV micro-reset.** 60–90 seconds of coherent breathing ($\approx$ 6 breaths/min) prior to difficult conversations to increase vagal tone (Kok & Fredrickson, 2010).

3. Team-level rituals

- **Listening rounds.** Time-boxed turn-taking with no interruption; the listener summarises and checks for "What did I miss?" (Edmondson, 1999).

- **Respectful inquiry.** Leaders begin with open, curiosity-led questions (Schein & Schein, 2018; van Quaquebeke & Felps, 2018).

- **Psychological safety audit.** Pair perception checks with AEL scale items to track growth (Drollinger et al., 2006).

4. Equity and cultural humility

Listening "across difference" requires lifelong reflexivity about power and perspective (Tervalon & Murray-García, 1998). Chapter 25's guidance to slow down, ask, and verify understanding is ethically aligned with this literature.

Application in Heart Unbound 2.0

The Laughter chapter translates theory into accessible, heart-led practice:

- **Laugh-Reset Micro-Rituals (60 seconds):** Inhale–smile–exhale with a soft "haaa," relax jaw/shoulders, let three gentle laughs rise; use whenever stress spikes to flip the nervous system to safety.

- **Joy Reps (7-Day Sprint):** One deliberate laughter cue daily (call a witty friend, watch a clip, playful walk, gratitude-with-a-grin). Record mood before/after to wire the joy–resilience loop.

- **Laughter Meditation + Shake:** 5–10 minutes breath → intentional chuckle → natural laughter → whole-body shake → quiet rest to clear tension and restore presence.

- **Empathic Humour Agreements:** Guardrails for safe joy: humour that includes (never punches down), opt-in play, a shared "pause word," and quick repair if a joke mislands.

- **Light-Hearted Communication Drills:** Practise "clear-and-kind with levity", state the truth, add a warm reframe/shared absurdity, then one concrete next step.

- **Joy Map → Calendar:** Map people/places/activities that spark laughter and schedule two micro-joy dates each week; protect them with "no doom-scrolling" and end-of-day fun cues.

- **Play Blocks (10–20 min):** Time-boxed silliness (doodle, dance, improv prompts) to unstick rumination and re-open creativity.

- **Self-Compassion Reframe:** When the inner critic appears, soften with a smile and a kind quip ("Oh hello, Safety Officer, thanks, I've got it"), then choose the next gentle action.

- **Relational Laughter Pairs:** Weekly 15-minute check-in with a buddy: share one stressor, one funny lens on it, and one small experiment, strengthen bond and perspective-taking.

- **Levity-Led Leadership:** Team norms for psychological safety, one-word mood + emoji check-ins, micro-celebrations, "laugh & learn" debriefs, and a rotating "spark of the week."

These practices are personally healing and professionally transformative for emerging and senior leaders, and for anyone cultivating authentic, heart-led self-leadership grounded in the restorative power of laughter.

Practice capsule: A heart-led listening protocol (10 minutes)

1. **Arrive (1 min):** Coherent breathing; silently set the intention "understand before responding."

2. **Open (2 min):** One open question; no interruption.

3. **Reflect (3 min):** Paraphrase facts + name emotion; check accuracy.

4. **Explore (3 min):** Two respectful inquiries (e.g., "What feels most important about this?").

5. **Close (1 min):** Summarise what you heard; ask "What did I miss?" and "What support would help?"

Conclusion

Across disciplines, the verdict is consistent: listening changes minds, bodies, and systems. It down-regulates threat physiology, increases social bonding, and builds cultures of trust and learning. When embedded as daily practice, supported by micro-skills, co-regulation, and leader rituals, listening becomes a cornerstone of heart-led self-leadership and collective flourishing. Chapter 25 of *Heart Unbound 2.0* is therefore not ancillary but essential: the practice through which the program's inner work is audible, actionable, and sustained.

References

Bodie, G. D. (2011). The understudied nature of listening in interpersonal communication: Introduction to a special issue. *International Journal of Listening, 25*(1–2), 1–9. https://doi.org/10.1080/10904018.2011.536462

Drollinger, T., Comer, L. B., & Warrington, P. T. (2006). Development and validation of the Active Empathic Listening Scale. *Psychology & Marketing, 23*(2), 161–180. https://doi.org/10.1002/mar.20105

Edmondson, A. C. (1999). Psychological safety and learning behaviour in work teams. *Administrative Science Quarterly, 44*(2), 350–383. https://doi.org/10.2307/2666999

Goleman, D., Boyatzis, R., & McKee, A. (2013). *Primal leadership: Unleashing the power of emotional intelligence* (10th anniversary ed.). Harvard Business Review Press.

Greenleaf, R. K. (1977). *Servant leadership: A journey into the nature of legitimate power and greatness.* Paulist Press.

Itzchakov, G., Kluger, A. N., & Castro, D. R. (2017). I am a good listener: The effect of high-quality listening on speakers' attitude ambivalence and attitude–behaviour consistency. *Journal of Experimental Social Psychology, 70*, 189–200. https://doi.org/10.1016/j.jesp.2016.12.003

Itzchakov, G., Kluger, A. N., Castro, D. R., & Icekson, T. (2018). The listener sets the tone: High-quality listening increases attitude clarity and intentions to disclose. *Personality and Social Psychology Bulletin, 44*(5), 762–778. https://doi.org/10.1177/0146167217747885

Kabat-Zinn, J. (2003). Mindfulness-based interventions in context: Past, present, and future. *Clinical Psychology: Science and Practice, 10*(2), 144–156. https://doi.org/10.1093/clipsy.bpg016

Kok, B. E., & Fredrickson, B. L. (2010). Upward spirals of the heart: Autonomic flexibility, as indexed by vagal tone, reciprocally and prospectively predicts positive emotions and social connectedness. *Psychological Science, 21*(7), 1123–1129. https://doi.org/10.1177/0956797610370161

Kosfeld, M., Heinrichs, M., Zak, P. J., Fischbacher, U., & Fehr, E. (2005). Oxytocin increases trust in humans. *Nature, 435*(7042), 673–676. https://doi.org/10.1038/nature03701

Miller, W. R., & Rollnick, S. (2013). *Motivational interviewing: Helping people change* (3rd ed.). Guilford Press.

Neff, K. D. (2003). Self-compassion: An alternative conceptualisation of a healthy attitude toward oneself. *Self and Identity, 2*(2), 85–101. https://doi.org/10.1080/15298860309032

Porges, S. W. (2011). *The polyvagal theory: Neurophysiological foundations of emotions, attachment, communication, and self-regulation*. W. W. Norton.

Rogers, C. R. (1957). The necessary and sufficient conditions of therapeutic personality change. *Journal of Consulting Psychology, 21*(2), 95–103. https://doi.org/10.1037/h0045357

Rosenberg, M. B. (2015). *Nonviolent communication: A language of life* (3rd ed.). PuddleDancer Press.

Schein, E. H., & Schein, P. A. (2018). *Humble leadership: The power of relationships, openness, and trust*. Berrett-Koehler.

Thayer, J. F., & Lane, R. D. (2009). Claude Bernard and the heart–brain connection: Further elaboration of a model of neurovisceral integration. *International Journal of Psychophysiology, 73*(2), 123–132. https://doi.org/10.1016/j.ijpsycho.2008.12.004

Tervalon, M., & Murray-García, J. (1998). Cultural humility versus cultural competence: A critical distinction in defining physician training outcomes in multicultural education. *Journal of Health Care for the Poor and Underserved, 9*(2), 117–125. https://doi.org/10.1353/hpu.2010.0233

van Quaquebeke, N., & Felps, W. (2018). Respectful inquiry: A motivational account of leaders' asking questions and listening. *Organisational Behaviour and Human Decision Processes, 144*, 121–140. https://doi.org/10.1016/j.obhdp.2017.10.007

Weger, H., Castle, G. R., & Emmett, M. C. (2014). The relative effectiveness of active listening in initial interactions. *International Journal of Listening, 28*(1), 13–31. https://doi.org/10.1080/10904018.2013.813234

THE
UNBOUND
JOURNEY

26 - "Focus" as Devotion: A Scholarly Validation of Focus as a Powerful Modality for Transformation

Rationale for the Article

Focus is the hinge that converts inner work into outer change. Without trainable attention, practices elsewhere in the program,relaxation, listening, decluttering, struggle to consolidate. The evidence reviewed shows that heart-led focus down-regulates stress physiology, upgrades executive control, and fosters resonant leadership. Chapter 26 therefore provides the integrative capacity that organises, sustains, and amplifies the whole curriculum.

Abstract

This article positions focus as a form of devotion rather than mere discipline, arguing that what we repeatedly attend to sculpts emotional life, physiology, and leadership impact. We integrate classic and contemporary literatures on attention (James; Kahneman), executive functions and mind-wandering, and the neurophysiology of prefrontal control, vagal regulation and the locus coeruleus–norepinephrine system. Converging evidence shows that stress and digital overload fragment attention, whereas mindfulness, breath-paced vagal activation, values-based goal setting, and structured work rituals reliably strengthen stability of focus, emotion regulation, and performance. We translate these findings into a heart-led practice model aligned with *Heart Unbound 2.0*, including a five-minute focused-breath protocol, distraction audits, implementation intentions, and purpose-anchored time-blocking. We also extend the "I Am" methods from Chapter 3 to identity-level focusing practices for individuals and leaders. The paper advances a rigorous, evidence-informed rationale for treating focus as an inner leadership capacity that can be trained, one that protects well-being, restores relational presence, and enables values-driven action.

Keywords: attention; executive function; mindfulness; vagal tone; implementation intentions; deep work; leadership; emotional intelligence

Introduction

"Where attention goes, life follows." Chapter 26 of *Heart Unbound 2.0* invites participants to treat focus as a devotion to what matters, not a contest of willpower. This stance resonates with over a century of psychological science: attention is limited, trainable, and constitutive of experience (James, 1890; Kahneman, 1973). In contemporary life, chronic stress and pervasive digital stimuli pull cognition into task-switching and mind-wandering, degrading both performance and mood (Ophir et al., 2009; Smallwood & Schooler, 2006; Ward et al., 2017). Conversely, when attention is stabilised around meaningful goals, prefrontal circuitry strengthens, autonomic balance improves, and prosocial leadership behaviours become more reliable (Arnsten, 2009; Boyatzis & McKee, 2005; Tang et al., 2015).

This article synthesises psychological, physiological, and leadership literatures to validate the chapter's practices and to specify mechanisms by which a heart-led focus enhances resilience and relational presence.

Conceptual foundations: What is focus?

Attention, effort, and executive control

Classical accounts treat attention as the mind's selective lens (James, 1890) constrained by a limited pool of effort (Kahneman, 1973). Contemporary models locate focus within executive functions, working memory, inhibitory control, and cognitive flexibility (Miyake et al., 2000; Diamond, 2013). Interruptions and unresolved tasks create "attention residue," degrading subsequent performance (Leroy, 2009), while frequent media multitasking correlates with poorer selective attention and task switching (Ophir et al., 2009; Rubinstein et al., 2001).

Mind-wandering, flow, and meaning

Mind-wandering is ubiquitous and can incubate creativity, yet excessive drift predicts lower momentary well-being (Killingsworth & Gilbert, 2010; Smallwood & Schooler, 2006). In contrast, deep absorption in optimally challenging tasks, "flow", elevates performance and intrinsic motivation (Csikszentmihalyi, 1990). Focus that is value-congruent sustains motivation and persistence (Locke & Latham, 2002; Deci & Ryan, 2000).

Neurophysiology of focus: From stress reactivity to regulated presence

Prefrontal–limbic balance

Stress hormones and catecholamines impair prefrontal cortex (PFC) function while biasing habitual responding (Arnsten, 2009). An optimal arousal "window" supports PFC-mediated control (Yerkes & Dodson, 1908). The locus coeruleus–norepinephrine system tunes exploration vs. exploitation; moderate tonic activity with phasic bursts supports stable task engagement (Aston-Jones & Cohen, 2005).

Vagal regulation and heart–brain synchrony

Polyvagal and neurovisceral integration models link higher resting heart rate variability (HRV), a proxy for vagal tone, to superior emotion regulation and executive control (Porges, 2007; Thayer & Lane, 2000). Slow, coherent breathing and HRV biofeedback enhance vagal activity and attention (Lehrer & Gevirtz, 2014; Brown & Gerberg, 2005).

Plasticity through contemplative practice

Mindfulness and focused-attention meditation produce structural and functional changes in attention networks and the insula/anterior cingulate (Hölzel et al., 2011; Lutz et al., 2008; Tang et al., 2015). Even brief training reduces mind-wandering and improves working memory and GRE reading comprehension (Mrazek et al., 2013; Zeidan et al., 2010).

Psychological mechanisms that make focus durable

1. **Implementation intentions.** "If–then" plans automate goal pursuit and reduce distraction (Gollwitzer, 1999).

2. **Values-based goal setting.** Specific, challenging, value-aligned goals outperform vague intentions (Locke & Latham, 2002; Ryan & Deci, 2000).

3. **Single-tasking and context control.** Task switching carries measurable time and error costs (Rubinstein et al., 2001); environmental controls, removing smartphones from view, restore available cognitive capacity (Ward et al., 2017).

4. **Rest, sleep, and movement.** Sleep loss erodes sustained attention and PFC efficiency (Lim & Dinges, 2010). Aerobic exercise enhances executive function (Hillman et al., 2008).

5. **Temporal architecture.** Working in ultradian cycles ($\approx$90 min) with deliberate breaks leverages natural oscillations in alertness (Kleitman, 1963); time-boxed "deep work" protects attentional bandwidth (Newport, 2016).

Focus as inner leadership

Leader attention is contagious: it shapes climate, norms, and collective focus (Goleman, 2013). Resonant leaders cultivate mindful awareness and emotional attunement that protect against burnout and sustain high-quality connections (Boyatzis & McKee, 2005; Avolio & Gardner, 2005). Psychological safety, a precondition for team focus and learning, rests on leader behaviours such as presence, listening, and clear priorities (Edmondson, 1999). Purpose clarity further amplifies effort and persistence (Wrzesniewski et al., 2013).

Evidence-informed practices that operationalise Chapter 26

1) Five-Minute Focused Breath (physiology first)

Protocol: Inhale nasally for ~4–5s; exhale for ~6–8s; light attentional anchor at the heart space; 5 cycles per minute for five minutes.

Rationale: Extended exhalation increases vagal efference, improving HRV and prefrontal control (Brown & Gerbarg, 2005; Lehrer & Gevirtz, 2014).

2) Distraction audit and context design

Protocol: Track interruptions for 2–3 days; remove phones from desk (or into another room); batch notifications; create "focus blocks" of 25–50 min with recovery micro-breaks.

Rationale: Eliminating ambient phone presence and reducing switches recovers working memory and fluid reasoning (Ward et al., 2017; Rubinstein et al., 2001).

3) Implementation intentions + WOOP

Protocol: For each focus block, write an **if–then** plan (e.g., *If* I open the browser, *then* I immediately return to the manuscript) and a WOOP sequence, Wish, Outcome, Obstacle, Plan (Oettingen, 2014).

Rationale: Automatises cue-response links and anticipates obstacles (Gollwitzer, 1999; Oettingen, 2014).

4) Meaning and flow design

Protocol: Align one daily priority with signature strengths and challenge-skill balance; enter with a 90-minute time-box and end with a reflective "learning line."

Rationale: Intrinsic motivation and flow increase persistence and well-being (Csikszentmihalyi, 1990; Ryan & Deci, 2000).

5) Recovery habits

Protocol: Protect sleep opportunity (7–9 h), brief movement snacks, and green-time breaks.

Rationale: Sleep and exercise reliably enhance attention and emotion regulation (Lim & Dinges, 2010; Hillman et al., 2008).

Application in Heart Unbound 2.0 - Focus

The Focus chapter translates theory into accessible, heart-led practice:

- **Attention-Reset Micro-Rituals (60–120s):** Three balanced breaths or a "notice–name–return" cycle to interrupt drift and re-anchor in the present.

- **Heart-Anchor Intention (AM):** One line each morning—*"Today I give my best energy to ____ because ____."* Set 1–3 meaningful intentions that reflect your values.

- **Deep-Work Sprints:** Protect 25–50 minute single-task blocks (with 5 minute recovery). Begin with a breath + focus cue; end by capturing the very next action.

- **Mindful Transitions:** 90-second close/clear/center ritual between activities (exhale, tidy the surface, log next step) to prevent cognitive carryover.

- **Focused Intention Statements (On-Demand Regulation):** Short self-coaching phrases, *"I choose steadiness." "One thing, right now."* paired with the 5-Minute Focused Breath.

- **Environmental Design for Clarity:** Prepare a "focus stage" (clean surface, lighting, water, playlist, timer). Remove one friction and add one cue before each session.

- **Recovery & Rhythm:** Honor ultradian cycles, brief movement, sunlight, hydration, and eye-rest every 90 minutes to keep the prefrontal cortex online.

- **Weekly Review & Recommit (15 min):** *Wins • Drifts • Lessons • One Focus for Next Week.* Realign tasks, boundaries, and blocks to purpose.

- **Boundary Agreements:** Personal non-negotiables that safeguard attention (no-meeting mornings, email windows, DND status) so presence can sustain performance.

- **Team Focus Norms (Leadership Application):** Agenda-led meetings, deep-work windows for all, async-first updates, and quick "repair rituals" when priorities or boundaries slip.

These practices make focus a compassionate devotion rather than a grind, personally centering and professionally transformative for emerging and senior leaders, and for anyone cultivating authentic self-leadership.

Practical protocol: A week of heart-led focus

1. **Morning (≤10 min):** Five-Minute Focused Breath → write the day's "Why/One Thing" → if–then plan.

2. **Work cycles:** Two 50–90 min focus blocks; phone out of sight; finish with a one-minute learning line.

3. **Mid-day reset (5 min):** Breath + identity statement.

4. **Evening (5 min):** Brief reflection. Where did attention serve values? What obstacle to plan for tomorrow?

Conclusion

A century of scientific work converges with contemplative traditions on a simple claim: attention is destiny. By treating focus as devotion, stabilised by vagal, supportive breathing, values-based intentions, and context design, *Heart Unbound 2.0* equips participants and leaders to convert compassion into consistent action. In doing so, Chapter 26 becomes not just another technique but the nervous-system and narrative scaffold for a life lived on purpose.

References

Arnsten, A. F. T. (2009). Stress signalling pathways that impair prefrontal cortex structure and function. *Nature Reviews Neuroscience, 10*(6), 410–422. https://doi.org/10.1038/nrn2648

Aston-Jones, G., & Cohen, J. D. (2005). An integrative theory of locus coeruleus-norepinephrine function. *Annual Review of Neuroscience, 28*, 403–450. https://doi.org/10.1146/annurev.neuro.28.061604.135709

Avolio, B. J., & Gardner, W. L. (2005). Authentic leadership development. *The Leadership Quarterly, 16*(3), 315–338. https://doi.org/10.1016/j.leaqua.2005.03.001

Boyatzis, R. E., & McKee, A. (2005). *Resonant leadership.* Harvard Business Press.

Brown, R. P., & Gerbarg, P. L. (2005). Sudarshan Kriya yogic breathing in stress, anxiety, and depression. *Journal of Alternative and Complementary Medicine, 11*(4), 711–717. https://doi.org/10.1089/acm.2005.11.711

Csikszentmihalyi, M. (1990). *Flow: The psychology of optimal experience.* Harper & Row.

Deci, E. L., & Ryan, R. M. (2000). The "what" and "why" of goal pursuits. *Psychological Inquiry, 11*(4), 227–268.

Diamond, A. (2013). Executive functions. *Annual Review of Psychology, 64*, 135–168. https://doi.org/10.1146/annurev-psych-113011-143750

Edmondson, A. (1999). Psychological safety and learning behaviour in work teams. *Administrative Science Quarterly, 44*(2), 350–383.

Gollwitzer, P. M. (1999). Implementation intentions. *American Psychologist, 54*(7), 493–503.

Goleman, D. (2013). *Focus: The hidden driver of excellence*. HarperCollins.

Hillman, C. H., Erickson, K. I., & Kramer, A. F. (2008). Be smart, exercise your heart. *Nature Reviews Neuroscience, 9*(1), 58–65.

Hölzel, B. K., et al. (2011). Mindfulness practice leads to increases in regional brain gray matter density. *Psychiatry Research: Neuroimaging, 191*(1), 36–43.

James, W. (1890). *The principles of psychology*. Holt.

Jha, A. P., Stanley, E. A., Kiyonaga, A., Wong, L., & Gelfand, L. (2010). Examining mindfulness training. *Emotion, 10*(1), 54–64.

Kahneman, D. (1973). *Attention and effort*. Prentice-Hall.

Killingsworth, M. A., & Gilbert, D. T. (2010). A wandering mind is an unhappy mind. *Science, 330*(6006), 932.

Kleitman, N. (1963). Sleep and wakefulness (Rev. ed.). University of Chicago Press.

Lehrer, P. M., & Gevirtz, R. (2014). Heart rate variability biofeedback. *Frontiers in Psychology, 5*, 756.

Leroy, S. (2009). Why is it so hard to do my work? *Organisational Behaviour and Human Decision Processes, 109*(2), 168–181.

Lim, J., & Dinges, D. F. (2010). A meta-analysis of the impact of short-term sleep deprivation on cognitive variables. *Psychological Bulletin, 136*(3), 375–389.

Locke, E. A., & Latham, G. P. (2002). Building a practically useful theory of goal setting and task motivation. *American Psychologist, 57*(9), 705–717.

Lutz, A., Slagter, H. A., Dunne, J. D., & Davidson, R. J. (2008). Attention regulation and monitoring in meditation. *Trends in Cognitive Sciences, 12*(4), 163–169.

Miyake, A., et al. (2000). The unity and diversity of executive functions. *Cognitive Psychology, 41*(1), 49–100.

Mrazek, M. D., Franklin, M. S., Phillips, D. T., Baird, B., & Schooler, J. W. (2013). Mindfulness training improves working memory and GRE performance while reducing mind-wandering. *Psychological Science, 24*(5), 776–

781.

Newport, C. (2016). *Deep work*. Grand Central.

Oettingen, G. (2014). *Rethinking positive thinking*. Current.

Ophir, E., Nass, C., & Wagner, A. D. (2009). Cognitive control in media multitaskers. *Proceedings of the National Academy of Sciences, 106*(37), 15583–15587.

Porges, S. W. (2007). The polyvagal perspective. *Biological Psychology, 74*(2), 116–143.

Rubinstein, J. S., Meyer, D. E., & Evans, J. E. (2001). Executive control of cognitive processes in task switching. *Journal of Experimental Psychology: Human Perception and Performance, 27*(4), 763–797.

Ryan, R. M., & Deci, E. L. (2000). Intrinsic and extrinsic motivations. *Contemporary Educational Psychology, 25*(1), 54–67.

Smallwood, J., & Schooler, J. W. (2006). The restless mind. *Psychological Bulletin, 132*(6), 946–958.

Tang, Y.-Y., Hölzel, B. K., & Posner, M. I. (2015). The neuroscience of mindfulness meditation. *Nature Reviews Neuroscience, 16*(4), 213–225.

Thayer, J. F., & Lane, R. D. (2000). A model of neurovisceral integration in emotion regulation and dysregulation. *Journal of Affective Disorders, 61*(3), 201–216.

Ward, A. F., Duke, K., Gneezy, A., & Bos, M. W. (2017). Brain drain: The mere presence of one's own smartphone reduces available cognitive capacity. *Journal of the Association for Consumer Research, 2*(2), 140–154.

Wrzesniewski, A., Dutton, J. E., & Debebe, G. (2013). Interpersonal sensemaking and the meaning of work. *Research in Organisational Behaviour, 33*, 143–165.

Yerkes, R. M., & Dodson, J. D. (1908). The relation of strength of stimulus to rapidity of habit-formation. *Journal of Comparative Neurology and Psychology, 18*(5), 459–482.

Zeidan, F., Johnson, S. K., Diamond, B. J., David, Z., & Goolkasian, P. (2010). Mindfulness meditation improves cognition. *Consciousness and Cognition, 19*(2), 597–605.

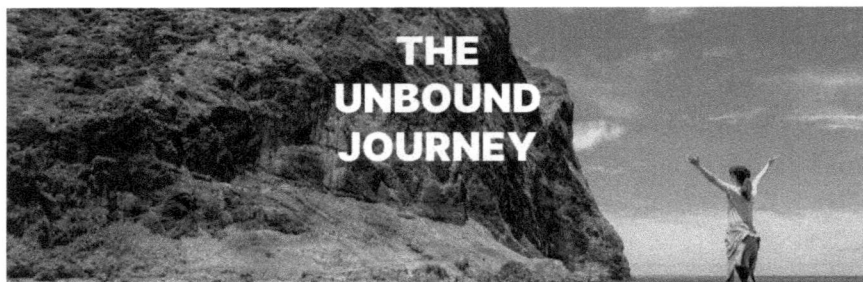

THE
UNBOUND
JOURNEY

27 - "Spontaneity" in Heart-Led Development: Psychological, Physiological, and Leadership Foundations for *Transfortmation*

Rationale for the Article

Participants often arrive with well-rehearsed coping strategies, control, rumination, and self-censorship, that keep them safe but small. Spontaneity loosens over-control without abandoning discernment. It restores play, curiosity, and values-aligned risk-taking, the same ingredients that predict well-being, creativity, and adaptive leadership. In program terms, Chapter 27 operationalises "freedom with responsibility": it teaches learners to sense the moment, trust inner guidance, and act congruently with values, thereby consolidating gains made in prior chapters (focus, listening, declutter, laughter) into a living, relational practice.

Abstract

This article examines spontaneity as a learnable capacity that supports authentic living and adaptive leadership in *Heart Unbound 2.0*. Drawing on psychological science (psychological flexibility, self-determination, emotion-regulation flexibility), neurophysiology (polyvagal theory, reward neurochemistry, heart-rate variability), and organisational research (improvisation, psychological safety), we distinguish spontaneity from impulsivity and show how spontaneous, values-aligned action broadens cognition, strengthens resilience, and deepens connection. We translate the evidence base into practices and assessments suitable for personal change and leadership development, including mindful "micro-experiments," improv-based exercises, and rituals that integrate the program's *I Am* chapter (mirror work, journaling, daily affirmations, leadership alignment). We conclude that cultivated spontaneity is not recklessness; it is disciplined freedom: a heart-led responsiveness that is neurologically coherent, psychologically flexible, and organisationally generative.

Keywords: spontaneity; psychological flexibility; polyvagal theory; heart-rate variability; reward neurochemistry; improvisation; psychological safety; self-determination; emotional intelligence; positive leadership

Introduction

Spontaneity is widely romanticised and widely misunderstood. In psychological terms it is best conceived as flexible responsiveness, actions that arise in the present, informed (not dominated) by plans, values, and context (Kashdan & Rottenberg, 2010). This stance differs from impulsivity, which reflects action without adequate consideration of goals or consequences (Dickman, 1990; Whiteside & Lynam, 2001). Across disciplines, spontaneity correlates with autonomy and intrinsic motivation (Deci & Ryan, 2000), positive emotion and broadened cognition (Fredrickson, 2001), and adaptive performance in uncertain environments (Vera & Crossan, 2005; March, 1991). We synthesise these literatures and translate them into practices compatible with *Heart Unbound 2.0*.

Conceptual foundations

Spontaneity ≠ impulsivity

Functional spontaneity is marked by awareness, values-alignment, and context sensitivity. By contrast, dysfunctional impulsivity is characterised by urgency, poor premeditation, and sensation seeking independent of goals (Whiteside & Lynam, 2001). Emotion-regulation research shows that healthy adults flexibly up- or down-regulate emotions to match situational demands, "regulatory flexibility" (Bonanno & Burton, 2013). Spontaneous action can therefore be both fast and wise when supported by attentional control and values clarity.

Psychological flexibility and autonomy

Acceptance and Commitment Therapy (ACT) frames psychological flexibility as contacting the present moment and choosing behaviour in service of values (Hayes et al., 2016). This maps closely to *Heart Unbound's* heart-led responsiveness. Self-Determination Theory adds that spontaneity flourishes when autonomy, competence, and relatedness needs are met (Deci & Ryan, 2000, 2017). Together, these frameworks validate spontaneity as disciplined freedom rather than anti-structure.

Positive emotion and play

The broaden-and-build theory predicts that joy and interest widen attention, enhance exploratory behaviour, and build durable resources (Fredrickson, 2001). Adult playfulness, an individual difference linked to creativity and social connection, captures a readiness to frame situations in a non-serious, innovative way (Proyer, 2012). Spontaneity operationalises this readiness in everyday life.

Neurophysiology of spontaneous action

Neurovisceral integration and safety

Heart-rate variability (HRV) indexes flexible parasympathetic control and is tied to executive functioning and emotion regulation (Thayer & Lane, 2000; Thayer et al., 2012). Polyvagal theory further explains how cues of safety enable social engagement and play (Porges, 2007). In practice, spontaneity emerges reliably when the nervous system is in a ventral-vagal (safe-and-connected) state.

Reward and bonding chemistry

Dopaminergic prediction signals energise exploration and learning (Schultz, 1998). Social laughter elevates endorphins, increasing pain thresholds and bonding (Dunbar et al., 2012), while oxytocin supports trust and affiliative behaviour (Carter, 2014). Spontaneous play and shared humor thus have measurable analgesic, motivational, and relational benefits.

Creative brain networks

Improvisation recruits coordinated activity across default-mode (generative), executive control (goal-maintenance), and salience networks (Beaty et al., 2015). Jazz-improvisation studies show down-regulation of self-monitoring with preserved goal direction, neural correlates of unguarded yet coherent expression (Limb & Braun, 2008). These mechanisms explain why trained spontaneity feels effortless but is not random.

Spontaneity in leadership and teams

Improvisation under uncertainty

Organisations thrive when people can explore, adapt, and learn in real time (March, 1991). Team improvisation, action without full pre-planning but within minimal structures, predicts innovative performance (Vera & Crossan, 2005). Leaders cultivate conditions for "enlightened looseness": enough scaffolding to coordinate, enough latitude to create (Crossan, 1998).

Psychological safety and authenticity

Spontaneous contribution requires interpersonal risk-taking; psychological safety makes this risk tolerable (Edmondson, 1999). Positive leadership practices (vision, compassion, relational energy) further enlarge the "zone of permission" for creative, prosocial spontaneity (Cameron, 2011). Even leader humor can catalyse flexibility and connection when used inclusively (Yam et al., 2018).

Mindful presence

Mindfulness training enhances attentional control and reduces reactivity (Kabat-Zinn, 2013; Langer, 2014). Mindfulness and spontaneity are complementary: presence loosens over-control while values keep behaviour grounded.

Practice: translating evidence for *Heart Unbound 2.0*

A. Micro-practices that build spontaneous capacity

1. **Physiological "green-light":** two minutes of coherent breathing (≈ 6 breaths/min) before creative conversation or play; target increased RMSSD HRV (Thayer et al., 2012).

2. **Values cueing:** name the guiding value for the next hour (e.g., curiosity, kindness). This couples ACT's choice point with SDT autonomy (Hayes et al., 2016; Deci & Ryan, 2017).

3. **"Yes, and ..." loops:** 5-minute improv rounds to train additive listening and low-stakes risk-taking (Vera & Crossan, 2005).

4. **Play sprints:** brief, agenda-free moments of movement, doodling, or humor to elicit broaden-and-build effects (Fredrickson, 2001; Proyer, 2012).

5. **Safe-to-try experiments:** small, reversible experiments that favor exploration over prediction (March, 1991).

B. Distinguishing spontaneity from impulsivity in practice

Use the *choice check*: Is my body in *safe* physiology? Is this action linked to a value? Can I articulate a minimal boundary? If yes, act. If not, pause. (Maps to regulatory flexibility; Bonanno & Burton, 2013; Porges, 2007.)

C. Assessment options for programs and research

- **Psychological flexibility:** Acceptance and Action Questionnaire-II.

- **Trait playfulness:** Short Measure of Adult Playfulness (Proyer, 2012).

- **Mindfulness:** Five-Facet Mindfulness Questionnaire.

- **Affect:** PANAS.

- **Physiology:** short-term HRV (RMSSD/SDNN) pre-/post-play or improv sessions.

- **Team climate:** Edmondson Psychological Safety Scale.

- **Leadership behaviours:** Authentic Leadership Questionnaire; observer-rated improvisation/learning scales (Vera & Crossan, 2005).

Application in Heart Unbound 2.0 - Chapter 27: Spontaneity

This chapter translates the science and spirit of spontaneity into accessible, heart-led practice:

- **"Yes Breath" Micro-Rituals:** 30–60 seconds to pause, feel, and ask "What would feel alive right now?" Take one tiny, safe-to-try action, no overthinking.

- **Spontaneity Sparks (Daily Acts):** Keep a living list of 10+ playful, low-stakes ideas; choose one each day and journal the mood/energy shift.

- **Serendipity Windows:** Protect short calendar blocks with no agenda; follow curiosity in the moment. Close with a 3-question debrief (What arose? What felt good? What did I learn?).

- **Improv "Yes, and…" Labs:** 5–10 minute pair or team drills that practice accepting offers, building trust, and creating together without a script.

- **Body-Led Decisions:** Use the Breathe-Feel-Act check: regulate, sense the body's "yes/no," then take the next kind step. Reversible, consent-based moves only.

- **2% Braver Experiments:** Replace big leaps with small, repeatable risk-light trials; review after each: keep, tweak, or drop.

- **Play Blocks:** Scheduled pockets for unstructured joy (movement, art, music). Outcome-free on purpose to re-train ease and creativity.

- **Unscripted Connection:** Micro-gestures that spark warmth, spontaneous voice notes, compliments, surprise appreciation, tracked over seven days.

- **Loose–Tight Planning:** Tight on values, boundaries, and safety; loose on method and timing. Build "wiggle room" into plans to welcome the unexpected.

- **Safety & Consent Guardrails:** Simple checks for budget, time, impact, and consent so spontaneity stays kind to self and others.

These practices are personally liberating and relationally enlivening, useful for individuals, partners, and teams who want more creativity, resilience, and authentic connection without sacrificing care or accountability.

Discussion

The evidence indicates that spontaneity, when rooted in values and physiological safety, is an adaptive competency. It widens cognitive scope, encourages exploration, and fortifies social bonds through positive emotion and bonding neurochemistry (Fredrickson, 2001; Carter, 2014; Dunbar et al., 2012). In leaders and teams, structured spontaneity (minimal rules, maximal learning) improves innovation under uncertainty (Vera & Crossan, 2005; March, 1991). Programs should therefore pair heart practices (breath, affirmation, compassion) with micro-improvisations and genuine play. This dual track, *settle the body, free the voice*, protects against the two common risks: over-control (rigidity) and under-control (impulsivity).

Limitations and future research

Many studies draw on WEIRD samples; more culturally diverse work is needed. HRV is a useful but nonspecific biomarker; multimodal indices (e.g., pupillometry, respiration) could sharpen inference. In organisations, randomised field trials comparing different reflective rituals (AARs vs. premortems vs. compassion letters) would clarify mechanisms and cost-effectiveness.

Conclusion

Spontaneity is not the opposite of discipline; it is discipline's liberating partner. By cultivating nervous-system safety, clarifying values, and practicing playful risk-taking, *Heart Unbound 2.0* participants can act in the moment with coherence and courage. The result is a style of self-leadership that feels alive and trustworthy to self and others, exactly the stance needed to love well, work wisely, and lead in uncertainty.

References

Beaty, R. E., Benedek, M., Silvia, P. J., & Schacter, D. L. (2015). Creative cognition and brain network dynamics. *Trends in Cognitive Sciences, 19*(8), 435-443. https://doi.org/10.1016/j.tics.2015.05.004

Bonanno, G. A., & Burton, C. L. (2013). Regulatory flexibility: An individual differences perspective on coping and emotion regulation. *Perspectives on Psychological Science, 8*(6), 591–612. https://doi.org/10.1177/1745691613504116

Cameron, K. S. (2011). *Positive leadership: Strategies for extraordinary performance* (2nd ed.). Berrett-Koehler.

Carter, C. S. (2014). Oxytocin pathways and the evolution of human behaviour. *Annual Review of Psychology, 65*, 17–39. https://doi.org/10.1146/annurev-psych-010213-115110

Csikszentmihalyi, M. (1990). *Flow: The psychology of optimal experience.* Harper & Row.

Deci, E. L., & Ryan, R. M. (2000). The "what" and "why" of goal pursuits: Human needs and the self-determination of behaviour. *Psychological Inquiry, 11*(4), 227–268. https://doi.org/10.1207/S15327965PLI1104_01

Deci, E. L., & Ryan, R. M. (2017). *Self-determination theory: Basic psychological needs in motivation, development, and wellness.* Guilford Press.

Dickman, S. J. (1990). Functional and dysfunctional impulsivity: Personality and cognitive correlates. *Journal of Personality and Social Psychology, 58*(1), 95–102. https://doi.org/10.1037/0022-3514.58.1.95

Dunbar, R. I. M., et al. (2012). Social laughter is correlated with an elevated pain threshold. *Proceedings of the Royal Society B, 279*(1731), 1161–1167. https://doi.org/10.1098/rspb.2011.1373

Edmondson, A. C. (1999). Psychological safety and learning behaviour in work teams. *Administrative Science Quarterly, 44*(2), 350–383. https://doi.org/10.2307/2666999

Fredrickson, B. L. (2001). The role of positive emotions in positive psychology: The broaden-and-build theory. *American Psychologist, 56*(3), 218–226. https://doi.org/10.1037/0003-066X.56.3.218

Hayes, S. C., Strosahl, K. D., & Wilson, K. G. (2016). *Acceptance and commitment therapy: The process and practice of mindful change* (2nd ed.). Guilford Press.

Heifetz, R., Grashow, A., & Linsky, M. (2009). *The practice of adaptive leadership.* Harvard Business Press.

Kabat-Zinn, J. (2013). *Full catastrophe living* (Rev. ed.). Bantam.

Kashdan, T. B., & Rottenberg, J. (2010). Psychological flexibility as a fundamental aspect of health. *Clinical Psychology Review, 30*(7), 865–878. https://doi.org/10.1016/j.cpr.2010.03.001

Langer, E. J. (2014). *Mindfulness* (25th-anniversary ed.). Da Capo.

Limb, C. J., & Braun, A. R. (2008). Neural substrates of spontaneous musical performance: An fMRI study of jazz improvisation. *PLOS ONE, 3*(2), e1679. https://doi.org/10.1371/journal.pone.0001679

March, J. G. (1991). Exploration and exploitation in organisational learning. *Organisation Science, 2*(1), 71–87. https://doi.org/10.1287/orsc.2.1.71

Porges, S. W. (2007). The polyvagal perspective. *Biological Psychology, 74*(2), 116–143. https://doi.org/10.1016/j.biopsycho.2006.06.009

Proyer, R. T. (2012). Development and initial assessment of a short measure for adult playfulness. *Personality and Individual Differences, 53*(8), 989–994. https://doi.org/10.1016/j.paid.2012.07.018

Schultz, W. (1998). Predictive reward signal of dopamine neurons. *Journal of Neurophysiology, 80*(1), 1–27. https://doi.org/10.1152/jn.1998.80.1.1

Thayer, J. F., & Lane, R. D. (2000). A model of neurovisceral integration in emotion regulation and dysregulation. *Journal of Affective Disorders, 61*(3), 201–216. https://doi.org/10.1016/S0165-0327(00)00338-4

Thayer, J. F., Åhs, F., Fredrikson, M., Sollers, J. J., & Wager, T. D. (2012). A meta-analysis of heart-rate variability and neuroimaging studies: Implications for neurovisceral integration. *Neuroscience & Biobehavioural Reviews, 36*(2), 747–756. https://doi.org/10.1016/j.neubiorev.2011.11.009

Vera, D., & Crossan, M. (2005). Improvisation and innovative performance in teams. *Organisation Science, 16*(3), 203–224. https://doi.org/10.1287/orsc.1050.0126

Weick, K. E. (1998). Improvisation as a mindset for organisational analysis. *Organisation Science, 9*(5), 543–555. https://doi.org/10.1287/orsc.9.5.543

Whiteside, S. P., & Lynam, D. R. (2001). The Five-Factor Model and impulsivity. *Personality and Individual Differences, 30*(4), 669–689. https://doi.org/10.1016/S0191-8869(00)00064-7

Yam, K. C., Christian, M. S., Wei, W., Liao, Z., & Nai, J. (2018). The mixed blessing of leader humor. *Academy of Management Journal, 61*(1), 348–369. https://doi.org/10.5465/amj.2016.0941

THE UNBOUND JOURNEY

28 - Quiet Mirrors: The Science and Practice of "Reflection"

Rationale of the Article

Reflection is the integrator of the entire curriculum. It converts the program's practices (breath, values, compassion, courage) into durable habits through metacognition and implementation intentions, while HRV-supportive breathing provides the physiological footing to do so safely. Without structured reflection, gains remain episodic; with it, participants build a renewable cycle of insight-action-learning that supports authentic self-leadership.

Note on Chapter 27 (Spontaneity). Spontaneity and Reflection are complementary: compassionate reflection reduces fear and perfectionism, creating the psychological safety in which playful spontaneity can flourish; spontaneous experiments, in turn, provide fresh data for reflective learning loops.

Abstract

Many leaders and learners arrive at reflection as if it were a mirror they fear might magnify their flaws. Yet when reflection is approached as steady attention, curious, compassionate, and oriented to action, it reliably strengthens clarity, emotional balance, and ethical leadership. This article synthesises core psychological, physiological, and leadership literatures to validate *Heart Unbound 2.0*'s Chapter 28 (Reflection) as a rigorously grounded, heart-led practice. We locate reflection within experiential learning (Kolb), reflective practice (Schön), and transformative learning (Mezirow); distinguish constructive reflection from maladaptive brooding; and summarise mechanisms that include metacognition, self-distancing, cognitive reappraisal, and self-compassion (Gross; Kross & Ayduk; Neff). Physiological evidence shows reflection is supported by neurovisceral integration among the prefrontal cortex, anterior insula, anterior cingulate, and autonomic pathways indexed by heart-rate variability (Thayer & Lane; Craig; Porges; Lehrer & Gevirtz). In leadership, reflection underpins authentic leadership, psychological safety, and performance learning loops such as after-action reviews (Avolio & Gardner; Edmondson; Ellis & Davidi). We propose a three-part "ATTUNE–APPRAISE–ACT" model and translate it into short, repeatable protocols (journaling, self-distanced writing, HRV-supported breath practices, values clarification, and implementation intentions) congruent with Heart Unbound's heart-led ethos. We outline measurement options (e.g., Self-Reflection and Insight Scale; MAIA; HRV RMSSD), ethical cautions, and future research directions. The evidence converges on a simple claim: when reflection is compassionate and purposeful, it is not rumination, it is renewable inner leadership.

Keywords: reflective practice; metacognition; emotion regulation; heart-rate variability; psychological safety; authentic leadership; journaling; implementation intentions

Introduction

Reflection is the disciplined capacity to turn attention toward experience, derive meaning, and translate that meaning into wiser action. It anchors experiential learning (Kolb, 1984), professional judgment (Schön, 1983), and adult development (Mezirow, 1991). In *Heart Unbound 2.0*, Reflection (Chapter 28) is framed as a heart-led practice: present-moment awareness, compassionate appraisal, and values-aligned action. This article examines the scientific basis for that framing and offers applied protocols suitable for individuals, teams, and leaders.

Conceptual Foundations

Reflection within learning and development

Classic models converge on iterative cycles: experiencing, sense-making, and experimenting (Boud, Keogh, & Walker, 1985; Kolb, 1984; Schön, 1983). Transformative learning adds critical reflection on assumptions, enabling perspective shifts (Mezirow, 1991). In organisational contexts, structured reflection (e.g., after-action reviews) accelerates learning and performance (Ellis & Davidi, 2005; Senge, 1990; Weick, 1995).

Constructive reflection vs. rumination

Not all inward attention helps. "Brooding" rumination predicts distress, whereas reflective processing can be adaptive (Treynor, Gonzalez, & Nolen-Hoeksema, 2003). Constructive reflection is marked by curiosity, self-compassion, and action planning (Neff, 2003; Pennebaker & Chung, 2011), while rumination is repetitive, evaluative, and non-solution-focused (Gross, 2015). Heart Unbound's emphasis on kind awareness and forward movement intentionally shifts reflection toward the adaptive pole.

Psychological Mechanisms

Metacognition and self-distancing

Reflection recruits metacognitive monitoring and perspective-taking. Self-distancing, recounting experiences from a third-person vantage, reduces affective reactivity and supports meaning-making (Kross & Ayduk, 2011). Socratic, open-ended inquiry similarly elicits insight without defensiveness.

Cognitive reappraisal and self-compassion

Reappraisal changes the meaning of events and is among the most effective emotion-regulation strategies (Gross, 2015). Self-compassion practices reduce self-criticism and buffer threat, enhancing learning from mistakes (Neff, 2003; Neff & Germer, 2013). These processes align with Heart Unbound's "gentle truth-telling" stance.

Expressive writing and insight

Brief, structured writing about emotionally salient events improves mental and physical health, likely via exposure, cognitive processing, and narrative coherence (Pennebaker & Chung, 2011). Adding values prompts magnifies effects by restoring a coherent self-view.

Physiological substrates of reflective practice

Neurovisceral integration and HRV

The neurovisceral integration model posits coordinated regulation among prefrontal regions, the anterior cingulate, and the autonomic nervous system, measurable through vagally mediated heart-rate variability (HRV) (Thayer & Lane, 2000). Higher resting HRV predicts better executive control and emotion regulation, capacities central to reflective functioning.

Interoception and the insula

Interoceptive accuracy and awareness, supported by the anterior insula, inform "felt-sense" appraisal and compassionate decision-making (Craig, 2009). Reflection that includes body cues (e.g., breath, heartbeat) integrates this channel of intelligence.

Polyvagal perspective and safety

The polyvagal theory emphasises cues of safety that enable social engagement and flexible regulation (Porges, 2007). Slow-paced breathing and HRV biofeedback can increase vagal tone and facilitate calm reflective states (Lehrer & Gevirtz, 2014).

Brain networks and the "reflective toggle"

Healthy reflection likely entails flexible switching between the default mode network (self-referential processing) and task-positive networks (cognitive control), mediated by salience systems (Raichle, 2015). Mindfulness practice enhances that flexibility.

Reflection in Leadership

Authentic leadership and moral clarity

Authentic leadership requires self-awareness, internalised moral perspective, balanced processing, and relational transparency, capacities cultivated through regular reflection (Avolio & Gardner, 2005).

Psychological safety and learning loops

Teams with high psychological safety engage in speaking up, learning from error, and structured debriefs (Edmondson, 1999). After-action reviews (AARs) and premortems are reflective rituals that measurably improve subsequent performance (Ellis & Davidi, 2005).

Sensemaking under uncertainty

Leaders interpret ambiguous signals and enact meaning (Weick, 1995). Reflection provides the pause in which sensemaking becomes deliberate rather than reactive.

An integrative model for Heart Unbound 2.0

We synthesise the literature into the **ATTUNE-APPRAISE-ACT** model:

1. **ATTUNE** (state-setting): establish physiological safety and present-moment awareness (paced breathing ~6 breaths/min; brief body scan; self-compassion cue). Supports vagal tone and metacognitive readiness (Lehrer & Gevirtz, 2014; Neff, 2003).

2. **APPRAISE** (meaning-making): use self-distanced journaling and values clarification to reframe experience (Kross & Ayduk, 2011; Schwartz value theory; Gross, 2015).

3. **ACT** (translation): identify one behavioural experiment and an *implementation intention* ("If situation X, then I will do Y"), which reliably increases follow-through (Gollwitzer, 1999). Close with a micro-AAR the next day.

Application protocols (individuals and teams)

- **The 3×3 Reflective Pause (daily, ≤10 minutes)**
  Attune: 60–90 seconds of slow breathing; note one body sensation.
  Appraise: Answer three prompts. What happened? What mattered? What is learned?
  Act: Name three "next right moves" (one tiny, one relational, one restorative).

- **Self-distanced compassion letter (weekly)**
  Write to yourself using your own first name from the perspective of a wise, kind mentor; close with one implementation intention. Combines self-distancing, reappraisal, and values fit (Kross & Ayduk, 2011; Neff & Germer, 2013).

- **Team Micro-AAR (10–15 minutes)**
  What did we intend? What actually happened? Why? What will we try next? Psychological-safety norms: curiosity before critique; share credit; own improvements (Edmondson, 1999; Ellis & Davidi, 2005).

Measures for practice and evaluation

- **Self-Reflection and Insight Scale** (Grant, Franklin, & Langford, 2002).

- **Brooding/Reflection subscales** (Treynor et al., 2003) to monitor rumination.

- **MAIA - Multidimensional Assessment of Interoceptive Awareness** (Mehling et al., 2012).

- **HRV (RMSSD)** as a state marker during breath-supported reflection (Thayer & Lane, 2000).

- **Team climate/psychological safety** check (Edmondson, 1999).

Safeguards and common pitfalls

Reflection can drift into self-criticism or perseveration. Safeguards include time-boxing, self-compassion language, self-distanced framing, and explicit action steps. When trauma is present, reflective exercises should be titrated and, where appropriate, guided by qualified clinicians.

Application in Heart Unbound 2.0 - 28: REFLECTION

The Reflection chapter translates theory into accessible, heart-led practice:

- **Micro-Pauses for Neural Integration:** 3-breath reset (hand to heart, "inhale: I welcome this light / exhale: I release what dims it") to shift from autopilot to presence, used before meetings, after triggers, and at day's end.

- **"Mirror of the Heart" Mini-Meditation:** 5 minutes to revisit one luminous moment from the journey, name the emotion it evokes, and distil a **one-word anchor** (e.g., Courage, Belonging) you carry on a card or phone lock-screen.

- **Heart–Mind Integration Journal (10 min):** Write by the triad **What happened? → What did I feel? → What did it mean?** Add a quick check, **"Am I looping or listening?"**, to pivot from rumination to compassionate contemplation.

- **Rumination → Contemplation Switch (L-O-V-E): Label** the pattern, **Observe** sensations, **Validate** the feeling ("makes sense that

---

I feel…"), **Envision** one kind next step. A fast protocol to turn insight into motion.

- **Gratitude × Forward-Vision (3-3-1):** Each evening list **3 gratitudes, 3 learnings**, and **1 heart-led intention** for tomorrow. Closes the day with coherence and opens the next with direction.

- **Integration Circle / Solo Debrief:** Share or journal **3 key learnings, 2 emotional shifts, 1 intention**; seal with a breath ritual. Repeat weekly to convert experience into embodied wisdom.

- **Values-Aligned Decision Lens:** Before commitments, ask: **Is it aligned with who I'm becoming? Is it kind to present and future me? Is it sustainable?** Choose the **one next true step** only.

These practices consolidate growth, prevent rumination, and anchor heart-led clarity, personally healing and professionally transformative for emerging and senior leaders, practitioners, and anyone committed to living from an integrated, unbound heart.

Discussion

The literatures reviewed converge on a coherent picture: reflection works when it is embodied, compassionate, and actionable. Physiological state (vagal tone) enables psychological flexibility; metacognition and self-distancing shape narrative meaning; and small, values-aligned experiments translate insight into impact. This arc, state, story, step, is precisely what *Heart Unbound 2.0* operationalises.

Limitations and future research

Many studies draw on WEIRD samples; more culturally diverse work is needed. HRV is a useful but nonspecific biomarker; multimodal indices (e.g., pupillometry, respiration) could sharpen inference. In organisations, randomised field trials comparing different reflective rituals (AARs vs. premortems vs. compassion letters) would clarify mechanisms and cost-effectiveness.

Conclusion

Reflection is not a mirror for self-blame but a quiet instrument for wiser living. When paired with physiological safety and purposeful action, it deepens self-knowledge, steadies emotion, and strengthens leadership. In *Heart Unbound 2.0*, Chapter 28's practices are therefore not ancillary, they are the hinge that turns experience into growth.

References

Avolio, B. J., & Gardner, W. L. (2005). Authentic leadership development: Getting to the root of positive forms of leadership. *The Leadership Quarterly, 16*(3), 315–338.

Boud, D., Keogh, R., & Walker, D. (Eds.). (1985). *Reflection: Turning experience into learning.* Routledge.

Craig, A. D. (2009). How do you feel Now? The anterior insula and human awareness. *Nature Reviews Neuroscience, 10*(1), 59–70.

Edmondson, A. (1999). Psychological safety and learning behaviour in work teams. *Administrative Science Quarterly, 44*(2), 350–383.

Ellis, S., & Davidi, I. (2005). After-event reviews: Drawing lessons from successful and failed experience. *Journal of Applied Psychology, 90*(5), 857–871.

Gollwitzer, P. M. (1999). Implementation intentions: Strong effects of simple plans. *American Psychologist, 54*(7), 493–503.

Grant, A. M., Franklin, J., & Langford, P. (2002). The Self-Reflection and Insight Scale: A new measure of private self-consciousness. *Social Behaviour and Personality, 30*(8), 821–836.

Gross, J. J. (2015). Emotion regulation: Current status and future prospects. *Psychological Inquiry, 26*(1), 1–26.

Kabat-Zinn, J. (1990). *Full catastrophe living.* Delacorte.

Kolb, D. A. (1984). *Experiential learning: Experience as the source of learning and development.* Prentice-Hall.

Kross, E., & Ayduk, Ö. (2011). Making meaning out of negative experiences by self-distancing. *Current Directions in Psychological Science, 20*(3), 187–191.

Lehrer, P. M., & Gevirtz, R. (2014). Heart rate variability biofeedback: How and why does it work? *Frontiers in Psychology, 5*, 756.

Mehling, W. E., Price, C. J., Daubenmier, J. J., Acree, M., Bartmess, E., & Stewart, A. (2012). The Multidimensional Assessment of Interoceptive Awareness (MAIA). *PLoS ONE, 7*(11), e48230.

Mezirow, J. (1991). *Transformative dimensions of adult learning.* Jossey-Bass.

Neff, K. D. (2003). Self-compassion: An alternative conceptualisation of a healthy attitude toward oneself. *Self and Identity, 2*(2), 85–101.

Neff, K. D., & Germer, C. K. (2013). A pilot study and randomised controlled trial of the Mindful Self-Compassion program. *Journal of Clinical Psychology, 69*(1), 28–44.

Pennebaker, J. W., & Chung, C. K. (2011). Expressive writing: Connections to physical and mental health. In H. S. Friedman (Ed.), *The Oxford handbook of health psychology* (pp. 417–437). Oxford University Press.

Porges, S. W. (2007). The polyvagal perspective. *Biological Psychology, 74*(2), 116–143.

Raichle, M. E. (2015). The brain's default mode network. *Annual Review of Neuroscience, 38*, 433–447.

Schön, D. A. (1983). *The reflective practitioner: How professionals think in action.* Basic Books.

Senge, P. M. (1990). *The fifth discipline: The art and practice of the learning organisation.* Doubleday.

Thayer, J. F., & Lane, R. D. (2000). A model of neurovisceral integration in emotion regulation and dysregulation. *Journal of Affective Disorders, 61*(3), 201–216.

Treynor, W., Gonzalez, R., & Nolen-Hoeksema, S. (2003). Rumination reconsidered: A psychometric analysis. *Cognitive Therapy and Research, 27*(3), 247–259.

Weick, K. E. (1995). *Sensemaking in organisations.* Sage.

THE
UNBOUND
JOURNEY

29 - "Homecoming": Psychological, Physiological, and Leadership Foundations for Returning to the Authentic Self

Rationale for the Article

As a capstone, *Homecoming* prevents "workshop decay" by marrying insight to embodiment and action. It (a) consolidates autonomy, relatedness, and competence (Deci & Ryan, 2000); (b) stabilises regulation through vagal/HRV mechanisms (Porges, 2011; Thayer & Lane, 2000); (c) builds self-compassion and meaning (Neff & Germer, 2013; McAdams, 2001); and (d) converts inner safety into outer leadership behaviours that foster psychological safety and high-quality connection (Edmondson, 1999; Dutton & Heaphy, 2003). In short, *Homecoming* is the integrative bridge from program learning to a sustainable way of living and leading.

Abstract

This article explores *Homecoming*, the culminating chapter of *Heart Unbound 2.0*, as an evidence-based process of returning to one's authentic self. We integrate psychological theory, psychophysiology, and leadership science to clarify how practices of breath, stillness, reflection, gratitude, and values-aligned action consolidate learning and support durable change. A narrative, integrative review synthesises foundational and contemporary literature on self-determination, self-compassion, emotion regulation, interoception and autonomic regulation, and authentic/compassionate leadership.

Homecoming can be conceptualised as the convergence of autonomy, relatedness, and competence (self-determination theory) with self-congruence (humanistic psychology) and belonging (social connection). Psychophysiological mechanisms include ventral-vagal engagement and heart-rate-variability-supported regulation, oxytocin-mediated bonding, attentional control via prefrontal networks, and broaden-and-build effects of positive emotion. Evidence-based exercises, values affirmation, expressive writing, slow breathing and mindfulness, identity work, and gratitude, strengthen this return "home" by cultivating self-acceptance, coherent identity narratives, and prosocial behaviour. In organisations, these same mechanisms underpin authentic leadership, psychological safety, and high-quality connections.

As a capstone, *Homecoming* integrates insight with embodiment. It offers a rigorously supported framework for sustaining personal healing and professional effectiveness through practices that anchor autonomy, compassion, and purpose.

Keywords: authenticity; self-determination; polyvagal theory; heart-rate variability; self-compassion; values affirmation; narrative identity; authentic leadership; psychological safety; belonging

Introduction

Homecoming names a developmental movement from striving and self-evaluation to grounded authenticity and belonging. The concept resonates with classic humanistic ideas of self-congruence (Rogers, 1961) and with contemporary views of eudaimonic well-being (Ryff, 1989; Ryan & Deci, 2001). In *Heart Unbound 2.0*, the chapter consolidates earlier skills (breath, awareness, courage, connection) into daily rituals that return participants to an inner "home" of safety and integrity. This paper defines *Homecoming* as both psychological integration and physiological regulation, and as a leadership stance that advances relational trust.

We address three questions: (a) What theories best explain the experience of coming home to oneself? (b) What neurophysiological pathways support this return? (c) How does *Homecoming* translate into leadership practices that are compassionate, values-aligned, and high-performing?

Conceptual foundations: authenticity, belonging, and eudaimonia

Self-congruence and self-determination

Humanistic psychology holds that growth involves movement toward authenticity, alignment of self-concept and experience (Rogers, 1961). Self-determination theory (SDT) specifies the basic psychological needs, autonomy, competence, and relatedness, that underwrite intrinsic motivation and vitality (Deci & Ryan, 2000). *Homecoming* can be framed as a state in which these needs are simultaneously honored: one acts volitionally (autonomy), effectively (competence), and in connection with self and others (relatedness).

Belonging and narrative identity

The need to belong is a powerful, general drive (Baumeister & Leary, 1995), while narrative identity supplies continuity and meaning across life chapters (McAdams, 2001). Practices that help participants "re-author" their stories, e.g., expressive writing and reflective dialogue, support *Homecoming* by integrating wounds and wisdom into coherent life narratives (Pennebaker, 1997).

Self-compassion and emotionally intelligent regulation

Self-compassion, mindfulness, common humanity, and kindness toward self, predicts resilience, lower psychopathology, and adaptive motivation (Neff, 2003; Neff & Germer, 2013). Together with emotion-regulation skills (Gross/Ochsner's cognitive reappraisal; Ochsner & Gross, 2005) and acceptance- and values-based methods (Hayes et al., 2012), self-compassion enables a stable "felt sense" of being at home, even amid difficulty.

Eudaimonia and broaden-and-build

Eudaimonic well-being emphasises purpose, self-acceptance, and personal growth (Ryff, 1989; Ryan & Deci, 2001). Positive emotions broaden cognitive–behavioural repertoires and build durable resources (Fredrickson, 2001), creating upward spirals that strengthen social connection and physiological regulation (Kok & Fredrickson, 2010). These literatures jointly explain why gratitude, joy, and awe are central rituals in *Homecoming*.

Psychophysiology of "home"

Autonomic safety and social engagement

Porges' polyvagal theory proposes that ventral-vagal activation enables calm, social engagement and co-regulation (Porges, 2011). Higher resting heart-rate variability (HRV) indexes flexible self-regulation and adaptive emotion processes (Thayer & Lane, 2000). Slow diaphragmatic breathing and coherent breathing protocols increase HRV and reduce stress (Brown & Gerbarg, 2005). These mechanisms give biological traction to the felt sense of "I am safe here."

Interoception, oxytocin, and mindful attention

Interoceptive accuracy supports emotional awareness and grounded decision making (Critchley & Garfinkel, 2017; Craig, 2009). Oxytocin systems facilitate trust and affiliation (Carter, 2014), while mindfulness training alters prefrontal–default mode dynamics in ways consistent with reduced rumination and enhanced presence (Brewer et al., 2011; Hölzel et al., 2011). Together, these findings validate embodied approaches, hand-to-heart, breath pacing, mindful stillness, as mechanisms of *Homecoming*.

Practices that operationalise Homecoming

Values affirmation and identity work

Values affirmation buffers stress and preserves executive functioning under pressure (Creswell et al., 2005), consistent with Steele's (1988) self-affirmation theory. Identity journaling helps revise limiting self-beliefs and integrates experience (Pennebaker, 1997). These practices directly support the "I am enough/I belong to myself" stance emphasised in the chapter.

Gratitude and positive relational practices

Daily gratitude exercises reliably increase well-being and prosociality (Emmons & McCullough, 2003; Seligman et al., 2005). In teams, high-quality connections, characterised by mutual positive regard, trust, and vitality, build resilience and learning (Dutton & Heaphy, 2003; Stephens et al., 2012). Cultivating gratitude and micro-moments of connection is therefore both personally and organisationally reparative.

Breath, stillness, and reflective cadence

Mindfulness-based stress reduction and allied contemplative protocols reduce distress and improve self-regulation (Kabat-Zinn, 1990; Hölzel et al., 2011). A "heart-anchor" routine, hand-to-heart posture, slow breathing (5–6 breaths/min), brief open monitoring, and a closing gratitude statement, maps cleanly onto autonomic and attentional mechanisms reviewed above (Brown & Gerbarg, 2005; Brewer et al., 2011).

Homecoming as leadership: authenticity, safety, and purpose

Authentic and resonant leadership

Authentic leadership links self-awareness, internalised moral perspective, balanced processing, and relational transparency to follower engagement and trust (Avolio & Gardner, 2005; Walumbwa et al., 2008). Resonant leadership emphasises mindful, hopeful, and compassionate emotional tone (Boyatzis & McKee, 2005). Leaders who have "come home" regulate themselves well and extend that safety outward.

Psychological safety and high-quality connection

Team learning thrives when interpersonal risk-taking is safe (Edmondson, 1999). Leaders' authenticity and compassion predict climates of psychological safety and high-quality connections (Dutton & Heaphy, 2003). In practice, the *Homecoming* repertoire, centering breath before meetings, reflective check-ins, gratitude rounds, and values-aligned decision rules, creates conditions where candor, error voice, and innovation are more likely.

Identity work and sustainable performance

Leadership transitions require experimentation with "provisional selves" before a new, coherent identity consolidates (Ibarra, 1999). Homecoming stabilises this process by anchoring identity in values rather than impression management, thereby reducing depletion and supporting sustainable, purpose-driven performance (Kahn, 1990; Ryan & Deci, 2001).

An evidence-informed "Homecoming Protocol"

1. **Arrive (somatic safety).** Two minutes of slow breathing (5–6 cycles/min) with hand-to-heart; notice interoceptive cues (Brown & Gerbarg, 2005; Critchley & Garfinkel, 2017).

2. **Name and normalise (self-compassion).** Label present-moment experience; offer a brief compassion phrase (Neff & Germer, 2013).

3. **Re-author (values + narrative).** 5-10 minutes of values-affirming expressive writing oriented to "Who am I when I am most myself?" (Creswell et al., 2005; Pennebaker, 1997).

4. **Re-align (purposeful action).** Identify one near-term behaviour that expresses a core value; schedule it (Hayes et al., 2012).

5. **Extend (relational practice).** Offer a gratitude or appreciation micro-gesture to a colleague or loved one (Emmons & McCullough, 2003; Dutton & Heaphy, 2003).

Suggested outcomes to monitor include HRV (physiological regulation), the Self-Compassion Scale (Neff, 2003), Basic Psychological Needs satisfaction (Deci & Ryan, 2000), and brief team psychological safety measures (Edmondson, 1999).

Application in Heart Unbound 2.0 - Homecoming

The Homecoming chapter becomes lived experience through these simple, heart-led practices:

- **Home-Anchor Micro-Rituals** A 60-second reset done at thresholds (waking, before calls, bedtime): hand to heart, three slow breaths, inner mantra, *"I am home. I am whole. I am free."* Repeat whenever you notice self-abandonment or strain.

- **Belonging Audit & Release** A daily two-prompt check-in: *"Where am I seeking approval?"* and *"What truth will I honor instead?"* Name one tiny act of return (e.g., speak honestly, decline kindly, choose rest) and do it before day's end.

- **Unmask One Thing** Choose one place to drop performance: say the real no, share the real yes, or reveal one feeling without over-explaining. Celebrate the relief, authenticity is your proof of home.

- **Inner Sanctuary Design** Create a tangible "home within" cue: a 10-minute quiet window, a nook with a candle/journal, or a device-free *Sabbath hour*. Add a doorway ritual (touch heart, breathe, arrive) when entering work or home.

- **Wholeness Pages (Weekly Integration)** Once a week, write three lines: *"I am whole because...," "This week I laid down...," "I will protect my light by..."* Close with one gratitude for your own becoming.

- **Boundaries as Belonging Agreements** Draft three non-negotiables that keep you self-connected (sleep, movement, creative time). Pair each with a kind script: *"To stay aligned with my heart, I'm choosing... and I won't be available for..."*

- **Repair & Return Protocol (Relationships)** When misaligned: Pause → Breathe → Own impact → Name need → Offer repair. Use clear-is-kind language (e.g., *"I withdrew there; what I needed was quiet. I'm back now, can we reset?"*).

- **Culture of Home (Teams & Families)** Establish brief rituals that convert belonging into shared practice: 2-minute arrivals (name feeling + intention), values check-ins on decisions, and quick repair rituals after tension. Make "no masks needed" a norm.

- **Future-Self Wayfinding** Each Sunday, set one "home step" for the week (the smallest action that keeps you true). Pair it with a *When-I-Forget* plan: your chosen cue, anchor (breath/mantra), and first compassionate next step.

These practices make homecoming repeatable, tiny returns to your inner sanctuary that, over time, become your natural way of living and leading.

Conclusion

Homecoming is not sentimental closure; it is an empirically grounded state of self-congruence and social connectedness, supported by identifiable neural, hormonal, and autonomic processes. When practiced through a brief, repeatable protocol and linked to values-consistent behaviours, it becomes a reliable container for both personal well-being and collective performance. The literature suggests that "returning home" is less a destination than a daily discipline, one that unites heart, mind, and action.

References

Avolio, B. J., & Gardner, W. L. (2005). Authentic leadership development: Getting to the root of positive forms of leadership. *The Leadership Quarterly, 16*(3), 315–338.

Baumeister, R. F., & Leary, M. R. (1995). The need to belong: Desire for interpersonal attachments as a fundamental human motivation. *Psychological Bulletin, 117*(3), 497–529.

Boyatzis, R. E., & McKee, A. (2005). *Resonant leadership: Renewing yourself and connecting with others through mindfulness, hope, and compassion.* Harvard Business School Press.

Brewer, J. A., Worhunsky, P. D., Gray, J. R., Tang, Y.-Y., Weber, J., & Kober, H. (2011). Meditation experience is associated with differences in default mode network activity and connectivity. *Proceedings of the National Academy of Sciences, 108*(50), 20254–20259.

Brown, R. P., & Gerbarg, P. L. (2005). Sudarshan Kriya yogic breathing in the treatment of stress, anxiety, and depression: Part I-Neurophysiologic model. *Journal of Alternative and Complementary Medicine, 11*(2), 189–201.

Carter, C. S. (2014). Oxytocin pathways and the evolution of human behaviour. *Annual Review of Psychology, 65*, 17–39.

Craig, A. D. (2009). How do you feel Now? The anterior insula and human awareness. *Nature Reviews Neuroscience, 10*(1), 59–70.

Creswell, J. D., Welch, W. T., Taylor, S. E., Sherman, D. K., Gruenewald, T. L., & Mann, T. (2005). Affirmation of personal values buffers neuroendocrine and psychological stress responses. *Psychological Science, 16*(11), 846–851.

Critchley, H. D., & Garfinkel, S. N. (2017). Interoception and emotion. *Neuron, 93*(3), 662–673.

Deci, E. L., & Ryan, R. M. (2000). The "what" and "why" of goal pursuits: Human needs and the self-determination of behaviour. *Psychological Inquiry, 11*(4), 227–268.

Dutton, J. E., & Heaphy, E. D. (2003). The power of high-quality connections. In K. S. Cameron, J. E. Dutton, & R. E. Quinn (Eds.), *Positive organisational scholarship* (pp. 263–278). Berrett-Koehler.

Edmondson, A. C. (1999). Psychological safety and learning behaviour in work teams. *Administrative Science Quarterly, 44*(2), 350–383.

Emmons, R. A., & McCullough, M. E. (2003). Counting blessings versus burdens: An experimental investigation of gratitude and subjective well-being in daily life. *Journal of Personality and Social Psychology, 84*(2), 377–389.

Fredrickson, B. L. (2001). The broaden-and-build theory of positive emotions. *American Psychologist, 56*(3), 218–226.

Hayes, S. C., Strosahl, K., & Wilson, K. (2012). *Acceptance and commitment therapy: The process and practice of mindful change* (2nd ed.). Guilford Press.

Hölzel, B. K., Lazar, S. W., Gard, T., Schuman-Olivier, Z., Vago, D. R., & Ott, U. (2011). How does mindfulness meditation work? Proposing mechanisms of action from a conceptual and neural perspective. *Perspectives on Psychological Science, 6*(6), 537–559.

Ibarra, H. (1999). Provisional selves: Experimenting with image and identity in professional adaptation. *Administrative Science Quarterly, 44*(4), 764–791.

Kabat-Zinn, J. (1990). *Full catastrophe living*. Delacorte.

Kahn, W. A. (1990). Psychological conditions of personal engagement and disengagement at work. *Academy of Management Journal, 33*(4), 692–724.

Kok, B. E., & Fredrickson, B. L. (2010). Upward spirals of the heart: Autonomic flexibility, as indexed by vagal tone, reciprocally and prospectively predicts positive emotions. *Biological Psychology, 85*(3), 432–436.

McAdams, D. P. (2001). The psychology of life stories. *Review of General Psychology, 5*(2), 100–122.

Neff, K. D. (2003). The development and validation of a scale to measure self-compassion. *Self and Identity, 2*(3), 223–250.

Neff, K. D., & Germer, C. K. (2013). A pilot study and randomised controlled trial of the Mindful Self-Compassion program. *Journal of Clinical Psychology, 69*(1), 28–44.

Ochsner, K. N., & Gross, J. J. (2005). The cognitive control of emotion. *Trends in Cognitive Sciences, 9*(5), 242–249.

Pennebaker, J. W. (1997). Writing about emotional experiences as a therapeutic process. *Psychological Science, 8*(3), 162–166.

Porges, S. W. (2011). *The polyvagal theory: Neurophysiological foundations of emotions, attachment, communication, and self-regulation*. W. W. Norton.

Rogers, C. R. (1961). *On becoming a person*. Houghton Mifflin.

Ryan, R. M., & Deci, E. L. (2001). On happiness and human potentials: A review of research on hedonic and eudaimonic well-being. *Annual Review of Psychology, 52*, 141–166.

Ryff, C. D. (1989). Happiness is everything, or is it? Explorations on the meaning of well-being. *Journal of Personality and Social Psychology, 57*(6), 1069–1081.

Seligman, M. E. P., Steen, T. A., Park, N., & Peterson, C. (2005). Positive psychology progress: Empirical validation of interventions. *American Psychologist, 60*(5), 410–421.

Steele, C. M. (1988). The psychology of self-affirmation: Sustaining the integrity of the self. In L. Berkowitz (Ed.), *Advances in experimental social psychology* (Vol. 21, pp. 261–302). Academic Press.

Stephens, J. P., Heaphy, E. D., & Dutton, J. E. (2012). High-quality connections. In K. S. Cameron & G. M. Spreitzer (Eds.), *The Oxford handbook of positive organisational scholarship* (pp. 385–399). Oxford University Press.

Thayer, J. F., & Lane, R. D. (2000). A model of neurovisceral integration in emotion regulation and dysregulation. *Journal of Affective Disorders, 61*(3), 201–216.

Walumbwa, F. O., Avolio, B. J., Gardner, W. L., Wernsing, T. S., & Peterson, S. J. (2008). Authentic leadership: Development and validation of a theory-based measure. *Journal of Management, 34*(1), 89–126.

Author note. This article translates the *Homecoming* chapter into a research-anchored framework for practitioners, coaches, and leaders implementing *Heart Unbound 2.0*.

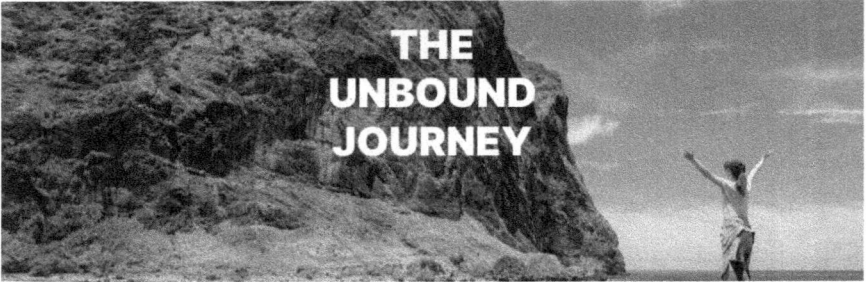

30 - "Living Invitations": Translating Heart-Led Development into Daily Micro-Practices

---

Rationale

This article is pivotal for *Heart Unbound 2.0* because it demonstrates that the program's closing chapter is not a "wrap-up" but a scientifically grounded transfer protocol. By linking each invitation to well-validated mechanisms (SDT, implementation intentions, HRV-based regulation, self-compassion, gratitude, and psychological safety), it supplies participants and organisations with a rigorous blueprint for sustaining change, measuring progress, and scaling heart-led leadership.

Abstract

Heart Unbound 2.0 – Living Invitations proposes ten everyday "invitations" (remembering, gathering "heart codes," ritual, intention, companionship, self-kindness, curiosity, sharing, gratitude, and embodiment) as micro-practices that sustain change after a transformational program ends. This article situates those invitations in contemporary psychology, psychophysiology, and leadership science. We synthesise evidence on motivation and identity (self-determination and self-affirmation), planning and habit formation (implementation intentions and rituals), psychological flexibility and mindfulness, social support and gratitude, and autonomic regulation (vagal tone, heart-rate variability, and slow breathing). We then map these mechanisms to the ten invitations and to leadership outcomes, authenticity, psychological safety, and values-based action offering a theoretically coherent and testable framework for *Living Invitations*. A brief "Application in Heart Unbound 2.0" section (mirroring Chapter 3 *I Am*) shows how affirmations, journaling, and values alignment operationalise identity change. We conclude with suggestions for evaluation (e.g., HRV, validated psychometrics) and implementation in personal and organisational settings.

Keywords: Living Invitations; self-determination theory; implementation intentions; rituals; psychological flexibility; gratitude; heart-rate variability; authentic leadership; psychological safety.

Introduction: From peak experience to daily practice

Intensive personal-development programs often produce powerful experiences that fade without a structure for enactment. *Living Invitations* reframes integration as a series of small, repeatable choices that protect autonomy while guiding attention toward values-congruent action. This framing aligns with research showing that sustainable change is supported when interventions (a) satisfy basic psychological needs for autonomy, competence, and relatedness (Deci & Ryan, 2000; Ryan & Deci, 2020), (b) convert intentions into context-linked plans (Gollwitzer, 1999), (c) are practiced frequently in emotionally salient ways that consolidate neuroplastic change (Draganski et al., 2004), and (d) are reinforced within supportive relationships (Cohen & Wills, 1985; Baumeister & Leary, 1995).

Below we outline the theoretical and physiological mechanisms that validate *Living Invitations* and show how these mechanisms extend to leadership and collective flourishing.

Psychological mechanisms undergirding the Invitations

Autonomy, meaning and identity

Self-determination theory (SDT) predicts that change is durable when practices are freely chosen, build skillfulness, and are socially embedded (Deci & Ryan, 2000; Ryan & Deci, 2020). Identity processes strengthen this durability. Self-affirmation protects a valued, moral self-concept and reduces defensiveness, enabling behaviour change and receptivity to feedback (Cohen & Sherman, 2014; Steele, 1988). Identity-based motivation research likewise shows that "who I am" stories cue "what I do" in context (Oyserman, 2009).

Living Invitations leverage these principles by asking participants to name "heart codes," set heart-led intentions, and enact them in micro-moments that feel self-congruent.

Planning, habits, and rituals

Intentions become behaviour when linked to "if-then" cues (implementation intentions; Gollwitzer, 1999). Repetition in stable contexts gradually automatises action (Lally et al., 2010). Ritual studies show that personally meaningful, scripted sequences can increase self-control, reduce anxiety, and enhance performance, even when the ritual is created by the individual (Vohs et al., 2013; Norton & Gino, 2014). The invitations to weave daily rituals and to review weekly "Where did I live from my heart?" operationalise these mechanisms.

Psychological flexibility, mindfulness, and compassion

Acceptance and Commitment Therapy (ACT) frames well-being as values-based action in the presence of difficult thoughts and feelings, i.e., psychological flexibility (Hayes et al., 2006). Mindfulness training enhances attentional control and emotion regulation (Kabat-Zinn, 2003), and self-compassion buffers shame and predicts resilience and adaptive motivation (Neff, 2003; Neff & Germer, 2013). The invitations to hold oneself kindly, to stay curious, and to cultivate simple contemplative rituals (e.g., five mindful breaths) are therefore not ancillary but central to sustaining change.

Social connection, gratitude, and positive emotion

Social support exerts direct and stress-buffering effects on health and performance (Cohen & Wills, 1985). Gratitude practices improve well-being and reduce depressive symptoms (Emmons & McCullough, 2003; Wood et al., 2010). Loving-kindness/compassion practices broaden momentary mindsets and build durable resources (Fredrickson, 2001; Fredrickson et al., 2008). The invitations to "walk together," "share your journey," and "practice gratitude" create upward spirals of positive emotion and social resonance.

Psychophysiology of heart-led practice

Autonomic regulation and the "felt sense" of safety

Polyvagal theory proposes that the ventral vagal system supports social engagement when the organism detects safety (Porges, 2007). Slow-paced breathing and resonant-frequency biofeedback increase heart-rate variability

(HRV), indexing flexible parasympathetic regulation and improved stress tolerance (Lehrer & Gevirtz, 2014). Chanting, humming, or prayerlike repetition can also improve cardiorespiratory coupling and baroreflex sensitivity (Bernardi et al., 2001). These mechanisms validate the invitations to begin and end the day with brief breath-based rituals and to use hand-to-heart cues as somatic "home signals."

Neuroplastic consolidation

Repeated, emotionally salient practice strengthens synaptic pathways (Draganski et al., 2004). Gratitude, self-affirmation, and compassion elicit midline cortical and reward-system activity associated with valuation and self-relevance, increasing the likelihood of re-enactment (Cascio et al., 2016; Fredrickson et al., 2008). Thus, the program's micro-practices are not merely symbolic; they engage learning systems that translate insight into embodied habit.

Mapping the ten Living Invitations to evidence

1. **Remembering (reflective review).** Guided reflection converts experience into learning (Schön, 1983; Kolb, 1984) and expressive writing improves health markers (Pennebaker, 1997).

2. **Gathering heart codes (values cues).** Values clarification enhances persistence and well-being (Hayes et al., 2006); self-affirmation maintains integrity under threat (Cohen & Sherman, 2014).

3. **Weaving daily rituals.** Rituals improve self-control and reduce anxiety (Vohs et al., 2013; Norton & Gino, 2014).

4. **Lighting the path with intention.** Implementation intentions and mental contrasting with if-then plans increase goal attainment (Gollwitzer, 1999; Oettingen & Gollwitzer, 2010).

5. **Walking together (support/accountability).** Social support predicts resilience and adherence (Cohen & Wills, 1985).

6. **Holding oneself kindly (self-compassion).** Self-compassion is linked to adaptive coping and reduced psychopathology (Neff, 2003; Neff & Germer, 2013).

7. **Staying curious and open.** Psychological flexibility predicts mental health and behavioural change (Hayes et al., 2006).

8. **Sharing the journey (storying).** Disclosure and prosocial sharing strengthen meaning and belonging (Pennebaker, 1997; Baumeister & Leary, 1995).

9. **Practicing gratitude.** Increases well-being and sleep quality while reducing symptoms (Emmons & McCullough, 2003; Wood et al., 2010).

10. **Embodying learning (from intention to identity).** Habit formation curves show automaticity emerging with consistent repetition in stable contexts (Lally et al., 2010); identity congruence sustains enactment (Oyserman, 2009).

Leadership implications

Authentic, mindful, and compassionate leadership

Authentic leadership integrates self-awareness, relational transparency, and internalised moral perspective (Avolio & Gardner, 2005). Mindful leadership is associated with higher employee well-being and performance (Reb et al., 2014). Resonant leadership emphasises emotional contagion and renewal practices (Boyatzis & McKee, 2005). The invitations, especially intention setting, gratitude, sharing stories, and self-kindness are micro-behaviours that cultivate these capacities.

Team climate and psychological safety

Regular reflection, disclosure, and gratitude rituals strengthen psychological safety, a key predictor of team learning and performance (Edmondson, 1999). Values-behaviour alignment enhances person–organisation fit and commitment (Kristof-Brown et al., 2005). Leaders who model the invitations therefore create climates where courage and creativity can flourish.

Application in Heart Unbound 2.0

- **Mirror Work & Voice Activation.** Speaking affirmations with a hand-to-heart posture engages embodied self-affirmation (Cohen & Sherman, 2014) and vagal pathways via prosodic voice use, supporting calm engagement (Porges, 2007).

- **Identity Journaling.** Expressive writing helps integrate identity shifts and reduces rumination (Pennebaker, 1997); framing entries as "I am becoming…" links goals to identity (Oyserman, 2009).

- **Daily Affirmation Rituals.** Brief, repeated self-affirmations consolidate value-consistent neural appraisal and reduce threat responses (Cascio et al., 2016).

- **Leadership Alignment.** Weekly "values-to-behaviour" audits convert self-affirmation into implementation intentions for meetings, feedback, and decision-making (Gollwitzer, 1999; Avolio & Gardner, 2005). These practices are intentionally lightweight and scalable, making them both personally reparative and professionally transformative for emerging and senior leaders.

Implementation and evaluation

- **Dosage and cadence.** Adopt one to three invitations at a time, practiced daily for a minimum of 21 days to establish cue–routine–reward loops, while recognising mean automaticity horizons near 2 months (Lally et al., 2010).

- **Measurement.**

  o *Physiology*: resting HRV (RMSSD) or paced-breathing HRV sessions (Lehrer & Gevirtz, 2014).

  o *Psychometrics*: Basic Psychological Needs Satisfaction (SDT), Self-Compassion Scale (Neff, 2003), Five-Facet Mindfulness Questionnaire, Gratitude Questionnaire-6, and workplace *psychological safety* pulse (Edmondson, 1999).

  o *Behavioural*: "if-then" adherence logs and brief weekly reflection ("Where did I live from my heart? Where will I open next week?").

Limitations and future directions

The present framework synthesises robust but heterogeneous literatures. Not all invitations have been tested together as a closed intervention. Future work should employ randomised or stepped-wedge designs comparing *Living Invitations* with active controls, using multi-level modeling to examine leader-to-team spillover effects and physiological markers (e.g., HRV synchrony) in dyads.

Conclusion

The *Living Invitations* chapter translates evidence-based mechanisms need satisfaction, identity-affirmation, if-then planning, ritualisation, compassion, gratitude, and autonomic regulation into a humane set of micro-practices. When enacted consistently, these practices help individuals and leaders carry transformation from the workshop into daily life, deepening authenticity, resilience, and relational safety.

References

Avolio, B. J., & Gardner, W. L. (2005). Authentic leadership development: Getting to the root of positive forms of leadership. *The Leadership Quarterly, 16*(3), 315–338. https://doi.org/10.1016/j.leaqua.2005.03.001

Baumeister, R. F., & Leary, M. R. (1995). The need to belong: Desire for interpersonal attachments as a fundamental human motivation. *Psychological Bulletin, 117*(3), 497–529. https://doi.org/10.1037/0033-2909.117.3.497

Bernardi, L., Sleight, P., Bandinelli, G., Cencetti, S., Fattorini, L., Wdowczyc-Szulc, J., & Lagi, A. (2001). Effect of rosary prayer and yoga mantras on autonomic cardiovascular rhythms: Comparative study. *BMJ, 323*(7327), 1446–1449. https://doi.org/10.1136/bmj.323.7327.1446

Boyatzis, R. E., & McKee, A. (2005). *Resonant leadership: Renewing yourself and connecting with others through mindfulness, hope, and compassion.* Harvard Business School Press.

Cascio, C. N., O'Donnell, M. B., Tinney, F. J., Lieberman, M. D., Taylor, S. E., Strecher, V. J., & Falk, E. B. (2016). Self-affirmation activates brain systems associated with self-related processing and reward and is reinforced by future orientation. *Social Cognitive and Affective Neuroscience, 11*(4), 621–629. https://doi.org/10.1093/scan/nsv136

Cohen, G. L., & Sherman, D. K. (2014). The psychology of change: Self-affirmation and social psychological intervention. *Annual Review of Psychology, 65*, 333–371. https://doi.org/10.1146/annurev-psych-010213-115137

Cohen, S., & Wills, T. A. (1985). Stress, social support, and the buffering hypothesis. *Psychological Bulletin, 98*(2), 310–357. https://doi.org/10.1037/0033-2909.98.2.310

Deci, E. L., & Ryan, R. M. (2000). The "what" and "why" of goal pursuits: Human needs and the self-determination of behaviour. *Psychological Inquiry, 11*(4), 227–268. https://doi.org/10.1207/S15327965PLI1104_01

Draganski, B., Gaser, C., Busch, V., Schuierer, G., Bogdahn, U., & May, A. (2004). Changes in grey matter induced by training. *Nature, 427*(6972), 311–312. https://doi.org/10.1038/427311a

Edmondson, A. (1999). Psychological safety and learning behaviour in work teams. *Administrative Science Quarterly, 44*(2), 350–383. https://doi.org/10.2307/2666999

Emmons, R. A., & McCullough, M. E. (2003). Counting blessings versus burdens: An experimental investigation of gratitude and subjective well-being in daily life. *Journal of Personality and Social Psychology, 84*(2), 377–389. https://doi.org/10.1037/0022-3514.84.2.377

Fredrickson, B. L. (2001). The role of positive emotions in positive psychology: The broaden-and-build theory of positive emotions. *American Psychologist, 56*(3), 218–226. https://doi.org/10.1037/0003-066X.56.3.218

Fredrickson, B. L., Cohn, M. A., Coffey, K. A., Pek, J., & Finkel, S. M. (2008). Open hearts build lives: Positive emotions, induced through loving-kindness meditation, build consequential personal resources. *Journal of Personality and Social Psychology, 95*(5), 1045–1062. https://doi.org/10.1037/a0013262

Gollwitzer, P. M. (1999). Implementation intentions: Strong effects of simple plans. *American Psychologist, 54*(7), 493–503. https://doi.org/10.1037/0003-066X.54.7.493

Hayes, S. C., Luoma, J. B., Bond, F. W., Masuda, A., & Lillis, J. (2006). Acceptance and Commitment Therapy: Model, processes and outcomes. *Behaviour Research and Therapy, 44*(1), 1–25. https://doi.org/10.1016/j.brat.2005.06.006

Kabat-Zinn, J. (2003). Mindfulness-based interventions in context: Past, present, and future. *Clinical Psychology: Science and Practice, 10*(2), 144–156. https://doi.org/10.1093/clipsy.bpg016

Kolb, D. A. (1984). *Experiential learning: Experience as the source of learning and development*. Prentice Hall.

Kristof-Brown, A. L., Zimmerman, R. D., & Johnson, E. C. (2005). Consequences of individuals' fit at work: A meta-analysis of person–job, person–organisation, person–group, and person–supervisor fit. *Personnel Psychology,* *58*(2), 281–342. https://doi.org/10.1111/j.1744-6570.2005.00672.x

Lally, P., van Jaarsveld, C. H. M., Potts, H. W. W., & Wardle, J. (2010). How are habits formed: Modelling habit formation in the real world. *European Journal of Social Psychology, 40*(6), 998–1009. https://doi.org/10.1002/ejsp.674

Lehrer, P. M., & Gevirtz, R. (2014). Heart rate variability biofeedback: How and why does it work? *Frontiers in Psychology, 5,* 756. https://doi.org/10.3389/fpsyg.2014.00756

Neff, K. D. (2003). The development and validation of a scale to measure self-compassion. *Self and Identity, 2*(3), 223–250. https://doi.org/10.1080/15298860309027

Neff, K. D., & Germer, C. K. (2013). A pilot study and randomised controlled trial of the Mindful Self-Compassion program. *Journal of Clinical Psychology, 69*(1), 28–44. https://doi.org/10.1002/jclp.21923

Norton, M. I., & Gino, F. (2014). Rituals alleviate grieving for loved ones, lovers, and lotteries. *Journal of Experimental Psychology: General, 143*(1), 266–272. https://doi.org/10.1037/a0031772

Oettingen, G., & Gollwitzer, P. M. (2010). Strategies of setting and implementing goals: Mental contrasting and implementation intentions. In J. E. Maddux & J. P. Tangney (Eds.), *Social psychological foundations of clinical psychology* (pp. 114–135). Guilford Press.

Oyserman, D. (2009). Identity-based motivation: Implications for action-readiness, procedural-readiness, and consumer behaviour. *Journal of Consumer Psychology, 19*(3), 250–260. https://doi.org/10.1016/j.jcps.2009.05.008

Pennebaker, J. W. (1997). Writing about emotional experiences as a therapeutic process. *Psychological Science, 8*(3), 162–166. https://doi.org/10.1111/j.1467-9280.1997.tb00403.x

Porges, S. W. (2007). The polyvagal perspective. *Biological Psychology, 74*(2), 116–143. https://doi.org/10.1016/j.biopsycho.2006.06.009

Reb, J., Narayanan, J., & Chaturvedi, S. (2014). Leading mindfully: Two studies on the influence of leader mindfulness on employee well-being and performance. *Mindfulness, 5*(1), 36–45. https://doi.org/10.1007/s12671-012-

0144-z

Ryan, R. M., & Deci, E. L. (2020). *Self-determination theory: Basic psychological needs in motivation, development, and wellness.* Guilford Press.

Schön, D. A. (1983). *The reflective practitioner: How professionals think in action.* Basic Books.

Steele, C. M. (1988). The psychology of self-affirmation: Sustaining the integrity of the self. In L. Berkowitz (Ed.), *Advances in experimental social psychology* (Vol. 21, pp. 261–302). Academic Press. https://doi.org/10.1016/S0065-2601(08)60229-4

Vohs, K. D., Wang, Y., Gino, F., & Norton, M. I. (2013). Rituals enhance consumption. *Psychological Science, 24*(9), 1714–1721. https://doi.org/10.1177/0956797613482945

Wood, A. M., Froh, J. J., & Geraghty, A. W. A. (2010). Gratitude and well-being: A review and theoretical integration. *Clinical Psychology Review, 30*(7), 890–905. https://doi.org/10.1016/j.cpr.2010.03.005

Author note. This article validates and operationalises the *Living Invitations* of *Heart Unbound 2.0,* offering researchers and practitioners a coherent, evidence-based pathway from insight to sustained, heart-led action.

YOU ARE NOT ALONE

As you journey through *Heart Unbound 2.0* and *The Unbound Way* there may be moments when your heart feels heavy or your reflections stir emotions that feel hard to carry. This is part of healing, and yet, you are never meant to walk this path by yourself. Support is not just available, it is your right.

The organisations listed here are included for you, because sometimes the most courageous act of self-love is reaching out and saying, *"I need support."* These groups offer free, confidential help. They exist to listen, to guide, and to stand beside you when you need it most.

Whether you are in Australia, New Zealand, the United States, Canada, or the United Kingdom, there are people ready to hear you, day or night. Reaching out is not a sign of weakness. It is a sign of strength. It is a way of honouring your heart and choosing life, connection, and hope.

Take these resources as companions on your journey. If ever you feel overwhelmed, please remember: help is just one call or message away, and you never have to face this alone.

Free Support Services - You Are Not Alone

Wherever you are on your *Heart Unbound 2.0* journey, support is always close at hand. These services are free, confidential, and available to you whenever you need to reach out.

<u>Australia</u>

- **Lifeline Australia** – 13 11 14 (24/7 crisis support and suicide prevention)
- **Beyond Blue** – 1300 22 4636 (24/7 support for anxiety, depression, and mental health)
- **Kids Helpline** – 1800 55 1800 (24/7 for children and young people aged 5–25)
- **Suicide Call Back Service** – 1300 659 467 (24/7 counselling for people at risk of suicide and their carers)

New Zealand

- **Lifeline New Zealand** – 0800 543 354 or free text 4357 (24/7 support)
- **1737, Need to Talk?** – Call or text 1737 (24/7 to talk with a trained counsellor)
- **Youthline** – 0800 376 633 or free text 234 (support for young people)

United States

- **988 Suicide & Crisis Lifeline** – Call or text 988 (24/7 for anyone in crisis)
- **National Alliance on Mental Illness (NAMI) Helpline** – 1-800-950-NAMI (Mon–Fri, 10am–10pm ET)
- **Crisis Text Line** – Text HOME to 741741 (24/7 to connect with a crisis counsellor)

Canada

- **Talk Suicide Canada** – 1-833-456-4566 or text 45645 (24/7 support for suicide prevention)
- **Kids Help Phone** – 1-800-668-6868 or text CONNECT to 686868 (24/7 for young people)
- **Wellness Together Canada** – 1-866-585-0445 (mental health and substance use support, available 24/7)

United Kingdom

- **Samaritans** – 116 123 (24/7 support for anyone in emotional distress)
- **Mind Infoline** – 0300 123 3393 (mental health support and resources)

- **Shout Crisis Text Line** – Text SHOUT to 85258 (24/7 support via text)

Please keep this page close. Just as you turn to your breath, your journal, or your heart, you can also turn to these voices of compassion whenever you need them. Reaching out is a way of returning home to yourself.

A Final Word on Support

Reaching out for help is not a sign of weakness, it is one of the deepest acts of strength. When you choose to call, text, or speak to someone who is there to listen, you are honouring your heart's need for care and connection.

Remember, your *Unbound* journey is not meant to be travelled alone. Just as you are learning to listen to yourself with compassion, these services exist to listen to you too. They are lifelines in moments of heaviness, reminders that you are seen, valued, and never beyond hope.

Every time you take the brave step to reach out, you are not stepping back, you are stepping closer to your wholeness. You are choosing to live unbound: with courage, with tenderness, and with the quiet knowing that your heart is never alone.

ABOUT THE AUTHOR

Dr John McSwiney, PhD

Executive Leader | Professor of Law | Organisational Development Consultant | Governance and Culture Transformer | Author | Coach

Dr John McSwiney is an accomplished senior executive and consultant with more than 25 years' experience leading organisational development, cultural transformation, and governance across education, defence, government, and corporate sectors in Australia and internationally. He has held senior roles including Director of Technical Training for the Royal Australian Navy, CEO of Haileybury International School in Beijing, and Director of International Programs at the Victorian Curriculum and Assessment Authority.

As a **Professor of Law and Associate Professor/Lecturer in Business and Corporate Law**, John has taught at leading Australian higher education institutions, and his teaching portfolio spans Contract Law, Torts, Negligence, Corporate Law, Organisational Behaviour, Emotional Intelligence, and Leadership. A recognised course leader and curriculum designer, John has successfully redeveloped programs, assessments, and outcomes to meet national accreditation and TEQSA requirements, while inspiring thousands of international and domestic students to engage critically with law, leadership, and ethics.

John is also the **Founder and Managing Director of Time to Transform**, a leadership and personal development consultancy delivering evidence-based programs in emotional intelligence, resilience, and culture change. His flagship initiatives - *Heart Unbound: The Ultimate 28-Day Heart Connection Challenge* and *Heart Unbound 2.0 – The Journey Expands*, are fully aligned with AQF, ASQA, APS, and NSQHS frameworks, and have been delivered across universities, corporations, and government departments.

A prolific author and thought leader, John has published widely across law, governance, politics, spirituality, and personal transformation, including *The Journey of 100 Hidden Hearts*; *Heart Unbound*: The Ultimate 28 Day Heart Connection Challenge; *Heart Unbound 2.0*: The Journey Expands; and is currently completing his next book titled – *"The Power of What If?"* due for release in late 2025.

John holds a PhD in Politics, an MA in Political Science, from Monash University as well as an LLB in Law, a Bachelor (Social Science) and is also admitted as a Barrister and Solicitor of the Supreme Court of Victoria. He also holds a Diploma and Master Practitioner qualifications in Life Coaching, blending academic rigour with practical, heart-based coaching.

Across every role, John brings a unique combination of **strategic leadership, legal expertise, and heart-centred teaching**, enabling leaders and organisations to cultivate trust, resilience, and performance while honouring authenticity and human connection.